Left Politics in South Asia

Reframing the Agenda

Left Politics in South Asia
Reframing the Agenda

Edited by
Ravi Kumar

AAKAR

Left Politics in South Asia: Reframing the Agenda
Edited by Ravi Kumar

First Published 2019

ISBN 978-93-5002-586-4

Published by
AAKAR BOOKS
28 E Pocket IV, Mayur Vihar Phase I
Delhi 110 091 India
aakarbooks@gmail.com

Laser Typeset at
Arpit Printographers, Delhi

Printed at
D.K. Fine Art Press, Delhi

Contents

Acknowledgements

This volume emerges out of a conference that was organized by the Department of Sociology, South Asian University in collaboration with Rosa Luxemburg Stiftung (RLS), South Asia. Logistically, bringing together this volume would have been impossible without the support of RLS and I wish to express my thanks to Pragya and Stefan for lending their support. In a situation when universities are ceasing to be centres of dissent and dialogue it would have been impossible without the support of Sasanka Perera, Dean, Faculty of Social Sciences to undertake this exercise. It was not only his logistical support but also his belief that universities must remain places where ideas are debated irrespective of any prejudices that allowed this exercise to culminate into a volume. This could have been much richer in terms of its South Asian content but for many intellectuals who did not get time to resubmit their revised pieces. Finally, without the support of Atul, who was instrumental in organizing the whole process, this volume would not have seen the light of the day. I will always remain indebted to Mr. K.K. Saxena of Aakar Books to bear with my delays and be receptive to my ideas for the volume. I only hope that this volume becomes a source of debate. All these exercises come at the cost of time that I should have given to Marti, Ruskin and Rama. I cannot compensate for the lost time to them.

Ravi Kumar
South Asian University

1

Introduction
Left Politics in South Asia: Reframing the Agenda

Ravi Kumar

A Divine Tongue

I am angry enough
to sing a song of curses at all of you
I am angry enough to curse
that the hands that burnt my effigy
shall char in the same fire
That the words that flew at me
like poison-soaked arrows
shall turn back to go
and wound and kill
the stone hearts that sent them
I am angry enough to sing
Oh you guardians of morals
May the screens part
and expose your truths
May the lord of cremation grounds
dance, smearing the ashes
from your powdered bones
I am angry enough to sing
a song of curses
That lips that spout lies shall burn and wither
That crowds that gather quickly shall die
But my divine tongue has no words
for curses
Go away, live!

Perumal Murugan (*Songs of a Coward*, Penguin)

South Asia has become an interesting geographical space where the politics of the 21st century has taken a curious turn, compelling an urgent need to reflect on the politics of resistance. It is important to mention that one is referring here to a politics of resistance that is anti-systemic. Social movement studies have extensively debated the movements in classificatory terms and this is not the place to get into it but by and large as this volume is about left politics it is to be understood in the context of how the politics that seeks to go beyond the status quo created by capitalism will be defined. These are grim times for Left politics in general not only because of the diminished strength of anti-systemic resistances but also because of the gradual weakening of the theoretical enterprise of Marxism in academia.

Chibber argues that class analysis has rapidly declined in South Asian studies as has been a general decline in Marxism as "an intellectual and political force". Its place has been taken over by two tendencies: "On the Right, it is of course the revival of free-market ideology and, more broadly, neoliberalism as a political project. On the Left, it is the rise of post-structuralism and, in area studies particularly, postcolonial theory (the tandem is hereafter referred to as PSPC). Indeed, the proponents of PSPC have rather boldly laid claim to the mantle of radical theory in the wake of Marxism's retreat" (Chibber, 2006, pp. 237-38).There has been a redefinition of the political landscape as far as the nature of Left politics is concerned in both urban and rural areas. And this has been true for nearly all of South Asia with some variations owing to their historical contexts.

A quick look at some of the debates reveal that there has been a concern regarding the direction of the Left politics in the region. Bhusal, a Communist Party of Nepal (United Marxist Leninist) leader points out how the nature of Maoist politics has changed. He argues that using the theoretical framework of Maoism the "People's War" of the Communist Party of Nepal-Maoist (CPN-M) aimed at concluding "new democratic revolution" once state power was captured.

In 2006, the Maoist Party concluded that the "People's War" had reached

> the stage of "strategic counter attack" passing already through the stage of "strategic defence" and "strategic balance". According to the Party's claim, some 80 per cent of territory of Nepal was under the influence of the "new regime". What is meant was the CPN Maoist was then very close to a point to smash what they called the "old regime" and establish their "new regime". However, just a few years down the road, the same party descended to a point to dissolve the "People's War", hand over the "people's army" and their weapons, form a government in alliance with Madheshi political parties that champion identity politics, and face a split. Yet, it keeps claiming Maoism as its guiding principle despite its abandonment of the "People's War", which it based on the principle of Maoism (Bhusal, 2013, p. 86).

One of the issues, it has been argued, has been that "Nepal's communist parties have never discussed and debated issues around the character of society and class, which forms the bedrock of programmes of a revolution" (Bhusal, 2013, p. 87). The characterization of the Nepali society even today as 'semi-feudal' and semi-colonial' is only one illustration of how the communist movement is still stuck in the classifications that Mao made of the Chinese society. Scholars like Mishra (1987) argued while trying to underline the underdevelopment of Nepal that it was incorporated "within the capitalist world-and regional-system in terms of labour, commodities and capital/finance"; it had diminishing ability to "reproduce indigenous means of subsistence-production, combined with a diminishing or very low capacity to carry out expanded reproduction"; it had a "a comprador bourgeoisie (whose interests are closely tied with world and regional capitalism) and the state class which contains nationalist components but which cannot lead a national transformation because of its strong political alliance with the feudal and other traditional — i.e. pre-capitalist — structures and its rapidly-growing economic and financial ties with the comprador bourgeoisie"; that there were "serious problems of familial, community-based, regional and national integration arising out of peripheralization and marginalization on the one hand and on the other, the successful resistance kept up by the state, the feudal elements and the comprador bourgeoisie to mass-based political-developmental forms" (Mishra, 1987, pp. 106-07).

Writing in 2014, Mishra says that "Politically, now that the left and 'communist' political parties, ideologues and leaders have agreed that Nepal, in essence, constitutes a capitalist state, it remains to characterize this specific form of capitalism that Nepal finds itself embedded within…". He goes on to argue elsewhere (2013) that social democracy is a good alternative in the current phase for Nepal as it "enhances the workers' ownership of social democratic capitalism as well as a social-democratic state". He derives this conclusion based on the fact that the workers "earn in two ways. Capitalists pay them a wage for the work they do. The state provides them with support and services in return for the votes they cast and for their citizenship in a democratic and equity-promoting state" (p. 53). One can obviously raise questions on the way he understands government as a mediator between the capital and labour as if the government does not have a class character. In the debate relating to whether Nepal is feudal or capitalist Bhusal (2013) argues that "In terms of production, Nepal has either subsistence or commodity production. Neither of them relates to feudalism as there is no exploitation of unpaid labour, and commodity production is antithesis of feudalism" (p. 90). For him "by 1963, Nepal's economic base was basically capitalist, with its basic social character remaining no longer semi-feudal" (p. 91). Mishra (2014) argues that Nepal has to march into capitalism like China and India have done and invite private investment, more so because arguments for the demise of capitalism, historically, have been exaggerated.

The possibilities of making class central in politics and policy does not seem to be on the cards of the dominant Left at the moment. Undoubtedly the debate on the character of Nepali society is important because it would determine the struggle that the Left would wage but on paper or on ground there is not much which demonstrates the commitment of the Nepali Left towards building a strong people's movement to overthrow capitalism or even to ensure that some policies of welfare capitalism are implemented. If one looks at the agreement that was signed on February 3, 2011 between the Communist Party of Nepal-Unified Marxist Leninist (CPN-UML) and the Unified Communist Party of Nepal-Maoist

(UCPN-M) for support in the prime ministerial election it fails to generate any radical impression. It talks in the rhetoric of ending all forms of feudalism, protect national independence, be patriotic, ensure an inclusive democracy and develop a pro-people political order[1]. The alternatives to the status quo are not very clear in the agreement unless they were hastily drafted. May 2018 indicated a huge win for the Left in Nepal electorally as the Communist Party of Nepal (United Marxist Leninist) (CPN-UML) and Communist Party of Nepal (Maoist Centre) were unified as Nepal Communist Party. Prime Minister K.P. Oli outlined the agenda by saying that "It's a historical day for Nepal; it has entered a new era of prosperity. The party unification will help Nepal in upgrading from the least developed country and will help to achieve sustainable development goals and poverty alleviation, among others." On the other hand, Pushpa Kamal Dahal observed: "A new era of prosperity and good governance has started in the country. The major motive of this unification is to lead the country towards socialism and economic prosperity with social justice."[2]

The challenge for the landlocked country to move towards any alternative form of government will be huge. However, it will also face challenges on the front of retaining the agenda of a socialist future in its party programme and get reduced to a political force, which strives at making capitalism more human. In situations of this kind, the past tells us, challenges of how well can one keep the party away from the government in terms of the party being the movement, the mobilizer and the government being the instrument of implementing what the party professes will be greater. The challenge also remains about how the Left in Nepal addresses the gender question, the caste question and also remains sensitive to human suffering at the cost of development. This becomes specially true when one looks at the question of equal participation of women in leadership of the Left parties. "The Maoists' commitment to women's emancipation helped raise awareness. Large numbers of women joined the Maoist People's Liberation Army, especially from marginalized caste and ethnic groups. But the senior Maoist leadership has remained all men" (Baniya et al. 2017, p. 4). Many more challenges have been posed on how the Left addressed the women's question in the movement as well as after attaining power.

The situation in Bangladesh also presents an interesting picture wherein the Left tradition of a strong peasant and worker organization/mobilization has failed to sustain. In fact, senior Left intellectual Badruddin Umar argues that "in the situation obtaining in Bangladesh… there exist very small Communist organizations which operate outside the framework of ruling class politics… It is, therefore, no exaggeration to say that the left as a political force has long been ineffective in Bangladesh. What is known as left, particularly the traditional left, may be described as left of the ruling class"(Umar, 2015, p. 206). There are also analyses, which argue that in a situation of bitter divide between "'secularist' and 'fundamentalist' forces and violent street politics" did provide an opportunity for emergence of the Left but the opportunity has been missed (Sarkar). The Shahbag kind of uprisings, for such analysts, becomes a positive indicator for "broadening and revising the scope and vitality of the Left" (Sarkar, 2015, p. 239). The questions that remain important in the Bangladeshi context is whether a Left organizational movement is emerging or has even the possibility of emergence rooted in a class analysis of the widespread discontent against a variety of issues. In the recent past, people have come out on the streets indicating the discontent but they are misdirected and it destroys the possibility of any Left assertion when the organizations calling themselves Left become part of the state, which creates this discontent.

The political condition in India has taken a turn for the worse. The political regime has raised concerns of a different kind—while it has entrenched corporate capital behind it the idiom of nationalism, religious hatred and a systematic takeover of things considered 'public' at the same time characterize this regime. Ghosh (2016) argues:

> Let us not be mistaken, this political regime is not Fascism. It is something much worse and far more intractable. This regime, as we have maintained for a while now, is characterized by a hitherto unprecedented level of generalization of the state of exception. Much

> more than what was seen in Nazi Germany, Fascist Italy, or Imperial Japan—to say nothing of Francoist Spain or Salazarian Portugal. This unprecedented level of generalization, and thus normalization, of the state of exception is on account of the neoliberal conjunctural specificity of post-Fordism-induced uncontrollable all-round precarity; and India's historically unique location within it.

Given this situation the Left politics in India has not been very promising either. The Left is represented by the parties collapsed gradually and much faster post-1989. Analysts would attribute it to the collapse of the Soviet model and its impact across the globe and many would attribute it to the turmoil within the country, which complicated the questions of class as caste acquired new significance in the wake of the Mandal Commission movement. Some scholars attribute it to the process of "empiricization" which meant "the pursuit of a political praxis that is uninformed by the project of transcending capitalism" (Pattnaik, 2011, p. 12). Some scholars see systemic oppression of people who are oppressed by "feudal remnants" in "collusion with imperialism and native capitalism" not being addressed by the Left political forces (Gohain, 2011, p. 79). None of the Left forces fight for their rights except "in parliamentary fora and legislatures, cushioned from the actual circumstances ad stresses of struggle on the ground" (ibid., pp. 79-80). Charges are levelled against the Left for assimilating the attitudes of the ruling classes, for succumbing to the "capitalist paradigm of development" and so on.

Jal argues that "we have seen the fallacy of socialism that is built on the principles of the commodity and the state. We saw they became Frankenstein-like monsters, to borrow Marx's phrase "independent beings endowed with life"... We have also seen that the left in India has embraced these Frankenstein-like beings". He furthers his argument that the Left has not been able to conceptualise even caste "and how caste is inexorably linked to modern classes, political power and ideological hegemony" (Jal, 2012, p. 57). Within these evaluations of the nature of Left politics are also elements of a futuristic vision of the direction that the movement should take. While Ghosh (2016) takes a position which does not see much possibility in the way Left politics is oriented to understand and address the current situation, Bhattacharya (2011, p. 73) dwells on the possibilities from within the existing Left and argues that the way forward for some is to have "a radical realignment of Left forces on the basis of united struggle". Given that the disastrous consequences of neoliberalism are being felt by each section of society the Left needs to get "integrated with the developing resistance of various sections of the people" to generate "the momentum... for a resurgence of the Left."

Vanaik (2012) tries to balance the arguments of battles on the street and the parliamentarism. "...the balance between parliamentary-electoral pursuits and extra-parliamentary mobilization activity must always be tilted strongly towards the latter" (p. 13). He makes a case of how certain political aspects, which appear social democratic might be important in the battle against capitalism:

> The left must, of course, start with and propose various social democratic perspectives such as strong welfarism, full employment, green economics, greater social and cultural rights and more empowerment of ordinary people, not because it believes that these are fully or properly achievable within capitalism but precisely because they are not! Therefore, such demands and the struggle for their achievement can be the spur towards the creation of a much more radical understanding of the need to break with capitalism as soon as possible. In short, the Indian left even as circumstances and its own failings have put it more on the defensive than in its past, it must now be more radical in its programme and practice than ever before (p. 13).

It is a complicated situation wherein the discontent does not seem to be producing a rebellion against the system that produces the discontent, wherein capitalism invents a variety of mechanisms to either circumvent the attention from the actual conflicts and reasons for the discontent and the larger 'anti-systemic' mobilization seem to be motivated towards those momentary reliefs from one version of capitalism vis-à-vis the other version. Embedded in this situation are debates about how the questions of gender, caste and tribals would be addressed. In other words, the necessity to imagine a new politics that addresses these hitherto ignored questions within the

Left politics within the region have also emerged as attacks against writers, LGBT activists or 'rationalists' are getting killed across the region. At the same time the question of strategy acquires significance. Hence, will the Left battle be one in which it becomes part of the outrightly oppressive regimes such as in Sri Lanka (under Rajapakse) or in Bangladesh (under Sheikh Hasina) or will it be a battle that will address all these questions but locates the solution within the politics of transcending capitalism? Forging an alliance is not only a class question as pointed above in context of Bangladesh or India but it has its own complexities. Engels wrote way back in 1894 about one aspect of what alliance with bourgeois political forces might mean:

> After the joint victory we might be offered a few seats in the new government, but always in a minority. This is the greatest danger. After February 1848 the French socialist democrats (of the Réforme, Ledru-Rollin, L. Blanc, Flocon, etc.) made the mistake of occupying such seats. As a minority in the government they voluntarily shared the blame for all the foul deeds and betrayals perpetrated by the majority of pure republicans against the workers; whilst the presence of these gentlemen in the government completely paralysed the revolutionary action of the working class which they claimed to represent.

Connected to this question of alliance is also the identification of who will go along with the Left politics and till what stage[3]. Hence, emerges the complicated nomenclatures and universe of many leftists and communists. This had emerged significantly after the defeat of the CPI(M) in West Bengal. A statement signed by over 200 people had stressed that there were many Lefts in India apart from the parties. It said:

> ...*the Left in India is not the Left parties alone and therefore the defeat of the Left parties does not mean the defeat of the Left.* The Left in India has never been reducible to these large parliamentary fronts and party machines, much less to the groups embattled in the forests of India, but has always been a much wider spectrum of organizations, movements and forms of struggle that range from the hundreds of left-wing trade unions that exist in the country in all the major industrial centres, unions that are essentially independent of party control and seeking today to form a

national federation, down to the dozens of popular campaigns and the organizations connected with them" (Kafila, 2011).

Accepting that there needs to be a debate among these Left forces their categorization must *ultimately* emerge from the nature of politics that they are engaged in and more *importantly* whether their politics aims at transcending capitalism or not. Papers represent this sensibility of initiating a debate, widening the agenda for a Left politics and exploring the possibilities in terms of analysis and politics in the region. This also informs the range of issues that are covered within this volume.

NOTES

1. The seven-point agreement between the UCPN (Maoist) and UML, available at http://www.satp.org/satporgtp/countries/nepal/document/papers/cpm2011agreement.htm (accessed on February 10, 2018).
2. These leaders were quoted by the press after unification. More details can be found at Xinhua (May 18, 2018) Nepal's two major parties merge to form the Nepal Communist Party, available at http://europe.chinadaily.com.cn/a/201805/18/WS5afe2857a3103f6866ee9295.html (accessed May 19, 2018).
3. It is interesting to remember what Engels wrote in the preface to the 1888 English edition of the Manifesto of the Communist Party. He was trying to not only tell us the reason why he along with Marx used the word 'communist' but was also trying to discern the difference between the two terms:

   "…we could not have called it a socialist manifesto. By Socialists, in 1847, were understood, on the one hand the adherents of the various Utopian systems: Owenites in England, Fourierists in France, both of them already reduced to the position of mere sects, and gradually dying out; on the other hand, the most multifarious social quacks who, by all manner of tinkering, professed to redress, without any danger to capital and profit, all sorts of social grievances, in both cases men outside the working-class movement, and looking rather to the "educated" classes for support. Whatever portion of the working class had become convinced of the insufficiency of mere political revolutions, and had proclaimed the necessity of total social change, called itself Communist. It was a crude, rough-hewn, purely instinctive sort of communism; still, it touched the cardinal point and was powerful enough amongst the working class to produce the Utopian communism of Cabet in France, and of Weitling in Germany. Thus, in 1847, socialism was a middle-class movement, communism a working-class movement. Socialism was, on the Continent at least, "respectable"; communism was the very opposite. And as our notion, from the very beginning, was that "the emancipation of the workers must be the act of the working class itself," there could be no doubt as to which of the two names we must take. Moreover, we have, ever since, been far from repudiating it" (Engels 1888: 08).

REFERENCES:

Baniya, Jeevan et al. (September 2017) *Gender and Nepal's Transition from War*, Conciliation Resources: London.

Bhattacharya, Dipankar (November 19, 2011) 'For a Left Resurgence', *Economic and Political Weekly*, Vol. 46, No. 47, pp. 71-73.

Bhusal, Ghanashyam (2013) 'The Revolutionary Task of Left Parties in Nepal', in Bhusal, Ghanashyam and Shahi, Yogendra (eds.) *The Left Debate in Nepal: A Nepalese Discourse on Left Ideology, State Restructuring, Development Policies and Programmes*, Centre for Nepal Studies and Rosa Luxemburg Stiftung: Kathmandu.

Chibber, Vivek (2006) 'On the Decline of Class Analysis in South Asian Studies', *Critical Asian Studies*, 38:4, pp. 357-387.

Engels, Frederick (1894) *The Future Italian Revolution and the Socialist Party*, available at https://marxists.catbull.com/archive/marx/works/1894/01/26.htm (Accessed on January 20, 2017).

Ghosh, Pothik (February 23, 2016) 'Fascism or Dictatorship of Neoliberal Capital? The Need for a Correct Line', *Radical Notes*, available at https://radicalnotes.org/2016/02/23/fascism-or-dictatorship-of-neoliberal-capital-the-need-for-a-correct-line/ (Accessed January 12, 2017).

Gohain, Hiren (September 17-23, 2011) 'Decline of the Left: A Critical Comment', *Economic and Political Weekly*, Vol. 46, No. 38 , pp. 79-80.

Mishra, Chaitanya (1987) 'Development and Underdevelopment: A Preliminary Sociological Perspective', *Occasional Papers in Sociology and Anthropology,* Vol. 1, 1987, pp. 105-135.

Mishra, Chaitanya (2013) 'Social Democracy: The Most Progressive System' in Kattel, Mukunda (ed. 2013) *Debating Transformation*, General Federation of Nepalese Trade Unions (GEFONT): Kathmandu.

Mishra, Chaitanya (June 10, 2014) 'Nepal and Capitalism', *Kathmandu Post*, available at http://kathmandupost.ekantipur.com/printedition/news/2014-06-09/nepal-and-capitalism.html (Accessed on March 13, 2018).

Jal, Murzban (June 16, 2012) 'On Understanding the Decline of the Established Indian Left', *Economic and Political Weekly*, Vol. 47, No. 24, pp. 49-58.

Kafila (May 24, 2011) 'End of the Left' in India? Statement by Leftists After Recent Election Results', available at https://kafila.online/2011/05/24/end-of-the-left-in-india-statement-after-recent-election-results/ (Accessed on July 18, 2018).

Patnaik, Prabhat (July 16-22, 2011) 'The Left in Decline', *Economic and Political Weekly*, Vol. 46, No. 29, pp. 12-16.

Sarkar, Srimanti (2015) 'The Role of the Left in Bangladesh's Democracy: Challenges and Prospects', in Dasgupta, Subhoranjan (ed.) *Democratic Governance and Politics of the Left in South Asia*, pp. 228-244, Aakar Books: New Delhi.

Umar, Badruddin (2015) 'Left in Bangladesh: Past and Present" in Dasgupta, Subhoranjan (ed.) *Democratic Governance and Politics of the Left in South Asia*, pp. 198-206, Aakar Books: New Delhi.

Vanaik, Achin (October 13, 2012)'Future Perspectives for the Mainstream Indian Left', *Economic and Political Weekly*, Vol. 47, No. 41, pp. 12-14.

2

Power and Resistance in Modi's India

Radhika Desai

The dominant questions in Indian politics today concern Hindutva and the Modi government: What accounts for such success as it has enjoyed? How firm and lasting is its hold on power? And, more generally, what does it mean for Indian politics? Is it just a continuation of politics as before, with the BJP (Bharatiya Janata Party) and the Sangh Parivar simply replacing Congress as the 'dominant party'? Or do Modi's government and through it the proximity of the Sangh Parivar to state power represent something altogether more serious and fearsome, an unbridled turn under Hindutva's first majority government, to fascist modes of governance with all their authoritarianism, para-state violence and excoriation of public institutions? Either way, what does it portend for secular and democratic, let alone socialist, feminist and anti-casteist, forces seeking to oppose the present government and Hindutva in general?

Many commentaries, scholarly and journalistic, typically portray Hindutva as storming to power on episodic waves of irrational and violent mobilizations. While they undoubtedly play a role, Hindutva's march to power has, in fact, been decades long and powered by the creation of a distinct social base. It dates back at least to the days of 'non-Congressism' of the 1960s and the post-Emergency Janata experiment of the 1970s. Such success as the BJP enjoys today (and it is all-too-exaggerated by journalists and scholars alike, as we shall see below, and remains far short of what would be necessary for stable rule and repeated election victories) has had to overcome many obstacles, although it has also benefited from the shortcomings of competing and opposing political forces. Even after the rise of the Hindutva accelerated in the late 1980s, turbo-charged, no doubt, by the mobilizations surrounding various rath yatras and Ram Mandir agitations, its advance was interrupted by a decade of Congress-led United Progressive Alliance rule. In addition, while the Modi government certainly represents further advance, it is not sufficiently secure to guarantee it another Lok Sabha majority.

The literature on Hindutva, built up during its long march to power, provides a various of answers to the questions posed above. It is too extensive to cite here in full though key works, which my argument relies on or detracts from, will be referred to in what follows. However, practically all of it examines one or another phase or episode or regional aspect of the political and electoral progress of Hindutva. Such analyses are easy prey to simplistic assumptions and hype in the media that exaggerate Hindutva's power and dissimulates its dangers.

By contrast, beginning in the late 1990s, I have accumulated a body of work which has evolved a framework in which to track Hindutva's line of advance out of its original base in the upper-caste and middle class petty bourgeoisie of Hindi heartland towns to most of India's states over the decades (Desai 1999, 2004a, 2004b, 2004c, 2010, 2011, 2014, 2016). The framework sets Hindutva's advance first and foremost against an account of India's changing political economy, particularly the turn towards more neoliberal or marketist policies beginning already in the late 1960s and the social changes to India's caste and class structure it set in train (2007, 2010b, 2017b and 2017c). The result is a framework for analysing the evolution of Indian politics as a complex picture composed of three trends, all halting, geographically uneven and deeply intertwined. Of these, the rise of Hindutva is one; the other two are the long-term decline of Congress and the rise of Parties of the Provincial Propertied Classes (PPPCs). The last belong to the grab-bag category loosely labelled 'regional parties' in scholarly and journalistic discourse but actually constitute a distinct part of it. The PPPCs are parties based primarily on dominant caste propertied groups in the states. These parties have proliferated since the late 1960s, successfully won state power in many of them and, between 1989 and 2014 were critical to holding power in New Delhi.

Each Lok Sabha election this century has been analysed in the same framework (2004a, 2010a and 2014) as has every State Assembly election in Gujarat, modelling how this framework can be applied at the state level (Desai 2004, 2010 and 2012). While there have been some other attempts at producing an overall framework for what one may call a 'comparative politics of Indian states' (see Harriss 1999, for example), my framework is distinctive in seeking to analyse Indian politics at the national and state levels in a consistent and historical materialist fashion. This requires taking account of the concurrent dynamics of political economy, the social structure of caste and class and the political party systems that gave rise to in India's states and at the national level. My work draws much of its inspiration from, but also seeks to systematize, extend to the present and to the national level the work on state level politics done in Francine Frankel and M.S.A. Rao's important two-volume edited collection, *Dominance and State Power in Modern India* (1989).

A final key distinction: unlike the vast bulk of the literature on the BJP and the Sangh Parivar, and against many who deny it (Jaffrelot 1993, Vanaik 1994), this framework is able to give due consideration to the fascist character of the Sangh Parivar (Desai 2014, 2016, 2017a). It understands the BJP as a fascist party as well as India's 'normal' party of the right. The BJP demonstrated its fascist character amply whenever it has assumed power, in the NDA coalition between 1998 and 2004 at the national level and in the states it has ruled so far. Its distinctive signatures include undermining and saffronizing public institutions, intimidating minorities, ethnically cleansing uppercaste and middle caste neighbourhoods, assaulting secular culture, its movements and activists, and deploying para-state violence, most spectacularly in the 2002 genocide of Muslims in Gujarat but also elsewhere against lower castes, women, Adivasis, minorities and political opponents. Today the Modi government rules without the hindrance of an effective opposition, let alone potentially troublesome coalition partners, having been handed that prize by a corporate class that practically singlehandedly created a sense of economic crisis under the previous government (Ghatak et al., 2014) and funded Modi's campaign to an extent practically unmatched anywhere (Vardharajan 2014).

Recognizing Hindutva's fascist character matters because it is not just a question of labels but fundamental to understanding its dynamics in power, to the even greater dangers this government could lead the country to. As an exceptional form of bourgeois rule, Fascism is distinctive in having its own autonomous political force with the means of violence—such as the fascist or Nazi movements or the RSS—which it offers as a supplement to state force in the service of bourgeois interests. This makes taking the fascist option—which a capitalist class may do out of desperation or a foolhardy choice—inherently dangerous. Whether the capitalist classes that took this option recognize it or not, as Ian Kershaw pointed out, it contains the possibility of fascist forces asserting their autonomy vis a vis the social forces—the propertied or capitalist classes—that brought them to power. As I observed it in 2014,

> Whether the Modi government crosses the bounds of constitutionality or the norms of bourgeois rule—which in India, with its everyday police brutality, judicial malfeasance and executive and legislative corruption, are admittedly rather wide in any case—to become an exceptional state, and whether it supplants or supplements state force with Sangh Parivar goons, and does so in ways that assert their autonomy from its capitalist backers remains to be seen. Events may (is one being too hopeful?) unfold in ways that sidestep these possibilities. That the new government contains these possibilities is not in doubt (Desai 2014: 48).

There could be any number of circumstances in which the Sangh Parivar would end up asserting its autonomy in dangerous, violent, war-like and unpredictable ways: attempting to avert a looming loss at the polls by creating a national or international emergency is certainly one of them. The ways in which this could be executed

> include excessively zealous repression and persecution of opposition forces and minorities and, of course, implementation of Hindutva's 'core agenda'–a uniform civil code attacking the country's Muslim minority, abrogation of Article 370 of the Indian constitution giving special status to the Union's only Muslim majority state, and construction

> of a Ram temple at the site still disputed by Muslims. Any and all of these can be guaranteed to result in acute political problems and/or considerable violence, with or without external implications (Desai 2016: 74).

If and when such strategies are pursued by the Sangh Parivar, the country, will be transported from the frying pan into the fire and the full scale of the dangers to which India's corporate capitalist classes have exposed the country for no other reason than their preference for a government devoted entirely to the pursuit of their interests over one that needed to offer a few concessions to the vast masses of the poor in order to maintain a stable electoral base, will be fully revealed.

The Evolution of Party Politics in Independent India

For a historical materialist account of Indian politics and its evolution in recent decades, it is important to place three critical elements into a single picture: the shift in India's political economy from planning to increasingly marketist or neoliberal policies; how it has shaped the combined caste and class structuring of Indian society, particularly the rise of the provincial propertied classes (PPCs); and how this is manifest in politics, changing India's party-political landscape over the decades as Congress declined, new parties of the provincial propertied classes (PPPCs) emerged and Hindutva advanced. Understanding this makes it clear that the Modi government represents an overshooting of the potential for Hindutva's advance that they contained.

It is hardly necessary to rehearse the progressive liberalization of economic policy in India in recent decades (Chandrashekhar and Ghosh 2004). The key point to note is that it did not begin, as most assume, with the 1992 IMF Structural Adjustment programme but predated it by more than two decades. The key turning point was the adoption of the green revolution approach to raising production and productivity in Indian agriculture. For that decision marked the admission of the Congress government that it did not have the political capacity to carry through its strategy of planned industrialization. The Indian state would no longer attempt to engineer an agrarian transition which would be compatible with industrialization and an egalitarian path of growth with a broad and deep domestic market (as outlined, for instance, in Frankel 2005, Patnaik 1995). It was a final admission that the Congress did not have the political capacity to carry it through because its power rested precisely on the groups—regionally varied middle or 'dominant' caste peasants—who were most opposed to that plan. These groups shunted economic policy onto an increasingly liberal and marketist track.

It is important to identify this juncture as the critical turning point in the evolution of India's political economy because, compared to the policy changes after 1992, the decisions of the late 1960s affected a larger sector and far more people than those of the early 1990s. The socio-economic processes it set lose also resulted in widening and deepening political support for these policies without, of course, ever amounting to an electoral or social majority. Since then economic policy has been turning increasingly marketist, more and more neoliberal (Ghosh 1998) leading to higher levels of inequality and, as it constrains demand, to a self-limiting growth path (Patnaik 1995).

While the new green revolution strategy increased production with critical inputs from the state, it also exacerbated inequalities in the countryside and accelerated the development of capitalism there. This constituted a 'slow-motion counterrevolution' through which the upper and dominant caste propertied classes in the countryside executed an agrarian transition of their own:

> These originally landed groups, whose political power is still so seldom recognized, not only undermined the planners' vision of an egalitarian agrarian transition as the basis of an autonomous and self-sustaining process of industrialization, *they effected an agrarian transition of their own devising, on their own terms.* Refusing to surrender their surpluses to the state, demanding that, instead, the state facilitate their enrichment, *they invested the resulting surpluses outside agriculture themselves, expanding their fields of activity and prosperity* (Desai 2017).

Not only did green revolution policies accelerate the rise of an agricultural bourgeoisie, as that class made investments in urban and industrial sectors, it was transformed into a bourgeoisie as such, or rather into the many regional bourgeoisies whom K. Balagopal dubbed the 'provincial propertied classes'. Their rise and characteristics are now the subject of a burgeoning literature, scholarly and journalistic (see, for instance, Varma 1998, Mishra 1995, Stern 2003, Rutten 1995, Baru 2000, Damodaran 2013). These regional bourgeoisies constituted the single most important addition to India's 'proliferating' bourgeoisie (Patnaik et al. 1996). The PPCs were more successful in those parts of the country where capitalist economic development was relatively rapid and sustained, such as Gujarat or Andhra, and weaker where it was not, such as in Eastern UP and Bihar.

Politically, these groups formed the Congress's rural base but, as their economic success grew, they were decreasingly willing to accept their subordination to the upper caste Congress leadership. Beginning as early as the late 1960s, these groups had begun striking out on their own, forming new parties focused on assuming power in their respective states. These parties were initially focused on favourable fiscal and other policies towards agriculture and were part of larger farmers' movements. However, as their interests widened to include urban, industrial and service sectors, so did their politics. The resulting Parties of the Provincial Propertied Classes (PPPCs) have since become a fixture on the Indian political scene. Occasionally reversed here or there, the process has continued across the country and has left Congress in possession of a social base consisting of the country's lower castes and classes and minorities though its 'high command' remains in the hands of its notoriously upper caste and class leadership which is simply unable to accommodate the ambitions of its middle castes. These developments, the decline of Congress, the rise of the regional parties and the rise of Hindutva (as well as its monopolization of the space on the right) are clearly visible in the two charts indicating the seats they won in the Lok Sabha and the vote shares they commanded (Desai 2014):

Chart 1: Seats Won by Party Category

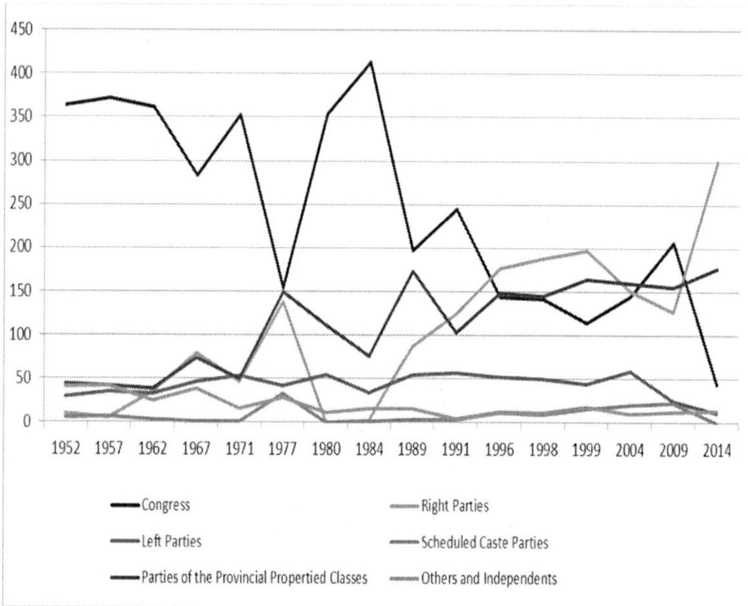

However, so far at least, as became clear in the 1990s in the fate of the V.P. Singh and Deve Gowda/Gujral governments, the PPPCs have been unable to constitute themselves into a national force and, in any case, they are susceptible to the charms of Hindutva. Indeed, as I have argued, Hindutva's purpose in a sense is to articulate new terms of inclusion of the middle castes into a pan Indian propertied class (Desai 2004c). Its power is stable precisely to the extent that it can accomplish this and it has accomplished this to greatest effects in some states where no PPPC has emerged and the provincial propertied class has been absorbed directly into the BJP (though the faultline between them and the upper castes remains active). Elsewehre, most PPPCs remained willing to ally with the BJP in state and national governments.

Chart 2: Vote Share by Party Category

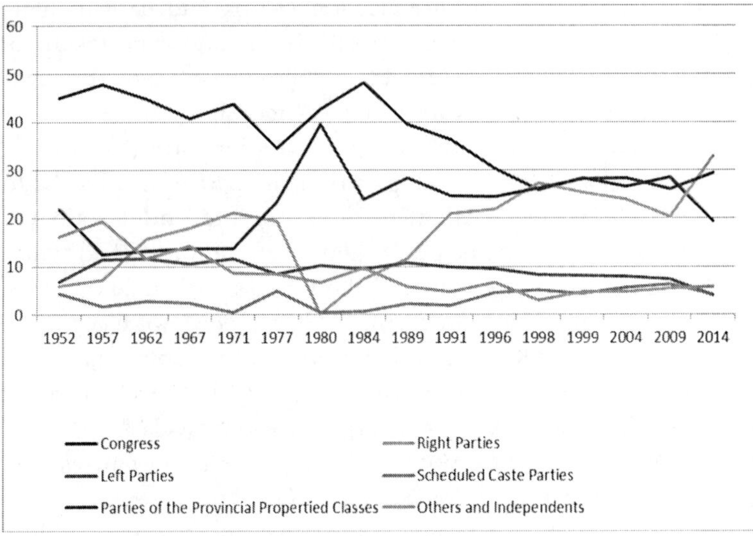

The Specificity of the Modi Government

Against this background, the Modi government is historically specific in a number of ways. It is not a simple continuation of the BJP's advance in recent years; that advance is still far short of what a parliamentary majority would require in normal circumstances. In 2014 Modi's parliamentary majority was so greatly in disproportion to the BJP's vote share that it is unlikely to be repeated (discussed below).

What electoral advance 2014 represented over previous elections was made possible by the corporate funding and backing Modi enjoyed. It was organized and articulated by the idea, dressed up as a theory by the likes of Jagdish Bhagwati and Arvind Panagariya, that the Congress government had become paralyzed and that Modi could galvanize government to clear projects proposed by big corporations and advance them by easing land acquisition, dealing with political resistance, etc. However, this 'theory' is inadequate as a tool of economic policy: even if it is carried out to the hilt it could fail to satisfy Modi's corporate backers, to produce enough growth, to say nothing of producing growth of a degree and quality that could secure and extend the support Modi enjoys to the extent necessary to give him another election victory and parliamentary majority. Thus Modi's re-election prospects cannot be taken for granted. As we shall see in the next section, this remains true even after the widely hailed victory in Uttar Pradesh.

However, the scale and enthusiasm of the corporate backing Modi enjoys does set the Modi government apart. While the NDA (National Democratic Alliance) governments under Vajpayee represented a complex electoral coalition of the propertied which included the small propertied and the professional middle classes, the Modi government represents the unalloyed power of a corporate capitalist class which is itself the result of the combination of decades of economic liberalism and the world-wide development of capitalism. Tensions between the corporate capitalist class and other, lesser capitalists have the potential to become important as they appear to have in the Patel agitation in Gujarat.

Another important point to bear in mind about the Modi government is that its rather precarious perch of governmental power has been made possible because both Congress and the left find themselves at the lowest ebb of their power. At the same time, any effective opposition to the fascist Sangh Parivar and Modi will require an alliance of all forces opposed to them in an alliance of the UPA sort or a 'Mahagathbandhan' of the sort that kept Bihar out of the BJP's grasp. While Congress's own decline has advanced far enough by the early 21st century that it could not return to power on its own, the rise in support for the left after six years of the BJP-led NDA government and with the support of key PPPCs the Congress was able to form two successive coalition governments. Whether this is possible today remains an open question and will certainly need to lure many more PPPCs.

This is, however, an obstacle that must be overcome for successful resistance to the Modi government because the political capacities of other, non-party, forces are simply not up to the challenge, despite the fetishization of the political capacities of NGOs, civil society organizations and small-scale social movements to effect progressive social change as opposed to political parties in recent decades. In a sense, they are the political counterpart of neoliberalism. While these forces are undoubtedly critical to maintaining high levels of political engagement, they can only effect change in conjunction with effective parties. They are simply too small, disparate and incoherent and, in themselves, reflect, rather than challenge, the hierarchies of civil society, that quintessentially capitalist social form.

Finally, as in most Western nations the professional middle classes have come to dominate the political life of India's national parties at least. Historically, alliances between these groups and popular classes (such as the alliance between intellectuals and workers in the social democratic parties of Europe) have been the political backbone of progressive politics. However, today, with the professionalization of politics, these classes dominate parties across the political spectrum and—like the Liberal Democrats in England or the AAP (Aam Admi Party) in India often form parties of their own. At the same time, however, they are more removed from the grass roots of politics than before, unable to reflect the priorities of ordinary people. The results can be seen in the waves of anti-establishmentarian politics from Sanders and Trump to Brexit. This phenomenon particularly afflicts the left and the national parties and constitutes a major obstacle in the advance of progressive politics and alternatives.

The Limits and Dangers of the 'Modi Magic'

What light does the preceding analysis shed on the Modi government's performance so far and its prospects in 2019? After elections in five states in early 2017, hard on the heels of the draconian demonetization experiment which wreaked havoc on the poorer sections of society (Ghosh et al., 2017), Modi's BJP was able to form the government in four. This fact was seized upon by some as underlining the unstoppable momentum behind Modi and his 'magic', with some even speaking of the BJP as India's 'second dominant party' (Palshikar 2017). This latter judgment rests on two key points. First, Palshikar argues that in 2014 the BJP 'inaugurated a new framework of party competition' in which

> The BJP clearly emerged as the dominant party not in mere numeric terms, but more substantively. It stretched to a large number of states, received support from a cross section of the society, placed the leadership factor at the centre of competitive politics and above all, set the tone for the political debates. Since then, but also during that election, the BJP and Modi made every effort to set aside the state-specific factors, make them less relevant and bring about an all-India imagination that dominated the electorate. This feature of the BJP's politics went against the established pattern of state-dominated competition (Palshikar 2017).

Secondly, according to Palshikar, the BJP redefined the ideological terrain. Without giving up Hindutva, the BJP injected the 'idea of development' into Indian political discourse, giving it a new meaning such that his 'new India' was 'a land of *opportunities rather than doles*' (Palshikar 2017).

In a slightly different argument, Yogendra Yadav also heralded a BJP 'hegemony' with three components: its 'brute power' unlike any other central government that includes the unconstitutional elements and para-state forces'; it's 'electoral dominance' which reached a new peak with the state assembly elections of early 2017; and 'moral and ideological acceptance of the regime by the people'. Yadav also noted three major limitations of this legitimacy: its exclusive character, barring minorities; the 'spin-doctoring' it entails; and the dearth of 'objective grounds for this popularity' given the economic slowdown', seemingly unaware of how these qualifications contradict his verdict of a BJP 'hegemony' (Yadav 2017). Of course, nothing succeeds like success and there were even those who were willing to argue that the demonetization debacle must have served Modi well: 'Despite its uncertain benefits and immediate toll on voters, demonetisation ... had great *signalling* value—the intended message was that only a very tough leader who is committed to controlling corruption can undertake a politically risky, disruptive, and potentially costly move like this' (Ghatak 2017).

However, there are many reasons to question such judgments of BJP strength. In this section we concentrate on those that emerge from the nature and extent of the 2014 victory and the BJP's electoral performance since. It is true, as Palshikar notes, that the BJP under Modi won the first single party majority in the Lok Sabha in three decades. However, he takes little note of the circumstances in which it was won and, more surprisingly for a political scientist, of the distorting effect of India's single member plurality or 'first-past-the-post' electoral system and its distorting effects. They require us to pay closer attention to the patterns of political partisanship.

Perhaps the most important thing about Modi's 2014 Lok Sabha election victory is that Modi secured the backing of India's powerful corporate classes by promising to bring the 'Gujarat Model' of development to New Delhi. In return, they supported Modi's campaign more fulsomely and munificently than any other (Vardharajan 2014). This support allowed the campaign to spare no expense. Modi's messages – about 'development' as well as the trademark communal ones – blared out of practically every media orifice that would be marshalled: hoarding, print, staged rallies and events, the holograms of Modi which characterized the campaign and, of course, TV. With the communal message was directed at the hard core of Sangh supporters, who were also treated to communal riots, as in Muzaffarnagar, and the 'development' message aimed at the rest, Modi campaigned with the usual Sangh Parivar 'forked tongue'. The Indian media, which had never distinguished itself in its principled opposition to Hindutva was now rendered even more pliant thanks to the corporate backing Modi had won. It now dutifully peddled the view that the Modi government had given up communalism in favour of development.

Despite the all-out effort that the Modi-led BJP was able to unleash, its election victory a considerably more modest achievement than the echo chamber of the mindless media celebration of the BJP's Lok Sabha majority seemed to believe. Modi was able to form the first single party majority government on a paltry 31 per cent of the popular vote. The next smallest share of the popular vote on which a single party majority government had proved possible in the past was Indira Gandhi's 1980 comeback. But even it was more than 10 per cent higher at 42.69 per cent. If we take into account the turnout, Modi's BJP had the support of only a quarter of the electorate as a whole. While the 'first past the post' system can usually be relied on to deliver disproportional results, the magnitude of the disproportionality in 2014 was unprecedented, a fluke unlikely to be repeated.

Moreover, the BJP's performance in the State Assembly elections during and after 2014 leaves much to be desired. Despite the well-funded campaign, the BJP's performance in the 5 State Assembly elections that took place alongside the 2014 Lok Sabha elections (Andhra Pradesh, Arunachal, Odisha, Sikkim and Telangana) left much to be desired. The BJP formed a government in coalition in only one state with Congress and various other PPPCs forming governments in the other four. Palshikar's idea that Modi has imposed a new national integration on India's politics clearly smacks of the sort of wishful thinking India's professional middle classes indulge in than objective analysis.

The BJP did go on to form governments in all four of the elections that followed later that year in Haryana, Jharkhand and Maharashtra, where the BJP had been strong for some time, and Jammu and Kashmir, where it formed an unprecedented coalition with the PDP (People's Democratic Party) in Jammu and Kashmir. However, in 2015 and 2016, the BJP was able to form a government in coalition in only one state, Assam, while losing the other states to local PPPCs (Tamil Nadu, West Bengal), the Left Democratic Front (Kerala) and Congress (Puducherry). Things became sufficiently serious to prompt Modi into a major cabinet reshuffle in the summer of 2016 but even here, his preference for control over performance, even electoral performance, means that it is unlikely to help his party's election prospects. Indeed, his repressive and controlling style may be accumulating discontents in the Sangh Parivar itself.

Those elections marked the half-way point of the BJP's term in office and clearly the BJP was treading water. It needed to regain and indeed, given the unlikelihood of a repeat of the 2014 translation of votes into seats, greatly extend its support if it was to have a chance at winning the 2019 elections. If the mainstream media and the political scientists cited above are to be believed the elections in early 2017, which led to the BJP forming governments in 4 (Goa, Manipur, Uttar Pradesh and Uttarakhand), ceding only Punjab to Congress, have delivered precisely that. Even here, however, things are not quite what they seem. Not only was the 'anti-incumbency' factor at work in all 5 elections, and not only did the BJP pull out all communal electioneering stops in Uttar Pradesh (Khare 2017), undoubtedly the jewel in the 2017 crown, despite these great exertions, the BJP scored a lower vote share in that state (39.7 per cent) than in the Lok Sabha elections of 2014 (42.63 per cent). Indeed, according to one rather insightful bit of number crunching, the BJP scored a higher share of the vote than in 2014 in only three of the last 16 State Assembly elections (Ray 2017). Finally, in the 2017 State Assembly elections, while the BJP had the majority in UP and Uttarakhand, only constitutionally questionable moves on the part of state governors allowed the BJP to form governments in Goa and Manipur, proving the utility of the spate of changes in governorships that Modi has undertaken.

This dismal electoral scorecard should not be surprising. In the nearly three years since assuming power the Modi government has amply demonstrated that not only did development not displace Hindutva on its agenda, such 'development' as it has pursued consists entirely of giving India's powerful corporate capitalist class what it wants as, indeed, its economic advisors had clearly indicated. However, this strategy has resulted, at best, in lacklustre growth, disappointing even the corporate classes who contributed so much to the Modi campaign, effectively buying him the Prime Ministership. A proper assessment of the government's economic performance is complicated by a major revision of the national accounts in 2014. They are impossible to compare with past years and most observers, including corporate sources, doubt the resulting numbers: the GDP growth rate of 7.4 per cent may place India at the top of the league tables of growth in major economies, it does not tally with the actual experience of economic slowdown, low credit growth and low inflation and a considerably lower Index of Industrial Production (Sridhar 2015). Given this actual economic experience on the ground, it is no wonder that the government's discontents are not confined to the usual suspects—workers and the poorer farmers, landless labourers, women and minorities. Today they include powerful constituencies, such as the Patidars in Gujarat, that are core components of the social base that the party of Hindutva had managed to consolidate over so many decades.

Coming amid this already troubled economic context, the demonetization debacle was, from the point of view of the Modi government, was surely at best an act of desperation and at worst the issue of a deathwish. The draconian experiment involved the sudden withdrawal of Rs. 500 and Rs. 1,000 notes from circulation, giving people limited time to deposit them in banks and/or exchanging them for notes of other denominations. With the overwhelming majority of the poor having no bank accounts and with practically no provision having been made for making notes of other denominations available, the measure could only have been the act of a government which held the vast majority of the country's people in supreme contempt. As various commentators have pointed out (Noorani 2017, Ghosh et al., 2017), not only did the measure make less sense even on its original justification of rooting out corruption—since 'black money' is rarely held in notes, since corrupton refers to illegal activities, not stocks of illegal funds, since the government was in any case promising to introduce new Rs. 2,000 notes—but the justification itself kept changing, culminating in the claim that it was meant to transform the Indian economy into a 'cashless' one. How this was to be done when vast swathes of India informal and petty producing sector operates only with cash and where the infrastructure of connectivity was lacking beggars the imagination.

The only rationale for the punitive and sadistic exercise that makes any sense given what we know about the BJP and Modi is that it was designed to deprive its political opponents of black money in State Assembly elections of early 2017, particularly in UP which the BJP had to win if a 2019 victory was to remain possible. In this the BJP may have succeeded but only by inflicting a level of harm on the people and the economy for so limited a partisan purpose that constitutes a shocking indictment of the government and telling sign of its desperation to gain some sort of electoral momentum in the runup to 2019 and also, perhaps, of its idiocy. For the entire effort to cloak the harm done by demonetization may be successfully through statistical jugglery (Sridhar 2017), the pervasive sense among people, business leaders and trade unions that it has exacted an enormous cost cannot be suppressed forever (Rajalakshmi 2017), a cost not likely to be forgotten or forgiven two years from now.

To this lacklustre economic performance, add mounting repression and unconstitutionality. The Modi government is engaged in both on economic issues such as appropriating land for the corporate sector or the Prime Minister besmirching the prestige of the second-highest office in the land with corporate endorsements. Both repression and unconstitutionality—on the part of the state and the Sangh Parivar forces of extra-state coercion that the Modi government commands—also pervade the actions and inactions of the government on matters relating to the saffronization of state and para-state structures including cultural and educational institutions, the heightening control of universities, the persecution of Dalits, Muslims and other minorities on arbitrary grounds, the murder of secular and left activists, the glorification of the army and the pursuit of an increasingly risky and dangerous strategy in relation to Kashmir and Pakistan chiefly in order to whip up support among the least salubrious elements at home. The list could go on.

Conclusion

All this should have been good news among centrist and left-of-centre forces had they not been a historic state of disarray. The project of resisting, let alone building an alternative to, Modi's BJP, is in far worse shape than the Modi government, electorally, politically and organizationally. The Congress is in a historic state of decline and disarray, barely able to maintain the pretence of viability as a national party under Sonia and Rahul Gandhi. While a number of Parties of the Provincial Propertied Classes in the country are unwilling to work with the BJP and the NDA, and Bihar's JDU (Janta Dal United) broke with the NDA precisely because it announced that Modi would be its prime ministerial candidate in 2013, all too many have become displaced by the BJP, such as the AGP (Assam Gana Parishad) or the various parties in Haryana, or remain willing to work with the BJP. While there has been an upsurge of protests against the Modi government, particularly those in India's public universities led by JNU (Jawaharlal Nehru University), they have failed to cohere into a single movement, let alone party. The left parties have suffered numerous setbacks in recent years and the CPI(M) (Communist Party of India (Marxist)) also finds itself internally divided whether the way forward lies in alliances with Congress just when the unprecedented weakness of Congress could be casting doubt on the viability of this option as was seen in the West Bengal State Assembly Elections this year which were swept by the Trinamool Congress for a second time. While substantial sections of the organized labour movement remain vigorous and progressive, while they are trying to reach out to the unorganized sector, while the network of NGOs and social movements seek to articulate various causes and positions even as they are persecuted in a variety of great and small ways by the government, no overall dynamic of resistance to Hindutva and Modi appears to be emerging.

REFERENCES

Balagopal, K. 1987. 'An Ideology for the Provincial Propertied Class', *Economic and Political Weekly*, Vol. XXII, Nos. 36 and 37, September 5-12. pp. 1546-7.

Baru, S. 2000. 'Economic Policy and the Development of Capitalism in India: The Role of Regional Capitalists and Political Parties' in F. Frankel, et al. (eds) *Transforming India*, New Delhi: Oxford University Press.

Byres, T.J. 1998. (ed). *The Indian Economy: Major Debates Since Independence*, New Delhi: Oxford University Press.

Chandrashekhar, C.P. and Jayati Ghosh. 2004. *The Market That Failed.* New Delhi: Leftword, 2nd rev. ed.

Damodaran, Harish. 2013. *India's New Capitalists: Caste, Business and Industry in a Modern Nation.* New Delhi: Permanent Black.

Desai, Radhika. 2017a. 'Hindutva and Fascism', A Review Essay on Jairus Banaji (ed), *Fascism: Essays on India and Europe*, *Economic and Political Weekly*, Vol. LI, No. 53, 31 December.

______. 2017b. 'The Slow-Motion Counterrevolution: Developmental Contradictions and the Emergence of Neoliberalism' in Kenneth B. Nielsen and Alf Gunvald Nilsen (eds). *Social Movements and the State in India: Deepening Democracy?* Basingstoke: Palgrave Macmillan.

______. 2017c. 'A BRIC Despite Itself: Sustained Growth versus Neoliberalism in India' in Richard Westra (ed). *The Political Economy of*

Emerging Markets Varieties of BRICS in the Age of Global Crises and Austerity. London: Routledge.

______. 2016. 'The Question of Fascism' in *Making Sense of Modi's India*, New Delhi, HarperCollins.

______. 2014. 'A Latter-Day Fascism?', *Economic and Political Weekly*, August 30, 2014, Vol. XLIX, No. 35, pp. 48-58.

______. 2012. 'India's New Right', *Frontline*, December 29, 2012, Vol. 29, Issue 26, http://www.flonnet.com/fl2926/stories/20130111292601900.htm.

______. 2011. 'Gujarat's Hindutva of Capitalist Development', *South Asia*, Vol. XXXIV, 3, December 2011, pp. 354-381.

______. 2010a. 'Hindutva's Ebbing Tide?' in Sanjay Ruparelia, Stuart Corbridge, John Harriss and Sanjaya Reddy (eds), *Great Transformations*, New York: Routledge, 2010, pp. 172-185.

______. 2010b. 'Is India Having a Good Crisis?' *Soundings*, 48, Winter 2010.

______. 2007. Dreaming in Technicolour: India as a BRIC Economy', *International Journal,* Autumn, pp. 779-803.

______. 2004a. 'Forward March of Hindutva Halted?', *New Left Review* 30, second series, November-December 2004, pp. 49-67. Reprinted in Arvind Sivaramakrishnan, *Short on Democracy: Issues Facing Indian Political Parties*, New Delhi: Imprint One, 2007.

______. 2004b. *Slouching Towards Ayodhya: From Congress to Hindutva in Indian Politics*, 2nd Rev. Edition, Three Essays, New Delhi, 2004, pp. xxv + 147.

______. 2004c.'The Cast(e) of Anti-Secularism' in Mushirul Hasan (ed.) *Will Secular India Survive?*, Imprint One, New Delhi, 2004, pp. 175-209.

______. 1999. 'Culturalism and the Contemporary Right: The Indian Bourgeoisie and Political Hindutva', *Economic and Political Weekly*, Vol. XXXIV, No. 12, March 20, pp. 695-712

Frankel, Francine, 2005. *India's Political Economy, 1947-2004: The Gradual Revolution,* 2nd ed., New Delhi: Oxford University Press.

Frankel, Francine and M.S.A. Rao (eds) (1989) . *Dominance and State Power in Modern India: Decline of a Social Order*, Delhi: Oxford University Press. 2 Vols.

Ghatak, Maitreesh, Parikshit Ghosh and Ashok Kotwal. 2014. "Growth in the Time of the UPA", *Economic & Political Weekly*, April 19.

Ghatak, Maitreesh. 2017. Demonetisation was bad economics but as an act of vigilantism it served Modi well politically. *The Wire*. 13 March. https://thewire.in/116124/demonetisation-bad-economics-clever-politics-modi/.

Ghosh, J. 1998. 'Liberalization Debates' in T.J. Byres (ed). *The Indian Economy:*

Major Debates Since Independence, New Delhi: Oxford University Press.

Ghosh, Jayati, C.P. Chandrashekhar and Prabhat Patnaik. 2017. *Demonetisation Decoded: A Critique of India's Currency Experiment.* Abingdon: Routledge.

Harriss, J. 1999. Comparing Political Regimes Across Indian States: A Preliminary Essay. *Economic and Political Weekly*, 34(48), 3367-3377.

Jaffrelot, Christophe. 1993. *The Hindu Phenomenon.* New Delhi: Viking.

Khare, Harish. 2017. 'The Consecration of a Hindu Vote Bank'. *The Wire* 13 March. https://thewire.in/116195/consecration-of-a-hindu-vote-bank-uttar-pradesh-election-2017/.

Mishra, P. 1995. *Butter Chicken in Ludhiana.* New Delhi: Penguin.

Noorani, A.G. 2107. 'The Decline of Modi'. *Frontline,* January 20.

Palshikar, Suhas. 2017. 'India's Second Dominant Party System'. *Economic and Political Weekly* Vol. 52, Issue No. 12, March 25, 2017.

Panagariya, Arvind. 2014. "The Promise of Modinomics", June 10, 2014. http://www.foreignaffairs.com/articles/141556/arvind-panagariya/the-promise-of-modinomics, accessed on June 28, 2014.

Patnaik, Prabhat. 1995. 'A Perspective on the Recent Phase of India's Economic Development', in *Whaltever Happened to Imperialism and Other Essays.* New Delhi: Tulika.

Patnaik, Prabhat, C.P. Chandrashekher and Abhijit Sen. 1996. 'The Proliferation of the Bourgeoisie and Economic Policy' in T.V. Satyamurthy (ed). *Class Formation and Political Transformation in Post-Colonial India,* New Delhi: Oxford University Press.

Rajalakshmi, T.K. 2017. 'Persistence of Misery'. *Frontline,* March 31, 2017.

Ray, Ashis. 2017. Is 2019 a done deal? Not if you look at the numbers. *National Herald,* April 5. http://www.nationalheraldindia.com/news/2017/04/05/is-2019-a-done-deal-not-if-you-look-at-numbers-16-state-elections-since-2014-bjp-failed-absolute-majority-in-13.

Rutten, M. 1995. *Farms and Factories: Social Profile of Large Farmers and Rural Industrialists in West India.* New Delhi: Oxford University Press.

Stern, R. 2003. *Changing India: Bourgeois Revolution on the Subcontinent,* Cambridge: Cambridge University Press, 2nd ed.

Sridhar, V. 2017. 'GDP Conundrum'. *Frontline,* March 31.

______. 2015. 'Rejigging Statistics'. *Frontline,* March 20.

Vardharajan, Siddharth. 2014. 'The Best Democracy Money Can Buy', *Economic Times,* April 30.

Yadav, Yogendra. 2017. Challenge to Indian Democracy. *The Wire,* March 15. https://thewire.in/116504/bjp-hegemony-power-democracy/.

Vanaik, Achin. 1994. 'Situating the Threat of Hindu Nationalism: Problems with the Fascist Paradigm'. *Economic and Political Weekly,* July 9.

Varma, P. 1998. *The Great Indian Middle Class.* New Delhi: Viking.

3

Reclaiming the Nation and Nationalism: A Marxist Praxis

V. Krishna Ananth

Notwithstanding the centrality that the nation and nationalism has assumed in the post-enlightenment era, Marxism, which essentially emerged as the most influential philosophy of this time had for long remained eclectic in its approach to this phenomena. While Marx himself seemed to gloss over this phenomenon, many Marxist scholars are guilty of having approached the nation and nationalism as merely a false consciousness.[1] Let it be stressed here that attempts to understand the nation and nationalism were made even during the times when Marx and Engels were engaged with the discourse on changing the world.

Ernest Renan's exposition of the nation as an exercise in everyday plebiscite (Renan 1982), perhaps the earliest one in a long series of attempts to explain the nation and nationalism, came at about the same time when Marx had critiqued capitalism in all its elements and a year before his death in 1883. Renan certainly rested his case on the historical experience of the French people, in the one hundred years between the Revolution of 1789 and the Paris Commune of 1871. Renan saw the nation as a *human collectivity* brought together by *will, consciousness* and *collective memory*.[2] It may be noted here that while Renan sought to explain the phenomenon from an entirely modernist premise, Bankim Chandra Chatterjee had, unintended, laid the premise for a nation on pre-modern foundations. His exposition of nationalism in *Anand Math* and the different meanings that were assumed by *Vande Mataram* (from a hymn in the novel to a battle cry and still later into an idiom for majoritarian communal politics) is only one illustration of how complex the concept of nation and nationalism is in the case of India. It is also necessary to stress that the nation and nationalism in India evolved in such a way to transform into a modern idea in the half century since Bankim with Dadabhai Naoroji, M.G.Ranade, Mahatma Gandhi and Jawaharlal Nehru infusing new thoughts (Bhattacharya 2011).

However, it may be stressed here that Renan was not attempting to define the philosophical foundations of nation and nationalism and hence failed to internalize J.G. Fichte and his arguments on the idea of nation, which was closely tied with the concept of the nation state (Fichte 2000).[3]

The important point to note here is that Renan's scheme was rooted in the Enlightenment philosophy as against Fichte's, which was grounded in the principles of Natural Rights, despite his ambitious attempt to re-conceive the foundations of Kant's *Critical Philosophy*.[4]

This important philosophical foundation of the nation, however, has come to play a critical role in the discourse on nationalism throughout the 20th century, manifesting in the two world wars and is dominating the discourse in our sub-continent at present. I shall come to this later in this paper. Meanwhile, it is relevant to briefly delve into the intervention by Joseph Stalin in the discourse on the nation in 1912, exactly thirty years after Renan attempted to describe the phenomenon. Stalin did seek to address some of the infirmities in Renan. The nation, in Stalin's view,

> is a historically constituted, stable community of people, formed on the basis of a common language, territory, economic life, and *psychological make-up manifested in a common culture* (Stalin 1912).

While Stalin's approach to the nation did not influence Marxist scholars in any significant way, it certainly influenced several practitioners of Marxist revolutionary principles. The commonality between Stalin's notion of the nation with Hitler's in the inter-war years (the anti-semitic ideology common to both in particular), undoubtedly did not last the war; the couple of years between Hitler's acts of invasion and the Soviet Union's entry into the war, nevertheless, witnessed Hitler and Stalin swallowing territories that lay between the east of Germany and west of the Soviet Union in a manner similar to the Treaty of Vienna in 1814. Similarly, the semblance of independence that the post-war Eastern European nations enjoyed was indeed the fallout of a new sense of independence that Hitler's defeat necessitated. The stress on 'a psychological make-up manifested in a common culture' which was central to Stalin's definition of the nation led to concerted efforts to secure homogeneity through a range of means including mass murders, forcible displacement of the people from their lands and colonization during the war years and subsequently (Gellner 1993).

Stalin's view on the nation and the national persisted even after his death in 1953 and the Soviet intervention, brutal in all senses of the term, in Hungary in 1956 when Soviet tanks rolled in to crush the people's movement was evidence of its fallacies. The Prague Spring of 1968, the Soviet Union's use of force to retain Czechoslovakia, as its satellite, was yet another example of the Stalinist notion of the nation.[5] Elsewhere, Communist China, under Mao Tse Tung sought to build upon the Stalinist notion of the nation as a 'Continental System' since the late 1960s (Anderson 1993).

The Stalinist impact on the Marxist discourse, however, was restricted. This did not persist with Marxist Praxis elsewhere and even with Mao in the context of China's liberation struggle. Mao, for instance, was also among those who located the potential for harnessing nationalism in a revolutionary sense in the struggle for the liberation in China. The roots of this lay in Lenin's approach to the national liberation struggles from a tactical point of view and espoused in the debates he had within the Communist International (Lenin 1978). Lenin's approach to nationalism was guided by the tactics of revolutionary praxis and had nothing to do with defining or describing what constituted the nation, from a Marxist premise, as Stalin sought to do. It was also an application of Marx's core idea of history that while men make history, they do so in circumstances imposed on them and not of their choice (Marx 1852). Lenin had before him Hobson's exposition of imperialism (Hobson 1901), which argued against colonialism and the imperative for Western capitalism to mend its ways, from a libertarian perspective. And then there was Rudolf Hilferding's exposition, posing the question as to whether Western capitalism can at all survive without the colonies (Hilferding 1910). These and Russia's backwardness in relation to the industrial West led Lenin to his seminal work on imperialism (Lenin 1916) and the debate he steered within the Communist International on the significance of the national liberation struggles in the East was drawn out of this understanding.

Mao certainly drew substantially from Lenin's prescriptions and the liberation war in China was indeed on these lines. It must be stressed here that all of it was tactics and did not evolve into a Marxist theory on the nation and nationalism. It was not very different from Ho-chi Minh in Vietnam, who held Lenin's contribution as immense and seminal.

Meanwhile, a Marxist approach to the nation and nationalism found expression in a far more forthright manner in the history of the struggle for independence in Algeria; Frantz Fanon's trenchant critique of French colonialism in Northern Africa (Fanon 1967) or the seminal contribution of Albert Camus, once again reflecting the churning that Marxist thinking had to go through in its engagement with the libertarian ideas (Camus 1953), rescued Marxism and thus contributed, in a substantive sense, to a Marxist praxis on the nation and nationalism.[6] Another substantive stream in this context is the resistance, in the cultural domain, to colonialism. Fanon set the stage for this again presenting the extent to which the *colonizer* rendering the *colonized* into an ally and foregrounding the necessity of decolonizing the mind of the colonized as well (Fanon 1952). Amilcar Cabral was among those who took this idea further in the African context (Cabral 1970). Edward Said, subsequently, put these in a conceptual frame and set a trail in the attempts to understand nationalism as not merely an economic category. Said's works underscored that the nation and nationalism cannot be seen in mere cultural terms and instead ought to be seem as a protracted movement (Said 1978; 1993).

While all these were attempts to locate the revolutionary potential in national liberation struggles and thus evolve a theoretical approach from within the concerns of the Marxist praxis, yet another round of studies to understand the phenomenon were produced in the early 1980s. Ernest Gellner, among them, came out with an analytical frame to hold that the nation and nationalism were essentially developments thrown up by modern society and sought to establish this as the outcome of the Industrial Revolution. In doing so, Gellner listed eight specific features of the industrial society, including the need for centralized administration, universalized training to ensure the technological changes were harnessed and that these were not possible in the pre-modern state of things (Gellner 1981).

The stress that Gellner gave to modernity in the Nation-nationalism discourse was criticized by Antony D. Smith holding that though the nation and nationalism were manifestations of the modern era, it was important to look for the ethnic origins of the phenomenon (Smith 1986). He drew a typology that may have helped describe the nation and nationalism, as they emerged outside the industrial West; Smith's contribution was that he classified nations on the basis of their origins and the typology he evolved threw up two substantive categories among the many: Territorial Nationalism and Irredentist Nationalism clearly lent a new dimension to the understanding of the phenomenon and thus added to the theory of nationalism.[7]

This, however, did not have any significant impact on the attempts, around the same time, by Marxist scholars as much as Gellner had on them. 'Haunted' by the prospect of a full scale war between the socialist states (in the context of the armed hostilities in Indo-China involving Vietnam, Cambodia and China during the late 1970s), Benedict Anderson conceded that nationalism was not merely the fallout, ugly as it may be, of capitalism (Anderson 1983). His analysis lent itself to approaching the phenomenon, evil it may have been, as something that one had to live with. Anderson paved the way to look at the Stalinist notion critically and open up a new trajectory from within the Marxist premise and away from seeing nationalism as merely a tactic in the course of the struggle against capitalism.

Eric J. Hobsbawm, a dyed-in-the-wool Marxist, however, seemed to put the clock back, holding on to Gellner's approach, wanting to wish away the nation and nationalism as the evil consequence of industrial capitalism and refusing to look at the nation and nationalism as having the potential to emancipate as much as it had to stall such emancipation. Notwithstanding the possibilities for such an elaboration, from the point where he raises the distinction between revolutionary nationalism as against official nationalism, Hobsbawm returns to his original position describing the nation and nationalism on the basis from which Gellner looked at the phenomenon (Hobsbawm 1990).

Hobsbawm, however, stuck in the notion of capitalism being the liberating machine from all pre-capitalist systems (and will be destroyed under its own weight of contradictions as Marx envisaged more than a hundred years ago), refused to acknowledge the potential for liberation in the nation and nationalism even where such assertions were registered by the oppressed nations and nationalities. Stressing the inevitability of the universality of the modern system to dismiss the assertions as merely 'an expression of conservative resistance to the inevitable advance of history', Hobsbawm simply condemns these acts as ones that are bound to 'retire from battle to become a repository of nostalgia and other sentiments...'[8]

The point here is that Marxist practitioners, as a rule, seemed to hold the nation and nationalism either as a feature of the capitalist development (in the sense Gellner sought to describe the phenomenon) or even when they conceded a role for nationalism in the revolutionary scheme, it was held merely as a tactical line (in the sense as Lenin sought to explain nationalism in the East) and such attempts by Fanon, Camus and Sartre did not impact the Marxist attempts to decode the phenomenon even as late as in the 1980s.

There is one element that is striking in all these attempts; and that is the absence of any reference to the making of the nation and nationalism in India.[9] It needs to be stressed here that unlike the Western European experience, where the emergence of the nation and the nation state took the gradualist route, or the ethnic basis as in such parts of Europe as in the Balkans where irredentism laid the foundation in the making of nations (Smith 1986; 1991), the process of the making of the Indian nation was *sui generis* and in many ways the Indian nation was a historical process. It may also be said, in a limited sense, that Renan's idea of the nation as an exercise in everyday plebiscite (Renan 1882) was very relevant in the case of the nation and nationalism in India. This process of everyday plebiscite was marked by a continuous engagement, sometimes antagonistic and otherwise in others, between the various social and economic groups in the colonial Indian society. In that sense, Otto Bauer's theorization of the nation, the nation-state and nationalism as a historical process, marked by two distinct aspects—first as an assertion against foreign rule and subsequently or concurrently as an assertion of the right to the development of the whole people—carried out simultaneously is relevant for us (Bauer 1924).

Bauer's work in 1924, perhaps, remains the most exhaustive treatment of the nation and nationalism hitherto. And yet this was not to be used by Marxists, both scholars and practitioners, across time and space. The reason for this was obvious. Bauer, incidentally, was banished in his own times for his forthright criticism of the way socialism was practised and more particularly because he raised this at the height of Stalinism. Bauer had also spelt out his opposition to Lenin's approach to nationalism as merely a tactical approach[10] and critiqued bourgeois nationalism to argue that the socialist society alone envisaged a nation that was 'no longer a rigid thing but a process of becoming,' and went on to define the scope of this becoming as 'the conditions under which people struggle for their necessities of life and to maintain themselves' (Bauer 1924: 56).

It will be appropriate to delve into Bauer's approach to the nation and nationalism in some detail at this stage. Bauer's discourse, as it was held in the context of the different approaches to the nation that ruled his times, began with questioning the two major positions of his times considering the 'nation' on the one hand 'as a natural community' and on the other 'as a community of culture'. These, he held, failed 'to focus on the various causes that determine national character' and went on to argue that 'human character is never explained by anything other than human destiny; national character is never anything but the precipitate of a nation's history.' As for the basis of the nation, consequently as a cultural community, Bauer stressed that it was important then to show 'how national character is determined by the common cultural values transmitted by earlier generations' and this indeed is a firmer basis according to him 'than if we seek to explain this community of character from the natural inheritance of physical properties' (Bauer 1924: 43).

Bauer then was categorical in locating the evolution of a national character in the historical processes that went into its emergence rather than any ethnic considerations. Proceeding from this, Bauer categorizes the nation and nationalism into three kinds and based on the various stages in the history of their evolution and existence:

1. In the immediate context of the post-feudal society, the nation is a collective of members, bound by common blood, are also linked up by common culture inherited from their ancestors.

2. The stage of development where the earlier nation disintegrates into communities that are divided on a socio-economic basis, the nation comes to be built on this foundation rather than on ethnic lines; the original common language then develops into various local dialects and in the wake of the different struggles for existence, they develop diverse kinds of culture. What holds the nation together, at this stage, is no longer the unity of blood and culture among the masses but the cultural unity of the ruling classes that dominate the masses and live off their labour. In place of the knights in the Middle Ages, the educated classes form the nation in this stage.

3. The socialist society of the future presents the third and final stage, once again uniting all fellow nationals into an *autonomous national unity*. It is no longer common descent, rather common education, work and cultural enjoyment that compose the nation... (Bauer 1924: 55-56).

The Marxist premise in Bauer's formulation is evident in two ways. One that his approach to the phenomenon from a historical perspective; an aspect that remained central to Marx. And second, and more significant, was the application of the principles of Historical Materialism to understand the three stages. Bauer, for instance, explains the causes for the fall of the nation in the first stage and also underscores the basis for the fall in the second stage. The ethnic nation, Bauer explains could not hold on with the advent of settled agriculture with the inherited features of unity breaking down and the appearance of locally differentiated tribes, the differentiation happening due to the differing conditions of their existence. 'The nation', he argues, 'thus bears within the germ of its decay.' Similarly, in the second stage, he argues that `the broad masses, by the work of whose hands the nation is maintained—peasants, artisans, workers—are simply left behind as far as the nation is concerned' and this is where the germs of its decay lies. Thus locating the cause for the collapse of the nation and nationalism in the first two stages, Bauer (like Marx posited the future transition from capitalism to socialism)[11] posited the end of the pre-history of the nation and nationalism (Bauer 1924: 55-56). Bauer's important contribution then will have to be seen in the departure he made from the Leninist approach to national liberation (which was one of the tactics) and more so in his break with the Stalinist notion of the nation.

Bauer also distinguished himself from the premises of Social Darwinism as much as he did from the Hegelian premise of the nation as being the product of the mystical popular will or the spirit and argued that the Materialist Conception of History 'can comprehend the nation as the never completed product of a constantly ongoing process' (which is where one can find in him a certain agreement with Renan's idea of the nation as an exercise in everyday plebiscite, which is a conjuncture and Bauer does not refer to Renan anywhere) and then goes on to stress that 'the ultimate driving force (of this process) is the conditions of human struggle with nature, the changes in human relations with labour.' This conception, Bauer argues makes the nation into a 'historical entity' (Bauer 1924: 57).

Such a resolution of the nation itself into a process, Bauer argues, takes us away from a history of struggles of nations to a perception in which 'the nation itself appears as the reflection of historical struggles' (Bauer 1924: 60-61). And he then proceeds to locate the conflict between the bourgeois notion to the nation and nationalism, that seeks to preserve the status quo in the guise of such sentiments as 'national specificity', when challenged by revolutionary movements seeking to overthrow the existing order of society. The working class, Bauer insists, 'is not yet a class of the nation...excluded from the enjoyment of cultural values' since these values are of no significance to it. 'Where others see the shining history of national culture, it sees the misery and serfdom of those on whose broad shoulders all national culture has rested since the decline of the old clan communism'. This then makes it imperative (and not merely a tactical position) for the working class to 'seek(s) its ideal not in the maintenance of national specificity, but rather in the overthrow of the former Constitution, which alone can make it into a member of the nation' (Bauer 1924: 66).

Bauer, certainly ought to be credited for evolving a Marxist understanding of the nation and nationalism and this is distinct from Hobsbawm's or Anderson's, notwithstanding that these were no less Marxists.

A Marxist theory on the nation and nationalism, however, could be seen evolving elsewhere in the context of the struggle against colonialism in India. It was in India that an attempt was made to bring about a synthesis of the libertarian perspective on freedom of the individual with that of the materialist approach to liberation. In other words, there was an attempt to make the nation such that that it could reconcile the larger good with the individual's rights. Meanwhile, it must be stressed here that the Marxist approach to the idea of nation and nationalism in India, in the Bauerian framework was not to be found in the tradition of the communist party. Notwithstanding the many struggles that the communists had launched and participated in the cause of Indian nationalism, they were guided by a Leninist approach to nationalism and hence it was more of a tactical approach. This was inevitable, in a sense, given the influence Lenin had on M.N. Roy and the early communists in India; and also the direct involvement of the representatives from the Communist Party of Great Britain—R.P. Dutt and Ben Bradley—on behalf of the Communist International in the affairs of the CPI since its inception in the 1920s.[12]

This, however, is not to convey that nationalism was merely a tactical line and for the communists in India sans conviction. The communists, in their own way, exerted a huge influence on the Indian National Congress and thus shaped its policies as well through the 1920s and in the making of the Karachi resolution defining freedom in terms of the rights of the workers and the peasants, in terms of the fundamental rights; it may be stressed here that the Fundamental Rights resolution at the Karachi session of the Indian National Congress (as early as in 1931), was an expression of what could be the Marxist praxis on nationalism and more specifically in the Bauerian sense.

This perspective, indeed, assumed a central position in the making of India into a Sovereign Democratic Republic in the Constitution as adopted on November 26, 1949. The Indian Constitution, to adapt Granville Austin's phrase, emerged into *the cornerstone of the nation* (Austin 1966). The Preamble to our Constitution set the national goals in three distinct but connected aspects of justice; social, economic and political. And in the six decades and more, it was found that what was adopted, after considerable debate and discussions in the Constituent Assembly, was inadequate and hence amended in a substantive sense. A close look at these amendments will reveal that at least a quarter of the 100 amendments involved elongating the scope of justice in the social, economic and political sense of the term; and these amendments were in conformity with the idea of India that evolved in the process of making of the nation.

Among them were the Constitution (First Amendment) Act, 1951, by which Article 15 (4) was added to enable reservation of seats for Scheduled Castes, Tribes and Other Backward Classes in educational institutions; and the Constitution (Ninety-Third Amendment) Act, 2005, to enable such reservations in educational institutions whether public funded or not. The more substantive set of amendments were in the domain of effecting land reforms and attacking private property beginning the Constitution (First Amendment) Act 1951 by which Article 31 (B) and the Ninth Schedule were added to the Constitution and culminating in the Constitution (Twenty-Fourth Amendment) Act, 1972 and the resolution of the idea of economic justice as it was in the Kesavananda case (AIR 1973 SC 1461); the Basic Structure Doctrine enunciated in this and the categorical assertion by Justice H.R. Khanna (whose judgment tilted the balance substantially in favour of the idea of India in this case) that the Right to Property guaranteed as a Fundamental Right (Article 31) did not constitute a Basic Structure led to the Constitution (Forty-Fourth Amendment) Act, 1978 which, apart from many more things, scrapped Article 31 of the Constitution (Ananth 2015).

The third substantive trajectory in this involved the Constitution (Forty-Second Amendment) Act, 1976 and the Constitution (Forty-Fourth Amendment) Act, 1978. Apart from the political import of these in the context of the Emergency and the importance of the latter amendment mentioned above in restoring the kernel of Constitutional Democracy and measures to ensure that the scheme was not reduced to a plaything by undemocratic forces, the substantial aspect of the Forty-Second Amendment was the insertion of the words *socialist* and *secular* to the Preamble of the Constitution. It is important to note that the Constitution (Forty-Fourth Amendment) Act, 1978, even though intended primarily to undo the Constitution (Forty-Second Amendment) Act, 1976, did leave such aspects as the insertions into the Preamble un-amended. That the Supreme Court of India upheld this in the Minerva Mills case (AIR 1980 SC 1789) was in essence an evidence of the evolution of the constitutional scheme consistent with the idea of India as envisaged by the makers of the Constitution.

In the midst of all this are such decisions by the highest court in India elongating the scope of the Right to Life (as not merely the right to exist but exist with dignity) in a catena of cases during the 1980s; or the shift insofar as political rights were concerned between the A.K. Gopalan case (AIR 1950 SC 27) and the Supreme Court's decision in the Bank Nationalization case (AIR 1970 SC 564) and further elongated in the Maneka Gandhi case (AIR 1978 SC 597).

It may, hence, be argued that the constitutional scheme of *justice*, resting upon the three pillars of *social, economic, political*, had fallen in place during the 1980s and the higher judiciary had settled several conflicts between forces of status quo and change by then. It must be added that this settlement was drawn in favour of the Idea of Justice (Sen 2009). The harmonious balance that the higher judiciary had struck between the Fundamental Rights and the Directive Principles of State Policy, which indeed was the essence of the judicial disputes since the Constitution came into force ensured justice in the *aspirational* sense of the term. The centrality that was accorded to Article 39 (b) and (c) in this trajectory involving the higher judiciary and Parliament can be seen as an important marker in the making of the Indian nation and nationalism; in other words the nation as a historical process in the Bauerian scheme.

This process, indeed, is sought to be altered, since the early 1990s, where the Indian state, in order to defend its shift towards neoliberal policies, is determined to break with the Nehruvian consensus to favour what is known as the Washington consensus. The definition of development in terms merely of shoring up exports and free-market principles (notwithstanding that history has taught us that capitalism has always depended on the state and its institutions to even stay afloat) has meant a return of the colonial system albeit the shift of manufacturing from the metropolis to the hinterland; a process of trans-national capital shifting production centres away from the metropolis in its quest for cheap and unorganized labour and raw material.[13] This will have to be seen as an integral part of the agenda that has remained unaccomplished, in the specific context of the WTO regime, since Seattle and Doha.

It then, makes sense to draw from the core of Bauer's 1924 text and locate nationalism in the violent as well as the non-violent resistance to the present day regime's measures such as privatization of the public space and resources in many parts of the country. The numerous deals involving the export of the natural resources, particularly in the state of Chhattisgarh since 2005 (when more than one hundred MoUs were signed between the state government and different corporate houses, including multinational firms, the terms of which were held secret) is a case in point where the nation and the national is traded off in the guise of development and economic progress. Yet another face of this era are the Special Economic Zones (SEZs) wherein the nation state gives up its sovereignty. In other words, the nation and nationalism assumes the shape that Bauer explains as in the second of the third stage in his thesis—a nation, held together, by the cultural unity of the ruling classes that dominate the masses and live off their labour—and any attempt to reclaim the nation on behalf of the majority of the people is then branded as anti-national.

This feature of the nation and 'nationality' is what Lord Acton held as one of the three subversive modern ideas (along with 'equality' and 'communism'). Acton, again a product of the Enlightenment era and a libertarian fundamentalist,[14] had seen this coming at least twenty years before Renan had formulated his notion that the nation was an act of everyday plebiscite. Acton pronounced his contempt for the idea of the nation and nationality in as many words when he held:

> Whenever a single definite object is made the supreme end of the state, be it the advantage of a class, the safety or the power of the country, the greatest happiness of the greatest number, or the support of any speculative idea, the state becomes for the time inevitably absolute' (Acton 1962).

The point is that the Constitution, in the shape it had assumed to ensure that the nation, as envisaged in the Karachi resolution, wherein *Swaraj* was defined by the Indian National Congress as not merely a political idea but in economic terms and foregrounding the concept of the citizen into the discourse. The resolution, which enlisted the Fundamental Rights of the citizens in free India, was a manifesto. It held, in as many words: 'In order to end the exploitation of the masses, political freedom must include real economic freedom of the starving millions' (Sitaramaya 1935: 463). Leaning on Bauer, it is imperative for Marxist praxis to reclaim the nation and nationalism from the side of the people who are fighting against the manifestations of globalization. In specific terms, the nation and nationalism ought to be liberated from those who rest their case on placing the productive forces, the material resources such as the mines, minerals, the forests and the water flowing in our rivers, at the disposal of trans-national corporations and their agents in our midst.

Such a battle is raging across the country: In Chhattisgarh and Jharkhand, for instance, to save the mineral wealth of the nation; in parts of North-Eastern India against the destruction of the forests and the mountains to build hydel power projects; elsewhere against GM crops; across the country against moves to privatize water bodies. These are, indeed, movements to reclaim the nation and nationalism and certainly not threats to the nation as held in some quarters. These are similar to Bob Marley asserting the rights of the blacks in America in *reggae* (Buffalo Soldier...). It rendered a new sense and direction to the civil rights movement in America in the 1980s and also defined the nation as the property of the productive forces. The point is the nation belongs to its productive forces and is neither a bourgeois construct nor is it an imagined community. This, indeed, is what Marxism holds for the present.

The argument will be left incomplete without addressing to the current discourse on nationalism in India; a resurgence of ethnic nationalism in many parts and especially in the margins of the country as well as the jingoism in response to this, once again resting its case on Hindu nationalism.[15] Both these variants, feeding on one another, are essentially undemocratic and belong to what Bauer described as the nation represented by a society based on differentiation of social classes and yet sought to be held together by the elite, the oppressing classes, by way of constructing a common culture. Such a construct, indeed, is only a fabrication and is designed to suit what the ruling groups want. The masses—the productive sections of the nation—and their aspirations are distorted and this variant of nationalism as much as sub-nationalism, as is ideology in the sense Marx held, is false consciousness.

Marxist praxis, then, warrants a programme to reclaim the kernel of nationalism rather than moving along with one or the other distortions. The kernel, insofar as the Indian nation and nationalism is concerned, is to be extracted from the historical process that brought this into existence; that is the idea of *Swaraj* as envisaged in the Karachi resolution and given concrete direction in the Republican Constitution. It is also necessary to hold on firmly to the principle of the nation as a historical entity. This, then, enables a Marxist praxis to formulate a programme to reclaim the nation and nationalism from cultural nationalism which serves as the basis for both Hindu-nationalism as well as sub-national movements in the various parts. Rather than deepening democracy, these contribute immensely to the weakening of democracy; while the sub-national movements invariably are rooted in feudal concepts such as clan and communal sentiments, the state response to those too are no different. The struggle to reclaim the nation and nationalism, then, will hence have to be a struggle to deepen democracy and unflinchingly anti-feudal.

This, rather than an approach based on Eric Hobsbawm's contempt for any nationalism as just bourgeois or that of Benedict Anderson to treat the nation as an imagined community (both of which continue to dominate Marxists and their thinking in India), is closer to Marxism and should be the basis for a Marxist Praxis.

NOTES

1. I am using this expression in the same sense as Marx used it to describe ideology as false consciousness. Karl Marx expounded this more particularly in *The German Ideology* (completed in 1846 but published in full as late as in 1932). In this virulent attack on Ludwig Feurbach, Marx makes the point that ideology seeks and succeeds in obfuscating the thoughts of men from understanding the basis of their thinking. This, subsequently, came to be taken up by various Marxist scholars/ practitioners of Marxist praxis such as Antonio Gramsci (the concept of hegemony-counter hegemony), Louis Althusser (Intellectual State Apparatus) and Michel Foucault (Surveillance and Control); and moving further from Marx, the Marxists did formulate ways to counter this false consciousness.
2. Renan's attempt to describe the phenomenon was found wanting for 1. It was premised sheer voluntarism (and thus help wide open the scope for nations without definite geographical frontiers and hence

as fluid categories that could be perceived on the basis of religious, racial and linguistic identities); 2. It presupposed the existence of a nation before the coming of nationalism as an ideological force; and 3. It sought to put under one category both homogeneous and heterogeneous communities (as for instance France as a nation as much as Yugoslavia or Czechoslovakia as nations) on the same plane.

3. Fichte's formulation of Rights in this work (which he did in 1795-96) were rooted in the principles of Ntural Right; in the second appendix to his work, Ficthe deals extensively with the Right of Nations and argues that
'every individual has the right to force any other individual he encounters either to enter into a state with him or to stay out of the sphere of his efficacy'; this proposition led him to hold that 'someone who does not live in a state can rightfully be coerced by the first state that encounters him either to subject himself to it, or stay away from it.' And since this formulation was rooted in the principle of natural rights, there existed the possibility of unity of people even if separated geographically as one nation; such a formulation, however, held nations as cultural categories. Interestingly, this formulation provided Adolf Hitler the basis to invade Poland, and Czechoslovakia in the late 1930s. Lest it is misconstrued, Fichte himself had espoused this in his infamus Addresses to the German Nation, which he was used to give from the podium at the University of Berlin through 1807 in the aftermath of the humiliating defeat of Prussia by Napoleon. In those lectures, he held the Latins and the Jews as decadent races and that the Germans alone possessed the possibility of regeneration and under them will blossom a new era in history. That Hitler too spoke that way was not mere coincidental and is the outcome of a theory of nationalism rooted in principles of Natural Rights. See William L. Shirer, *The Rise and Fall of the Third Reich*, London, 1998 for a brilliant exposition of this aspect in Hitler's rise.
4. See Editor's Introduction by Frederick Neuhouser to J.G. Fichte, *Foundations of Natural Right: According to the Principles of the Wissenchaftslehre*, CUP edition, 2000, pp. vii-xxviii.
5. While Hungary and the Prague Spring are mostly studied in the context of the undemocratic nature of the socialist regime, these are also important markers of the Stalinist notion of the nation, stressing on a psychological make-up manifesting in a common culture as necessary in the making of a nation. The Stalinist era also witnessed the manufacturing of such a common culture, where it did not exist in

order to make the Soviet Union into a national state. The collapse, in the late 1980s and the emergence of the Confederation of Independent States exposed the fallacious basis on which this idea of the nation was constructed.

6. It may be of interest here to recall that Camus came under a scathing attack from a number of French Marxist scholars for his position in *The Rebel.* A scathing critique that it was on Revolutionary strategies that were carried out under the 'command mode', Camus came under attack even from Jean Paul Sartre in that instance. *The Rebel*, however, can be the basis of a Marxist praxis and its relevance is all the more in the aftermath of the collapse of the socialist block in my view.
7. Territorial Nationalism, according to Smith is the nationalist movement led by one dominant nationality that brings in others into the nation as subservient people or subjugated people. One may consider the Sri Lanka experience as an example in this regard. It is also possible to look at East Pakistan until 1971 as another example. Irrredentist Nationalism, although similar in many ways, is, however, different in that it is about a sominant group of a national movement annexing an adjacent land from an adjacent territory. One can find this across the Balkan region and in West Asia.
8. It will be worthwhile to quote Hobsbawm on this in full: 'But, if the only historically justifiable nationalism was that which fitted in with progress, i.e. which enlarged rather than restricted the scale on which human economies, societies and culture operated, what could the defence of small peoples, small languages, small traditions be, in the overwhelming majority of cases, but an expression of conservative resistance to the inevitable advance of history? The small people, language or culture fitted into progress only insofar as it accepted subordinate status to some larger unit or retired from battle to become a repository of nostalgia and other sentiments—in short, accepted the status of old family furniture which Kautsky assigned to it...' (Hobsbawm 1990: 41-42)
9. Hobsbawm does refer to India but these are only in passing and fleeting. Anderson, whose concerns on the subject emerged from events in South East Asia does not even turn fleetingly towards the Indian experience, thus drawing criticism from Partha Chatterjee (Chatterjee 1993). I must, however, clarify that my criticism of Anderson is from an entirely different plane.
10. A brief biographical note on Otto Bauer will be in order in this context. Born in Vienna in 1881, Bauer emerged as an important theoretician

of the socialists in Austria and his first theoretical work was in 1907 dealing with Nationalism and Socialism. Bauer expressed his problems with the Bolshevik Revolution, even in its early days, and his concerns were around the problems of establishing socialism in a semi-feudal country since he apprehended that it will lead to the despotism of a small minority in his thesis titled *Bolschevismus oder Sozialdemokratie?* in 1920. He was forthright in denouncing Stalinist terror, the practice of annihilation of cultures in the cause of homogenization (Stalin's idea of a nation as constituting a common culture). Although the rise of fascism in Germany led Bauer to re-visit his association with the Soviet Union, he was not welcome there. Hitler's rise took him to Czechoslovakia and after the German invasion and the fall of Czechoslovakia, Bauer fled to France in 1938 and died soon after (Kolakowski 1978: 254-256).

11. I am referring here to his preface to *A Contribution to the Critique of Political Economy*, where Marx held: 'In the social production of their existence, men inevitably enter into definite relations, which are independent of their will, namely relations of production appropriate to a given stage in the development of their material forces of production... From forms of development of the productive forces these relations turn into their fetters. Then begins an era of social revolution. The changes in the economic foundation lead sooner or later to the transformation of the whole immense superstructure... The bourgeois relations of production are the last antagonistic form of the social process of production—antagonistic not in the sense of individual antagonism but of an antagonism that emanates from the individuals' social conditions of existence—but the productive forces developing within bourgeois society create also the material conditions for a solution of this antagonism. The pre-history of human society accordingly closes with this social formation' (Marx 1859: 25-26).
12. I must mention here that R.P. Dutt's *India Today*, published in the course of the final stages of the freedom struggle and updated subsequently after independence, ends up treating nationalism in a manner not too different from the way the Cambridge School did (in the 1960s) and a nuanced Marxist historiography of the National Movement had to wait until the 1980s. The communist movement too suffered from this approach, ending up with the Calcutta Thesis of 1948 (authored by B.T. Ranadive) and exposing its cadre to massacre. The Tactical Line adopted by the party in 1951 (in lieu of a programme) persisted with the Dutt-inspired line and after the CPI split in 1964, the CPI(M)

persisted with the fundamentals of the 1951 resolution. It was finally jettisoned in 1978 at the Salkia Plenum and the effect of this was further disastrous with the left in India swinging closer to nationalism of the bourgeois kind and ending up speaking, many times, for the unity and integrity of the nation. This lack of perspective was most evident when the mainstream left parties failed to condemn in an outright manner the Nuclear Weapons Programme that the Government of India set out in May 1998. I have discussed this elsewhere (Ananth 2003).

13. I must stress here that the call for 'make in India' by the present regime in India is essentially one that seeks to carry out this neoliberal agenda couched in some notion of nationalism. It is a different matter that the call has remained unheeded, coming as it did in the larger context of the crisis that global capitalism has landed since almost a decade.
14. I am using this phrase consciously and on purpose. It is a fact that libertarian ideas have raised more complex challenges against liberty than deepening democracy in a historical sense; as for instance, we have in our midst several well-meaning people to whom opposition to the nation-state is a necessary condition to liberal thoughts and thus end up supporting campaigns that threaten freedom in their own way. The fundamentalist premise on which the demand for a separate Khalistan nation was built was glossed over by a section of our liberal opinion is a case in point. There are numerous examples of this kind in our short history.
15. I am referring to the movements in Kashmir and in some parts of North-Eastern India as much as to the demand, in the 1980s, for Khalistan and Assam. It holds true of the violent campaign against the 'outsider' in Bombay by the Shiv Sena in the 1970s or the demand for a Tamil nation in Madras in the 1960s. It is not just incidental that the 1980s saw such enactments as TADA and POTA, subverting the fundamental rights as guaranteed by the Constitution in the guise of saving the nation from disintegrating, we are now in the grip of a jingoist campaign threatening the foundations of the nation and nationalism, reminiscent of the times when Fichte drew a large following when he addressed the nation from the podium in the University of Berlin after Prussia was defeated by Napoleon; or with the rise of Hitler in the inter-war years and the glorification of war and aggression.

REFERENCES

Acton, Lord (1862), Nationality, in *The Home and Foreign Review*, July 1, 1862, pp. 146-74 ((Reprinted in Gopal Balakrishnan (ed.) *Mapping the Nation*, Verso, London, 1996, pp. 17-38).

Anand, C.L. (2008). *Constitutional Law and History of Government of India*, Delhi, Universal Law Publishing Company (8th Edition).

Ananth, V. Krishna (2003) *The Politics of the Bomb: Some Observations on the Political Discourse in the Context of Pokhran II* in C. Ram Manohar Reddy and M.V. Ramanna (eds). *Prisoners of a Nuclear Dream*, Orient Longman, Hyderabad.

Ananth, V. Krishna (2015). *The Indian Constitution and Social Revolution: Right to Property Since Independence*, Sage, New Delhi.

Anderson, Benedict (1983). *Imagined Communities*, Verso, London.

Anderson, Benedict, Introduction to Gopal Balakrishnan (ed). *Mapping the Nation*, Verso, London, 1996, pp. 1-16.

Austin, Granville (1966). *The Indian Constitution: Cornerstone of a Nation*, Oxford University Press.

Bauer, Otto (1924). *Die Nationalitatenfrage und die Sozialdemocratie*, Vienna (Reprinted in Gopal Balakrishnan (ed). *Mapping the Nation*, Verso, London, 1996, pp. 39-77).

Bhattacharya, Sabyasachi (2011). *Talking Back: The Idea of Civilization in the Indian Nationalist Discourse*, Oxford University Press, New Delhi.

Cabral, Amilcar (1970). *History is a Weapon: National Liberation and Culture*, Eduardo Mondlane Memorial Lecture Series, Syracuse University, New York (http://historyisaweapon.com/defcon1/cabralnlac.html) accessed on September 30, 2016.

Camus, Albert (1953). *The Rebel*, London.

Chatterjee, Partha (1993). Whose Imagined Community? (Reprinted in Gopal Balakrishnan (ed.) *Mapping the Nation*, Verso, London, 1996, pp. 214-225)

Fanon, Frantz (1952). *Black Skin White Masks*, London (Reprinted 2008).

Fanon, Frantz (1961). *The Wretched of the Earth*, London (Reprinted in 1967).

Fichte, J.G. (1795), *Foundations of Natural Right: According to the Principles of the Wissenchaftslehre* (Reprint, Cambridge University Press, Cambridge, 2000).

Gellner, Ernest (1981), Nationalism in *Theory and Society*, Vol. 10, No. 6, pp. 753-776.

Gellner, Ernest, The Coming of Nationalism, Storiad'Europa, Vol. I, Turin 1993 (Reprinted in Gopal Balakrishnan (ed.) *Mapping the Nation*, Verso, London, 1996, pp. 98-145).

Hilferding, Rudolf (1910). *Finance Capital: A Study of the Latest Phase of Capitalist Development*, Vienna (Reprint, Routledge & Kegan Paul, London, 1981).

Hobsbawm, Eric J. (1990). *Nations and Nationalism Since 1780,* Cambridge University Press.

Kolakowski, Lesxek (1978), *Main Currents of Marxism*, Vol. 2, Oxford University Press.

Lenin, V.I. (1916). Imperialism the Highest Stage of Capitalism, *Lenin's Selected Works*, Vol. 1, 1963, Progress Publishers, Moscow.

Lenin, V.I. (1978). *Lenin and National Liberation in the East*, Progress Publishers, Moscow.

Marx, Karl (1852), *The Eighteenth Brumaire of Louis Bonaparte*, Moscow.

Marx, Karl (1859). *A Contribution to the Critique of Political Economy*, Moscow, Progress Publishers (Reprinted in 1970)

Renan, Ernest (1882). *Qu'est-cequ'une nation*, Paris.

Said, Edward (1978). *Orientalism*, Routledge & Kegan Paul, London.

Said, Edward (1993). *Culture and Imperialism*, Alfred A. Knopf, New York.

Sen, Amartya (2009). *The Idea of Justice*, Allen Lane.

Shirer, William L. (1998). *The Rise and Fall of the Third Reich*, London.

Sitaramayya, Pattabhi (1935). *The History of the Indian National Congress*, Vol. 1, Padma Publications, Bombay.

Smith, Antony D. (1986). *The Ethnic Origins of Nations*, Oxford University Press.

Stalin, Joseph (1913). Marxism and the National Question, *Prosveshcheniye*, Nos. 3-5 https://www.marxists.org/reference/archive/stalin/works/1913/03.htm accessed on September 30, 2016.

4

Neoliberal Capitalism, Resistance and Crisis of the Left in India

Ravi Kumar

Introduction

Neoliberal capitalism is no longer restricted to one geographical location. It is universal. Those who opposed the universal categories on grounds of it being undemocratic, homogenizing and limiting are confronted with the fact that capitalism is a universal phenomenon and the battle against it has to be fought through the universal category of class. Only a political struggle grounded in commitment to an exploitation free world can contest the callousness, aggression, arrogance and unimaginative world of capital. However, this struggle is not easy as the ruling class, today, has at its disposal technology and instruments that ensure maximization of profit and limit the realization that capitalists survive only because labour creates value that is unjustly appropriated by it. This was realized by Engels when he was writing the preface to *Wage, Labour and Capital*:

> In the present state of production, human labor-power not only produces in a day a greater value than it itself possesses and costs; but with each new scientific discovery, with each new technical invention, there also rises the surplus of its daily production over its daily cost, while as a consequence there diminishes that part of the working-day in which the laborer produces the equivalent of his day's wages, and, on the other hand, lengthens that part of the working-day in which he must present labor gratis to the capitalist.

Neoliberalism takes this whole process to a whole new level but also produces contradictions that threaten capital's own existence. These contradictions are generally latent and come to the surface when capitalism is in a crisis. Recent times have also shown that a crisis exists but capitalism successfully manages it, largely due to absence of a sharper and potent class consciousness. For instance, in recent times one has seen an extremely narrow understanding of the idea of privatization. The Indian state, in case of Indian Railways, has been trying to say that they would not hand it over to private capital but in reality components of its operation are being gradually privatized. In other words, contradictions are to be sharpened and made use of in order to defeat the rule of capital. This paper is an effort to briefly map the situation of pauperization and marginalization that contemporary capitalism has produced in India while a few keep getting richer and how it also produces possibilities of resistance from the Left which is somehow lacking.

About 296, 438 farmers have committed suicide in India between 1995 to 2013 (Sainath 2014). Almost 60 per cent of total health expenditure in India was paid by the common man from his own pocket in 2009 as over 39 million Indians get pushed to poverty because of illnesses annually. In fact, illness is one of the major causes of indebtedness in India as nearly 47 per cent and 31per cent of hospital admissions in rural and urban India, respectively, were financed by loans and sale of assets (Sinha 2012). Educationally, there has been a segmentation of schools wherein the poor, girls and other marginalized groups go to ill-equipped state run schools and those wanting a 'better' education go to the private schools. The drop-out rates are still huge apart from the issue of quality in education. The pauperization of teaching labour-force like any other site of production continues unabated.

On the other hand, poverty is increasing amidst the clamour of a high growth rate. In fact, the growth rate has been driven by the skewed wealth accumulation in a few hands. This skewed wealth accumulation, generally, has happened because of failure to share the fruits of rising productivity in the form of wages with workers. In fact, reports have indicated that the real wages have not grown at the same speed as the growth of labour productivity (ILO 2013: 46). In the last few decades the gap between rich and poor has increased in India. The larger picture shows that there is a vast gap between those having income under $10,000 and those having income above that. In fact, the difference between the richest 10 per cent and the poorest 10 per cent of population is huge.

Chart 1: High Net worth Individuals by Region and Country (Figure in $)

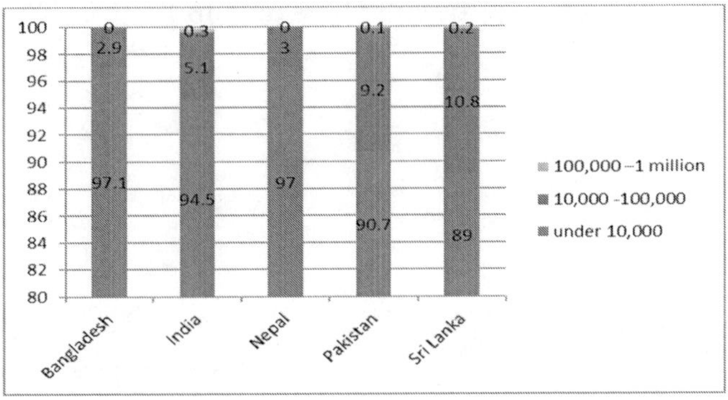

Source: Credit Suisse (2014)

There is a growing tendency of polarization between rich and poor in the society today. While productivity increases it does not translate into the improvement of conditions of the vast mass but rather in skewed accumulation of wealth as indicated by the figures below. In the recent past this has happened steadily.

Chart 2: Wealth Share of India's Top 10 Per cent Over Years

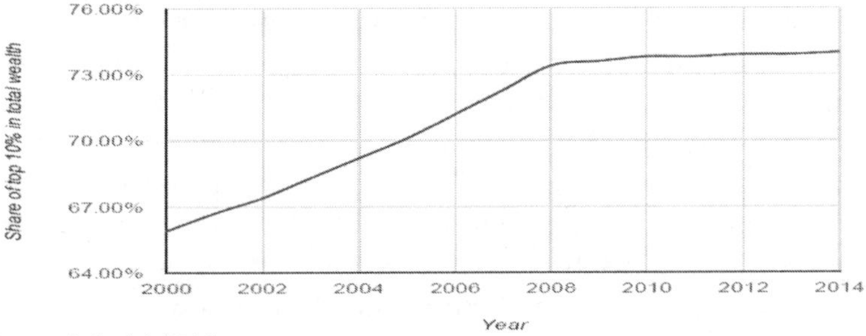

Source: Rukmini (2014)

This growth in the wealth of a few people has been obscene. In fact, it is so stark that the growth in their wealth leaves behind the growth of top 1 per cent richest people across the world. In the year 2000 India's richest 1 per cent had "a lower share of India's total wealth than the world's top 1 per cent held of its total wealth. That changed just before and after the global recession—though the world's superrich are recovering and India's top 1 per cent holds close to half of the country's total wealth" (Rukmini 2014).

Chart 3: Wealth Share of Top 1%

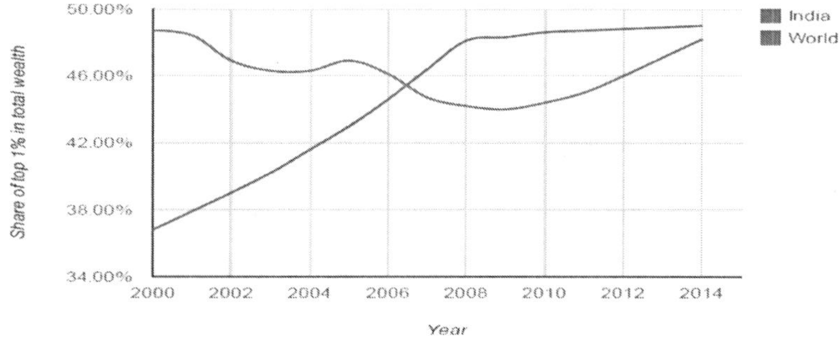

Source: Rukmini (2014)

The stark impoverishment of the vast mass of population is creating dehumanized living conditions for them. This dehumanization process emerges out of the social relations wherein the enhanced productivity of the workers is creating purchasing power for the owners of capital and not for workers. Undoubtedly capitalism is destined to be this skewed at this stage but the process of dehumanization created commodification of every sphere of our existence when purchasing power does not grow accordingly for everybody creates a situation of crisis–the starkness of an inhuman system. Capitalism is creating commodities out of education, health, social security but the consumers (every human is a potential consumer today) cannot buy it. The earlier avatar of the welfare state no longer exists as the state continues to withdraw from its responsibilities and subcontracts everything to the private capital. State managed enterprises are either sold off or the jobs are gradually subcontracted to private capital. Human resource companies are a major investment which supply workers to universities, ministries, banks, etc. This has pauperized the labour force by not only taking away their social and economic security but making them underpaid without any rights to question the employees. With the state already spending less on the social sector (Chart 4), it further decides to cut down the budget on the two basic human needs such as education by about 11,000 crores[1] and health budget by 6,000 crore rupees[2].

Apart from this over the past two decades one has seen pauperization of the labour force. Wherever possible the jobs have been contractualized–ranging from university faculty, school teachers, health staff, clerks to housekeeping staff. It is pertinent to remember that it is not merely about giving up *responsibilities* but giving away *business* to individuals at the cost of lives of a large mass of people that is reflected in this attitude of the state. This is what state withdrawal means–creating space for expansion of private capital in areas where it was not present.

Chart 4: State Expenditure on Health and Education of Gross Domestic Product

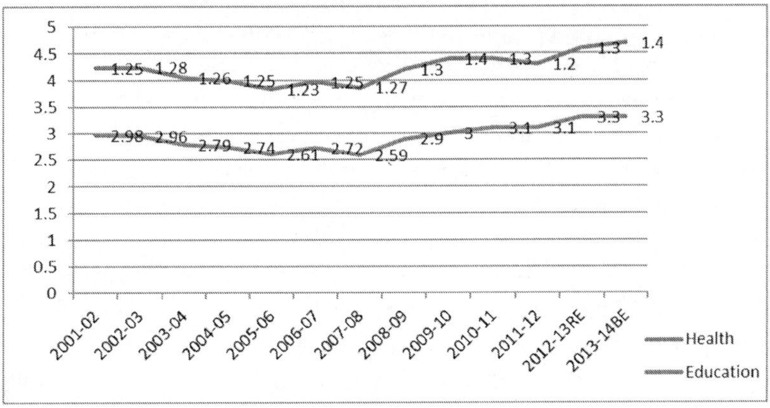

Source: Collated from different years of *Economic Survey*, Ministry of Finance, Government of India

The contractualization of labour force is not new, specifically when one confronts the agrarian economy, which contributed a greater share to the economy at one point of time. For instance, it contributed 51.9 per cent of the GDP in 1950-51, which is reduced now to 13.7 per cent in 2012-13[3]. This agrarian economy always had an ad hoc arrangement vis-à-vis employment and wage and the struggle of the landless workers historically bear a testimony to this. The landless agricultural labourers in most parts were at the mercy of the landed gentry as laws which existed were implemented half-heartedly.

Similar developments could be seen in the urban sphere where the trade union struggles did win many battles but all those gains are now being reverted back by the rule of capital. For instance, the idea of an eight-hour workday, which was achieved after great battles, hardly exists today as in some sectors technology takes *work* into a realm of timelessness and in some other sectors pauperization of the workforce compels them to work longer hours, for instance the security guards or factory workers. Another dimension of accumulating wealth of a few at the cost of pauperization of vast mass is reflected in the fact that "real worker wages have been stagnant in the three decades to 2013 while real productivity has increased at an annual average rate of 7 per cent. Real wage growth has languished at an average annual rate of 1 per cent between 1983 and 2013, lagging real productivity improvement" (Singh 2015). As private capital becomes aggressive, expands into new areas to sustain and maximize surplus accumulation through all means assisted by the state it has contributed to pauperization of the workforce. The situation becomes grim when one finds the state in collusion with private capital resorting to violence of the worst nature. This violence occurs across different workplaces—whether school teachers or university faculty are beaten up by mercenaries of private capital (the police and hired goons) in different cities or workers of different factories are beaten up and put behind bars for months and years.

The state-owned enterprises have been handed over to private capital—disinvestment of public firms, privatization of airports, freeze on regular employment in different spheres to dispensing with pension and bringing into the ambit of market basic necessities such as health—all have impacted the majority of masses in an unprecedented manner. This is what neoliberal capitalism does. It brings everything under the control of the market and state, hitherto seen as welfarist it sheds all its inhibitions to assist private capital in taking over whatever possible with the aim of accumulating as much wealth as possible.

This becomes visible when one sees a huge population working as contractual and casual workers with meagre salaries battling for survival and on the other hand a number of billionaires competing with their global counterparts. A survey of the world around us reveals the kind of life that the new economy has brought for most of the people. The informal sector that flourishes—from the delivery man of food-joints to the courier delivery person to the workers in restaurants to the subcontracted housekeeping staff and administrative personnel in the offices all are underpaid, struggling to survive, whereas the other side of the horizon has an inflow of massive wealth. Globally the accumulation of wealth in a few hands has happened. Unabashed exploitation of natural resources and exploitation of the vast mass of population has created such a situation that 1 per cent of the richest people in world own 40 per cent of the wealth (Randerson 2006).

It is interesting to note that the International Labour Organization while trying to show that there is a great discontent against the governments as indicated by the data does not show inequality as one of the major causes of this discontent. This became evident in the ILO *World of Work Report 2011: Making Markets Work for Jobs* wherein the possibility of social unrest emerges as a major concern (ILO 2011: 01).

Though it recognizes many factors as responsible for unrest across the world it does not look at the widening gap between the rich and poor across the world and in South Asia (*Financial Express* 2014) and therefore the question of distribution of wealth or the exploitative social relations that characterizes capitalism as the inevitable cause of social unrest even though it may not be very apparent in the unrests that have happened in some of the regions. The need to locate the social unrest or the increasing rich-poor gap within the capitalist production process and social relations becomes necessary and this can also be ascertained from the trend of declining share of labour's income in the economy in recent times as highlighted by The *ILO Global Wage Report 2012/13*. The reports points out that the view that the income of labour as well as capital will grow as countries become more prosperous is no longer valid as one finds the share of labour in income declining (2003: 41).

Today a huge proportion of wage and salaried population in India lives on $2 or below in India (ILO 2013: 30). There has been a trend globally to pay profits as dividends and an "increased pressure on companies to reduce the share of value added going to labour compensation" (ILO 2013: 44). On the other hand, "the top 10 per cent of wage earners now make 12 times more than the bottom 10 per cent, up from a ratio of six in the 1990s" as per an OECD report (TOI 2011).

Consequently, pauperization of the vast mass due to the informalization and contractualization of the economy combined with the predatory character of the corporate sector further pushes them to poverty and marginalization. It seems illogical as well that the economy which survives on commodification of each and every aspect of life does not pay much attention to the relationship between labour compensation and ability to consume. In the long term ignoring this relationship often leads to a crisis. However, the corporate sector proudly projects how the prospects for private capital will be better in the days to come. One estimate says that there is a vast potential for them in the heath sector due to the growing presence of private capital

Chart 5: Private Capital's Vision of the Health Sector

- Healthcare revenue in India is set to reach $ 280 billion by 2020
- Private sector's share in healthcare delivery is expected to increase from 66 per cent in 2005 to 81 per cent by 2015
- In India, private healthcare accounts for almost 72 per cent of the country's total healthcare expenditure
- Private sector's share in hospitals and hospital beds is estimated at 74 per cent and 40 per cent, respectively.

Source: IBEF (August 2014a)

The same think tank projects a rosy picture for the future of private capital in education :

Chart 6: Private Capital's Vision of the Education Sector

- The emergence of the un-organized private education sector in India has opened a door of opportunities for many companies
- With increased corporate investments in the sector, the share of private schools in the total number of schools have increased over the past few years
- The schooling segment in India is expected to be $44 billion
- The private education sector which was valued at $50 billion in 2008 is estimated to reach $115 billion by 2015

Source: IBEF (August 2014b)

Neoliberal Capitalism and Possible Resistance

It is apparent that the situation is grave – everything is being given to the private capital which works on only one primary premise– that of profiteering and accumulation of wealth for a few at the cost of the majority. This is happening when poverty, even by conservative estimates is around 29.5 per cent[4], and the cost of living has gone up while social security is non-existent and the economy appropriates surplus through lowering wages and substandard working and living conditions. These are neoliberal and darker times as human existence is constantly being forced to submit to the rule of capital. The idea of freedom, social collective and dissent are in decline as capitalism uses every individual against the self-concealing our self-defeating existence as the success of our individual lives. So profound and devious is the design of capital in our times, a stage termed neoliberal. There has been a substantial amount of literature that has debated the origins and nature of neoliberalism in general (Dumenil and Levy 2011; Harvey 2005; Saad-Filho and Johnston 2005) and there have been specific works locating its demonic character for the social sector. The following characteristics of neoliberalism can be found in India (Kumar 2014a):

1. The market becomes the organizing principle of all aspects of our life—political, economic, social, and cultural—as commodification pervades all of them.
2. The distinction between public and private diminishes/ vanishes as private takes over everything that is public,

including the 'sanctified' so-called security systems.

3. Politics increasingly and overtly becomes a domain of the ruling elite, as a number of millionaires and billionaires rise in formal democratic institutions. The Indian Parliament has become a place for them now as indicated by the figures.
4. While 'resource crunch' becomes an excuse for the state's inability to manage health, education, pension, etc., the state, simultaneously, doles out huge monetary benefits to corporate houses as tax waivers and subsidies.
5. Poverty increases in real terms (if not in definitional terms of the state, which manipulates its definitions and figures) and so does the gap between those who can afford to be buyers in the new commodified economy and those who cannot.
6. The market expands and creates monopolies in such a way as to give the impression that it can cater to everyone (according to their capacity and, thus, not ignoring any segment of population) trying to generate illusions about its predatory nature.
7. Through an unprecedented control over ideological apparatuses, the market creates a chimera of 'hope' and 'aspirations' that keep telling the masses about unlimited 'possibilities' under neoliberal capitalism. This temporal intoxication is broken by crises that the economy faces repeatedly.
8. By pumping into individual imagination illusory impressions of the world, it tries to push its darker side into oblivion (such as farmers' suicides, hunger deaths, malnourishment, environmental catastrophes, etc.) though they resurface time and again.
9. The idea of 'social justice' is destroyed as the state reduces its role and hands everything to the market, which believes in its criteria of 'competition' and mutilated notion of 'merit'. Social concerns and historical constructs are no longer factored in the idea of 'justice'.
10. There is growing intolerance towards *dissent* and *dialogue*. It

is seen as hampering the smooth functioning of the institution and is taken as an 'attack' on its endeavour to attain the goals that it has set for itself.

11. It is more aggressive in terms of governance. Hence, it not only manipulates the existing bourgeois democratic structures such as the Parliament or regulatory bodies such as the University Grants Commission but also resorts to physical violence against those who resist.
12. There is increasing surveillance of public as well as private lives. This emanates from the fear that private capital has come from the masses engaging in acts of resistance and subversion.
13. The ruling class has no respect for the rules of governance which it has created. It manipulates them to suit its own interests.

These characteristics create situations that facilitate the accumulation process of private capital under contemporary times. The result is an enormous disparity in the ability to consume (ironically in an economy that thrives on the idea of consumption):

Chart 7: Disparity in the Ability to Consume

- Nearly 40 per cent of the rural population of India had MPCE below Rs 800 and about 60 per cent had MPCE below Rs 1,000. About 10 per cent had MPCE above Rs 1,650
- 60 per cent of rural population had MPCE less than Rs 1,000 ($20)
- 10 per cent of rural population had MPCE over Rs 2,500 ($50)
- 60 per cent of urban population had MPCE less than Rs 1,600 ($32)
- 10 per cent of urban population had MPCE over Rs 5,800 ($116)

Source: GOI (2011)

This inequality is also epitomized in somebody living in a 27 storeyed residence[5] or a 2,000 crore residence[6] on one hand while the majority live in dilapidated housing and abysmal living conditions.

Chart 8: Housing and Living Conditions in India

- Around 62.3 per cent houses do not have bathroom facilities in rural India
- Around 59.4 per cent houses do not have latrine facilities in rural India
- Around 65.8 per cent houses in rural India are of pucca type[7]
- Around 59.4 per cent houses in rural India have a separate room for married couples and the figure for urban India is 57.6 per cent proving insufficiency of space in houses[8]

Source: GOI (2013)

There is not much that can be expected from a system which has increasingly been dominated by the bourgeoisie that has captured all instruments of what is termed the representative democracy. After all, most of the Members of Parliament today are millionaires and billionaires. "...The average assets per winner for 281 BJP winners analysed is Rs 11.59 crores, 44 INC winners have average assets of Rs 16.71 crores, 37 AIADMK winners have average assets worth Rs 6.47 crores and 34 AITC winners have average assets of Rs 2.51 crores" (ADR 2014 : 10). In this situation of heightened aggression of capital one finds the anti-capitalist forces being pushed to the margins–electorally as well as in terms of movements. In fact, absence of movements has led to their electoral decimation as well. This situation has not arisen suddenly but is a result of accumulated political deviations that characterized the left in the country and which continue to exist even today.

The Left in These Difficult Times

When the CPI(M) was defeated in West Bengal (in 2011) after over three decades of rule there was a sense of despair, especially with the exuberant bourgeois propaganda machine foretelling the end of the left in India. It did not end there. Prakash Karat, General Secretary of the CPI(M) after its defeat said that "Those who have written our epitaph will be proved wrong." The defeat of CPI(M) and the exuberance of media compelled over two hundred 'leftists' to issue a statement[9] saying that

> *The Left in India is not the Left parties alone and therefore the defeat of the Left parties does not mean the defeat of the Left* (emphasis original). The Left in India has never been reducible to these large parliamentary fronts and party machines, much less to the groups embattled in the forests of India, but has always been a much wider spectrum of organisations, movements and forms of struggle that range from the hundreds of left wing trade unions that exist in the country in all the major industrial centres, unions that are essentially independent of party control and seeking today to form a national federation, down to the dozens of popular campaigns and the organisations connected with them.

The signed document furthermore said that

> We feel that the defeat of the parliamentary left *should* mean space for a stronger left movement, a 'new left' if you like, that reflects the aspirations of the mass of people more creatively, with more imagination and greater integrity.

The collapse of the CPI(M) as an electoral force represents the inevitable—inevitability of *working class* politics becoming a bourgeois state and still claiming to retain its class character. This, undoubtedly, leads us to many complex questions such as what role does one take upon if participating in the parliamentary politics and to what extent can one immerse oneself in bourgeois practices.The collapse brought out debates about distinction that one needs to draw between the Left as a state and as a movement as well as the questions of coping with 'vices'/deviations that a bourgeois state carries within itself. For instance, being part of a state/government would one implement the policies and programmes of a bourgeois system, hence, carrying forward the lineages of class-based inequalities and perpetuating it? As an example would one not try to be innovative and subvert the bourgeois system by thinking of alternative banking systems or create education materials and policies that teach subversion rather than perpetuating the same ideas that capitalism asks one to do? If these questions were asked then some more clarity could be achieved in haziness that engulfed left politics owing to the diminishing distinction between the Party and the State. It also told us about the disconnections that the parties have developed over time with the masses by creating a distinction between party and movement, apart from the question of workings of the party (Kumar, 2014b). No doubt there has been a need to recognize the resistances against capital wherever it has been taking place but there is also a need to clearly outline the nature of politics that these places have carried within themselves. In other words, while often resistances become instrumental in not only exposing the malaise that capitalism carries within its womb but also in bringing forth the inner contradictions of capitalism as a system but how far do these resistances become effective instruments of working class struggle remains a point to be analysed in greater detail. Also, it remains to be seen as to what kind of new spaces have opened up for the left in the aftermath of the CPI(M)'s defeat though capitalism in its neoliberal avatar continues to be more and more inhuman, callous and inconsiderate albeit more sophisticated.

Recent times also saw a massive support from some kind of 'Left' to temporal assemblies against corruption, transparency and democracy, specifically in the city of Delhi through the new political formation called Aam Admi Party (AAP). It came like a wave when the Left of different hues and colours saw a tremendous transformatory potential in such a political formation, especially when it was getting a fovourable response from the population on the margins as well as the 'middle class'. The discontent brewing in society took populist overtones as bourgeois politics began exploring different vistas. The left was also seen trapped within this populism as its class politics seemed to be taking a backseat. The dilemma that it was confronted with was somewhat different (compared to that of the dominant bourgeois parties)—it found AAP taking a similar social democratic agenda that the left wanted to take up or was already taking up in different forms. These new political tendencies further added to the weakening of the parliamentary left.

Even the abject situation, as pointed above, which has been produced by capitalism, has not fomented a powerful Left assertion. It has largely been because of the failure of the dominant left to put working class politics before any other concern. The attack that neoliberal capitalism unleashes on the social sector has been rampant but an alternative to the project that bourgeois politics presents has also been lacking from the forces claiming to represent the working class. In other words, whether it has been about opposing the flawed Right to Education Bill (2009) in the streets or in the Parliament when it was being put through (even though the left had a huge presence inside Parliament) or whether it has been about resisting commodification of education and health the 'working class' failed; the required opposition to the privatization of the public sector also failed to generate any heat which could have forced the Indian bourgeoisie represented through the state to rethink its policies. Neoliberal politics has increasingly become aggressive and we are at a stage when it pushes its agenda of giving more and more space to the capitalists to not only use resources of the state (ideally belonging to the masses) but also seeks to hand them over whatever can get them profit. This happens when economic pauperization is widespread. Ironically, the working class stands marginalized along with the swelling discontent against the system.

At another level, historically, the Indian left fell prey to identity politics. It is not to deny the attention that caste as an important issue should have got but the left could not effectively differentiate itself among masses from the political formations which originated as caste-based formations but eventually ended being agents of certain segments of the Indian bourgeoisie and its politics. This became apparent when the left lost a sizeable mass base to political formations which flourished on issues of caste-based equality and justice. Undoubtedly, left also has to explain issues such as the absence of Dalits from its leadership, etc. Finally, it failed miserably at any effort to locate identity politics within a class-based transcendental politics. Linked also to this has been its (specifically the Parliamentary left) failure to conceptualize and understand the idea of the 'worker' itself thereby not able to make inroads when informalization of the economy happened on a mass scale. Hence, teachers or journalists could not battle it out in streets along with other workers as they believed themselves to be part of another class. All this weakened it further at a moment when the strength of the left would have really mattered against the aggression of neoliberal capitalism.

Lastly, the left needs to critically introspect about the way the Party has worked (Kumar 2014b). It has to reinvent organizational practice by de-hierarchizing it and establishing the idea of horizontal dialogue as a political practice not only within the party but between the party and the masses as well.The battle against neoliberal capitalism is passing through a weak moment but the upsurge is bound to happen as capitalism gets embroiled in its own contradictions–when economies no longer work simply through the success stories of a few rich while the vast mass gets impoverished; when promises cease to be electoral weapons; and when the *essence* becomes the reality.

NOTES

1. See Mehra, Puja (November 27, 2014) Social sector funds slashed, *The Hindu*, available at http://www.thehindu.com/news/national/social-sector-funds-slashed/article6637180.ece (Accessed November 28, 2014).
2. See NDTV (December 23, 2014) India Slashes Health Budget, Already Among World's Lowest: Report, available at http://www.ndtv.com/article/india/india-slashes-health-budget-already-among-world-s-lowest-report-638877 (Accessed December 24, 2014).
3. See *Economic Times* (August 30, 2013) Agriculture's share in GDP declines to 13.7% in 2012-13, available at http://articles.economictimes.indiatimes.com/2013-08-30/news/41618996_1_gdp-foodgrains-allied-sectors (Accessed October 10, 2013).
4. These are estimates of the Rangarajan Committee. For details see Singh (2014) and GOI (2014).
5. http://www.dailymail.co.uk/news/article-2053231/Worlds-expensive-house-Antilia-Mumbai-lies-abandoned.html (Accessed on June 20, 2014).
6. http://photogallery.indiatimes.com/celebs/celeb-themes/expensive-celebrity-homes/articleshow/34338130.cms (Accessed on June 20, 2014) as well as http://daily.bhaskar.com/news/ENT-inside-shah-rukh-khans-rs-2000-crores-bungalow-mannat-4368549-PHO.html (Accessed on June 20, 2014).
7. "A 'pucca structure' was one whose walls and roofs were made of materials such as cement, concrete, oven burnt bricks, hollow cement/ash bricks, stone, stone blocks, jack boards (cement plastered reds), iron, zinc or other metal sheets, timber, tiles, slate, corrugated iron,

asbestos cement sheet, veneer, plywood, artificial wood of synthetic material and poly vinyl chloride (PVC) material" (GOI 2013: 30).

8. This also relates to the fact that "overcrowding has various adverse effects to leading a healthy and undisturbed life and hence is considered as an important problem to be addressed by urban planning" (GOI, 2013: 33).
9. This can be found at http://kafila.org/2011/05/24/end-of-the-left-in-india-statement-after-recent-election-results/(Accessed June 20, 2013).

REFERENCES

ADR (May 18, 2014) *Analysis of Criminal Background, Financial, Education, Gender and Other Details of Winners*, Association for Democratic Reforms: Delhi.

Credit Suisse (October 2014) *Global Wealth Databook 2014*, Research Institute: Zurich.

Dumenil, Gerard and Dominique Levy (2011) *The Crisis of Neoliberalism*, Harvard University Press: Cambridge, MA.

Financial Express (October 03, 2014) 'Income inequality: Poor-rich gap growing in India, Asia-Pacific, says UNESCAP', available at http://archive.financialexpress.com/news/income-inequality-poorrich-gap-growing-in-india-asiapacific-says-unescap/1295313 (Accessed November 20, 2014).

Government of India (July 2011) *Key Indicators of Household Consumer Expenditure in India, 2009-2010*, National Sample Organization, Ministry of Statistics and Implementation: New Delhi.

Government of India (2013) *Key Indicators of Drinking Water, Sanitation, Hygiene and Housing Condition in India July 2012 - December 2012*, National Sample Survey Office, Ministry of Statistics and Programme Implementation: New Delhi.

Government of India (June, 2014) *Report of the Expert Group to Review the Methodology for Measurement of Poverty*, Planning Commission, Government of India: New Delhi

Harvey, D. (2005) *A Brief History of Neoliberalism*. Oxford: Oxford University Press.

International Labour Organisation (2011) *World of Work Report 2011: Making Markets Work for Jobs*, ILO and Academic Foundation: New Delhi.

International Labour Organisation (2013) *Global Wage Report 2012/13: Wages and Equitable Growth*, ILO: Geneva.

India Brand Equity Foundation (August 2014a) 'Healthcare' available at http://www.ibef.org/download/Healthcare-August-2014.pdf (Accessed on October 15, 2014).

India Brand Equity Foundation (August 2014b) 'Education and Training' available at http://www.ibef.org/industry/education-sector-india.aspx (Accessed on October 15, 2014).

Kumar, Ravi (2014a) *Education, State and Market: Anatomy of Neoliberal Impact*, Aakar Books: New Delhi.

Kumar, Ravi (2014b) 'Reimagining Democracy: Radicalising Dialogue and Dissent as an Organisational Practice within the Indian Left', in Dasgupta, Subhoranjan (ed.) *Democratic Governance and Politics of the Left in South Asia*, Delhi: Aakar Books, pp. 90-103.

Randerson, James (December 6, 2006) 'World's richest 1% own 40% of all wealth, UN report discovers', *The Guardian*, available at http://www.theguardian.com/money/2006/dec/06/business.internationalnews (Accessed October 12, 2014).

Rukmini, S. (December 8, 2014) 'India's staggering wealth gap in five charts', available at http://www.thehindu.com/data/indias%ADstaggering%ADwealth%ADgap%ADin%ADfive% ADcharts/article6672115.ece (Accessed on December 9 , 2014).

Saad-Filho, Alfredo and Johnston, Deborah (2005). Introduction. In Saad-Filho, Alfredo and Johnston, Deborah (eds.) *Neoliberalism: A Critical Reader*. London: Pluto Press, pp. 1-6.

Sainath, P. (August 01, 2014). 'How states fudge the data on declining farmer suicides', available at http://www.rediff.com/news/column/p-sainath-how-states-fudge-the-data-on-farmer-suicides/20140801.htm (Accessed on September 11, 2014).

Singh, Mahendra Kumar (July 7, 2014) 'New poverty line: Rs 32 in villages, Rs 47 in cities', *The Times of India*, available at http://timesofindia.indiatimes.com/india/New-poverty-line-Rs-32-in-villages-Rs-47-in-cities/articleshow/37920441.cms (Accessed on August 10, 2014).

Singh, Prabhat (January 21, 2015) 'Higher productivity equals higher wages? Not for the Indian industrial worker', available at http://www.livemint.com/Opinion/Vxmd5HHO8qeLuq YUiobbpM/Higher-productivity-equals-higher-wages-Not-for-the-Indian.html?utm_source=copy (Accessed on January16, 2015).

Sinha, Kounteya (May 17, 2012) 'India ranks 3rd in region in 'out of pocket' med spend', *The Times of India,* available at http://timesofindia.indiatimes.com/india/India-ranks-3rd-in-region-in-out-of-pocket-med-spend/articleshow/13178290.cms (Accessed January 19, 2014).

The Times of India (December 7, 2011) 'India's income inequality has doubled in 20 years' available at http://timesofindia.india times.com/india/Indias-income-inequality-has-doubled-in-20-years/articleshow/11012855.cms (Accessed on July 11, 2014).

5

Who is Afraid of Postcolonial Theory? Development, Accumulation and the Spectre of *Outside*

Dhritiman Chakraborty

Postcolonial theorists have spilled a great deal of ink tilting against windmills of their own creation. In so doing they have also given license to a massive resurgence of nativism and Orientalism.
–Vivek Chibber, 2013: 77

Postcolonial societies require such a theory of the outside so as not to remain altogether outside Theory any more. It is the theory of foreclosure (in Lacan) that offers postcolonial theories a way of not remaining foreclosed in Theory any longer.
–Anup Dhar, unpublished working paper, 2016

This chapter wants to argue why we need the theoretical rubric called 'postcolonialism' while talking of politics of resistance in India in particular and South Asia in general. In doing that it is guided by two kinds of critico-theoretical impulses: first the question of 'difference' which will be defined as an inalienable constitutive element of the political in a field overdetermined by heterogeneous socio-economic forces in relation to the global circuit of capital qua developmentalist regime in India, secondly this emphasis on 'difference' does not necessarily determine the object of its study as 'heavily oriented towards culturalism' (Chibber 2011), therefore placing political (as understood in the Marxian dialectic of class analysis) in a virtual cul de sac. On the contrary, this paper tries to re-engage with the question of class and surplus labour in the capitalist drive for accumulation in the South Asian context without eschewing the postcolonial emphasis on 'difference', refigured as a conceptual space of 'outside' which is both produced and repressed by the complex of capitalist and non-capitalist production processes. This discussion will partly try to answer the sharply polemical and consistent critique of postcolonialism (Parry 2004, 2012; Dabashi 2012; Chibber 2013; Gopal 2016; Lazarus 2011; Ahmed 1997; Purakayastha 2014 etc.), that at times posits this entire corpus as conceptually redundant as it blindly draws to post-structural tool kit to dismember the Eurocentric bias in epistemological and ideological formations. Hence questions are roundly raised as to the mistaken overlapping of Eurocentricism with capitalocentiricty and its so-called universalizing proclivities—"latent in the very term 'Eurocentricism' has been the fetish of 'Europe' or 'the West' (Lazarus 2004: 44). As a critic in a recent review of Vivek Chibber's 2013 title on what is considered as the most vitriolic attack on 'Subaltern Studies' till date has stated, 'postcolonial theory will survive not because of its unity but because of its *disunity*' (Watson 2013). Hence the latest in this bandwagon of charges has been the point of eclecticism, the accusation of inherent 'incoherence' and the rhizome-like expansionary paradigm that hardly answer for the materiality of subalternization, variegated forms of subordination in the contemporary plexus. Though it cannot be denied that postcolonial theory is in dire need of what Ania Loomba and others have called a kind of 'revivifying reflux' (2006: 9), new conceptual coordinates to re-politicize its foundational radical agenda, this hardly means that all questions of 'difference' should be erased for a neo-universalist project of Marxian political, that just because the neoliberal regime has entered an intense stage of depredation, all possible markers of otherness, ideological and political, should be permanently or temporarily debunked.

However, this is also a fact that some of these critical interrogations have in a profound way reshaped the contour of postcolonial studies, bringing in issues that were shelved on the backburner after its alleged 'culturalist/discursive turn' in the 1980s and the subsequent jettisoning of more fundamental issues of economic neo-imperialism. Now the point is instead of discussing the current phase of accumulation and exclusion in the singular logic of historical materialism and therefore reimagining the question of resistance in that single economico-political register, we need to continue the dialogue with postcolonial theoretical rubric for other possible materialist interpretations of multivalent forms of power discrimination in close alliance with the neoliberal capital. Moreover, we need to facilitate more critical and creative engagement to retain both the points of 'postcolonial difference' and the pressing necessity for a 'materialist critique' (Parry 2004). It would be a more productive contribution if we can rethink the question of postcolonial political within this double bind of maintaining the 'difference' question alongside more prodding issues of the exploitative capitalist production circuit based on continuing primitive accumulation and the resultant decimation of all markers of 'difference'. What further needs to be understood is that the proposition of 'difference' is not a derivative of any orientalist imagination for 'otherization' and 'ethnicization', it is rather produced by capital itself, its use of massive exploitative forces to sustain the increasing demand for accumulation. This has led to huge displacement, dislocation, forced migration, precarization of life, rampant informalization of jobs, crumbling infrastructure of distribution, land grabs by multinational corporations and the pitying state of postcolonial governance. Each of these instances of destitution is linked to the coordinated functioning of excessive accumulation of surplus that constantly destroys all its other, any alternative production system, any life-world that defies its hegemonic language-logic-experience-ethos. Hence the question that weighs on us is how to rethink of politics as emanating from these contingent spaces of destitution and disaffection. Should we shy away from complex nuances of economic forces that lead to this condition of depravity by simply calling it an expansion of the neo-imperial world system (can we for that matter undermine the role of the state in post-colonies like India?), or do we need to go beyond Hardt and Negri's postulations on the current age of Empire and the resistant politics of multitude to rethink the matrices of global capital and its postcolonial manifestation in India? What are the possible constituents of any such formulations that focus more on postcolonial specificities and the associated emphasis on 'difference' and 'alterity'? Do they warrant for a disclosure of any such space of 'outside', therefore looking for politics beyond the negotiable parameters that capital has opened up? Do we therefore need to rethink altogether a new dynamic of politics which exists, yet does not seem to be so, which is obscured and yet peeps out from the holes that perforate the sheet of capitalism? Is capitalism then a story of a perforated sheet (Arundhati Roy has called it a 'ghost story'), or a narrative that constantly conceals and invisibilizes this tattered texture of the sheet? What role can a postcolonial understanding of otherness/outside play in highlighting these holes, these interstices that ceaselessly undercut the otherwise triumphalist narrative of capitalist world-order? If the first quotation from Vivek Chibber at the very top of this paper hints at a radical departure from any engagement with 'outside' in consolidating the politics of anti-capitalism, the second quotation holds out a new signpost, prompting towards a necessity for making the shift from politics to political, from becoming foreclosed in the circuit of global capital to reappearing as a resistant, recalcitrant other. This essay is about undertaking this paramount journey, about grappling for new interpretations of Marxian politics which is not predefined or predisposed to any definite structure of telos, rather something which is constituent, which is in the process of emerging, *a-venir* from that space of the foreclosed, from multitudinous experiences of being-in-the-*outside*-world.

Lest this essay appears to be a belated apologia for postcolonial theory's obduracy with the cultural quotient, let me sum up the main argument here which is precisely to reposition the question of 'difference' in postcolonial theory in a radically different paradigm of class focused analysis of surplus labour. This retention of the point of 'difference' vis a vis postcolonial theory is not aimed after ferreting out an 'alternative to capital', but as 'outside to capital'. Any discussion on alternative willy-nilly refers to the capitalocentric development discourse that to follow Arturo Escobar (1995) is first rendering the other as 'primordial' and 'backward' to legitimizes its inclusion within the developmentalist regime. 'Outside-ness' in contrast is distinguished as both inside and yet outside; it is both produced and yet repressed and foreclosed. From the perspective of birthing a new framework of political, one has to secure this space of 'outside', its agential and dissident possibilities as differently elucidated in range of conceptual registers starting from 'subaltern' (Guha 1982), 'wretched of the earth' (Fanon 1963) 'world of the third' (Chakrabarti, Dhar and Cullenberg 2012, 2016), 'bare bodies' (Roy 2005), 'political society' (Chatterjee 2004), inhabitants of 'need economy' (Sanyal 2007) and so on.

Is Class a Misnomer in Postcolonial Theory? The Genealogy of Class Analysis in Postcolonial Studies in India

As it is evident from this brief introduction, postcolonial theory in recent years has been found wanting in adequately responding to the neoliberal condition and the current juncture of neo-imperial politics. The contention is that this has led to a crisis which is now both internally and externally dissected. If the internal response has been one of re-fashioning its original political matrix, externally it has been diagnosed as ill-equipped to unleash any legible anti-imperialist dissenting paradigm that can redress the capitalist policy imperatives. If we accept the external critique, some other equally pressing questions then come up: questions like how to define capitalist hegemony in India, what are the configuralities of this hegemony and whether they unqualifiedly tally with the logic of capitalist accumulation and its resultant production relation in the developed countries. If the answer is no, can we then say that there is still a space of difference/outside of capital in the non-West which has not been fully incorporated, therefore not reduced to its hegemony per se? What is the relationship between hegemony and this space of 'outside'? Alternatively, the question could also be on why do we need to imagine a space of 'outside' at a time of 'Empire'? What could be the implication of any such imaginary that does not affirm by the 'end-ist' logic of capital and still looks for ground that mark the limit to its experience-language-logic-ethos? To elaborate these arguments, we have to first define what we mean by 'Outside', whether there has been any epistemological tradition that decisively explored this space of 'outside' in the postcolonial theory coming from the non-West. To undertake any such critico-political interventions, one needs to once again engage in the theorizations of differential subjectivities in the postcolonial subaltern studies, the reconfiguration of the worker question in an economy which is largely disaggregated, and the problematization and possible expansion of the historical materialist discourses to include other questions of culture and historicity. Though it cannot be claimed that the following is an exhaustive study of this extremely vast and invigorating discipline of political-economy of postcolonial development in India, it however makes a basic point which corroborates the main argument of this paper: that 'difference' as an epistemic register also strongly figured in the discussion of political economy in India and therefore when postcolonial theory highlights the importance of 'difference', there is a possibility of a critical dialogue for futural emancipatory utopias. Such an engagement on a secondary level can then usher in a whole new way of looking at the fraught relationship of postcolonial theory vis a vis Marxism in South Asia.

Postcolonial theory begins with this injunction that Marxism alone cannot explain or eliminate all instances of marginalization in differential registers that are structured in complex intersections of historical and social forces. Therefore a great deal of intellectual investment has been made in exploring the social economy of the postcolonial materialities, its ambiguities and paradoxes. Postcolonial critique of all forms of discursive power henceforth promises to expand the horizon of radical critique to incorporate hitherto unaddressed sites of power constellations. And in highlighting all these different registers of oppressions, their 'Otherness', and the ineffectuality of the deterministic historical materialist approach to properly render all their nuances, the class as the singular critical entry point for a holistic discussion of range of exploitations appears incapacitated. This therefore marks what many recognize as the beginning of 'frame multiplication' (Ray and Katzenstein eds. 2005: 18). This is the larger tendency that Vivek Chibber holds culpable for the 'decline of class analyses' in the social sciences in India (2011: 368). The question of 'difference' and 'otherness' more prominently emerged in its place in almost all the fields of social and politico-economic studies of India. It was also evident in the mode of production debate in the 1970s and 80s that serially appeared in the pages of *Economic and Political Weekly* (EPW) and later in the contributions in forms of chapters in the Subaltern Studies collective that started in 1982. Ashok Sen, Ajit Choudhury, Amit Bhadury, Utsa Patnaik, Jairus Banaji and Partha Chatterjee are some of the hallowed names who participated in those debates to refashion the field of postcolonial political economy on lines of cultural and social specificities. Hence Althusser and Gramsci became the two most revered names that crop up in their deliberation to explicate the difference of the Indian context. Their cumulative discussions and disagreements lead to the following points which are extremely pertinent to this discussion–

a. India did not experience any bourgeois revolution of the sort and measure that happened in England in 1640 and in France in 1789.
b. As an outcome of this delayed and 'belatedness' of any classical sort of bourgeois revolution in India, the historical materialist trajectory is bound to be non-teleological and non-deterministic.
c. The whole transition hypothesis therefore stands contested as the transition within an ensemble of capitalist and non-capitalist production forces is virtually impossible. It therefore rejects all variants of linear hypothesis that vouches for any forms of transition either from pre-capital to capital or capital to socialist modernity.
d. Instead of a linear stagist history, the postcolonial historiography is detected to be a complex of synchronic formations that straddle various opposite binaries between elite/subaltern, Brahmin/Dalit, and bourgeois/proletariat and so on.
e. Therefore on the basis of these assumptions, the whole production of capital in the Indian economy cannot be merely discussed by focusing on the fundamental class processes comprising wage labour and the primitive

> dissociation of the means of labour from the labourer, rather it requires a greater scrutiny of other formal subsumption categories of the economy that functions along with caste and other remnants of feudal economy within a single commodity space.

What is evident from this enumeration is how recurrently the question of 'difference' returns in the problematization of the transition thesis and the political economy of a postcolonial nation (in this case it is India). Therefore to argue that the essentialization of 'difference' is only a hallmark of cultural studies is definitely glossing over the fact. In reality, Subaltern Studies can be read as a follow up of this mode of production debate that tried to address hordes of other seminal issues like the 'difference' of India's capitalist accumulation story, its variegated manifestation in the agricultural sector, in the land relation, the politics of patronage and the recalcitrance of the feudal elements in the economy. These discussions from the very beginning point to the limits of capital and the bourgeoisie's universalizing hegemonic project in India. Even though Subaltern Studies or for that matter postcolonial theory is often accused of celebrating unqualifiedly all aspects of subaltern existence to show the failure of capital and the bourgeoisie universal-liberal mission in India, a deeper scrutiny however can furnish a different interpretation of this failure narrative. One can also argue that by focusing on the limits of capital and its encompassing agenda, a space of 'outside' was perforce created which then nullifies the claim that there is one monolith of capital and everything is defined in conformity or in alterity to that monolith. Therefore this narrative of capital's faltered and incomplete journey in the non-Western context can be seen in a different, perhaps from a more radical perspective. Let me quote this paragraph at length from Sumit Sarkar's *Modern Times* (2014) that quite comprehensively offers a mapping of three main serialities of this mode of production debate and how each of them tried to negotiate with the question of difference in non-industrial, agriculture-based economy.

'The need was felt, therefore, to formulate categories to characterize and explain rural societies like the Indian, where many decades of intensive commercialization and some urban industrial capitalist growth had still not radically transformed the major part of the countryside.

Broadly, three kinds of positions emerged, with many variants for each. Some emphasized the colonial dimension as a principal barrier (even occasionally suggesting a distinct colonial mode of production), linking up with the widely current 'dependency' theories that sought to directly relate growth in the core capitalist world to the 'development of underdevelopment'(Gunder Frank's much-quoted phrase) in the subordinated colonial or semi-colonial periphery. Others, while not denying the evidently crucial nature of overall imperialist domination, felt that class relations within the colonized world also required more attention. The favoured formula, put forward for instance (with some internal differences) by Utsa Patnaik and Amit Bhaduri, was 'semi-feudal'. This stressed the continued domination of the Indian countryside by elements that needed to be characterized as basically pre-capitalist...not the full-scale capitalist appropriation of surplus value through a mastery of the production process. But there was also an alternative...put forward notably by Jairus Banaji in an influential paper in 1977. This used empirical details from the Maharashtra Deccan in the late nineteenth century to argue a case for a particular kind of capitalism in the countryside: one that amounted to a 'formal subsumption' of labour (where the production process has come under capitalist control, but has not been internally transformed), as distinct from the 'real subsumption' (which happens when the labour process is technologically revolutionized). Both in his view could be meaningfully considered capitalist.' (133-134).

What is so striking about this rendition is how in diverse and shifting registers like 'semi-feudal', 'formal subsumption', 'development of underdevelopment', a space of the 'difference' is implicated. This is the space that has made this otherwise holistic trajectory of capital's journey to the east slippery, therefore short of any encompassing supremacy it generally commands in the metropolitan centres. It on the other hand shows the perseverance of this space of the being-in-the-*outside*-world, the 'not-so-same

Other' that Capital has either to destroy or to co-opt to perpetuate its expansionary agenda. When Ranajit Guha in describing this space of the outside in the first volume of Subaltern Studies (henceforth SS) collective writes, 'What clearly is left out of this un-historical historiography is the *politics of the people.* For all parallel to the domain of elite politics there existed throughout the colonial period another domain of Indian politics in which the principal actors were not the dominant groups of the indigenous society or the colonial authorities but the subaltern classes' (italicized by the author himself) (1982: 4), he is rather eloquently making it clear how germane is this notion of the 'outside' that any engagement with postcolonial societies has to address in order to undertake any counter hegemonic agenda. There is no gainsaying in the fact that he took recourse to community, culture, tradition and other popular structures of faith and social convention to bring forth his understanding of, 'vast areas in the life and consciousness of the people which were never integrated into (the bourgeoisie's) hegemony' (Guha 1982: 5-6). Here we also need to highlight the background that led to this collective, the status of a failed state (the experience of Emergency days (1975-77) was quite fresh), the 'inadequacy of the bourgeoisie as well as the working class to lead into a decisive victory over colonialism' (Guha 1982: 7). The cultural question only came in the context of this particular background which was treated as an expedient call collectively shared across all disciplines of scholarships. It was therefore a collective endeavour to retrieve the polyphonous voices of political consciousness which have so far been only represented in the elite discourses of anti-colonial nationalism. Hence the SS collective can also be seen as part of the continuum that carried the thrust of forging a space of 'outside', an alternative language-logic-experience-ethos that tears into the dominant consensus of the capitalist development. Asok Sen's piece, 'Subaltern Studies: Capital, Class and Community' which has not drawn much attention in any critique of the SS reiterates the point that what SS wanted to do by highlighting the 'unrealized potential' (1987: 220) of the subaltern consciousness is primarily derived from the Gramscian understanding of radical politics and the subsequent critique of the passive role of the bourgeoisie. This essay is particularly important in showing how transformative potentials were not abandoned by the SS, rather by using the active and passive elements from Gramsci, how the SS collective was looking for molecular changes in the 'field of force' to imagine a counter hegemonic project. In his words, 'The wider historical outline of a non-capitalist transition, in which I have situated the revolutionary subject of Subaltern Studies, is inseparable from the task of Marxist mediation' (1987: 234). Therefore to claim that postcolonial theory has shunned questions of resistance, insurgency, and transformative political ideals is perhaps a reflection based on selective readings of some texts, whereas missing out on the large reservoir of other politically more significant contributions.

(Un)knowing the 'Other': Towards a Post-Oirentalist Political

What almost all these discrete and sometimes oppositional voices confirm is that the Indian scenario is different and an unqualified application of Marxian critique is counterproductive. What is also apparent from this analysis is the way the question of 'difference' crept into the whole discussion on mode of production and the dialectical interpretation of the social relation accordingly. However, what needs to be underlined is that their take on the issue of 'difference' is premised on a far more inclusive paradigm than the sole register of culture-ideology within which it has been predominantly addressed and analysed in the academic discourses of postcolonial theory at institutions in the West. Simultaneously, it cannot be denied that this aspect of 'difference' has for long been used and abused to mean a range of quasi political positions, from a critique of historiography to negating the enlightenment ethos to create a rupture in the Eurocentric knowledge discourses. As a consequence this assertion of 'difference' gradually gave in to random celebration of plurality of subjectivities, deferential possibilities of identity and subaltern assertion, and the uncritical acceptance of ideas like tradition, community and religion. According to Neil Lazarus, this ascendance of the cultural frame (precisely in the studies of cultural difference) in the overall critique of power and imperial domination then takes the form of civilizational critique.

Consequently, Europe as a categorical imperative was then generously equalled to a range of interpretations that strangely ignored the basic materialist factors which are responsible for Europe's domination over the globe. The Subaltern Studies collective also took recourse to some of these propositions of cultural difference which eventually occupied a central axial position in their enquiries (from Vol. 7 onwards). But what one also needs to mention is the way they keep theorizing this separate world of the subaltern as 'outside' (not necessarily a spatial marker), in distinction from the dominant elite/civil/privileged sphere. According to Ranajit Guha, these 'vast areas', that he calls the 'domain of the subaltern', constitute a space of 'outside' that shows limits to elite's hegemony. This divisioning of the domains which he alerts us against conceiving as 'hermetically sealed' (ibid) is pertinent to any discussion on 'difference' as a conceptual and ontological marker for birthing a new anti-capitalist political. Be it in the development critiques of Escobar, Ivan Illich, Teodor Shanin, to name just few, and in the post-development studies by Gibson-Graham, D.L. Seth, Majid Rahmena (one can consult Rahnema and Bawtree eds. 1997), in studies of Adivasi politics (Munshi 2012), this space of outside frequently returns and is reconceived in inventive and creative terminologies. In fact one can even pose this question on how politics is distinguished from political, should all imaginaries of otherness and differences are whittled out. What are we then left to imagine if all coordinates of political are reduced to mere negotiation within a hegemonic structure? By political what is meant here is an impulse to transcend the modalities of a structured possibility, of daring to imagine spaces that undermine that domain and delves deep into those nodes of (im)possibility which are present but yet absent, a kind of absence presence. In an introduction to one of the most seminal studies on class politics in South Asia (at least that is what Chibber has said about the book, 2013) this is what Ronald J. Herring and Rina Agarwala have to say:

> These indeterminacies are not overcome by a claim that identity politics has replaced class politics: we are equally unable to provide compelling theory on the conditions under which some identities will be chosen

> over others, or why answers vary over time. Nor do we know how some identities produce successful politics when others do not. We do know that such choices are embedded in structures of constraints and opportunities (2008: 23).

What needs to be pointed out here is how these 'structures of constraints and opportunities' are formed. Are they only based on governmental apparatus or do they include forces of culture and other popular mediations that cumulatively overdetermine the churnings of identity politics in South Asia? What is that (un)knowable element which controls this choice of some identities over other? To initiate any engagement in this realm of the (un)knowable, we have to come back to the question of 'outside', the domain of (im)possible political. The political edges of the postcolonial theory –something that this essay wants to strongly argue for - can be resuscitated by focusing on these spaces of 'outside' and 'difference'. To do that, we have to give shape to a new 'politics of outside' by first reinterpreting culture as a philosophy of life, a sense of 'shared environment' (Chakrabarti, Dhar and Cullenberg 2012: 177) that harbours and nourishes different forms of life, different levels of intimacies that cut beyond the hegemonic rationalist perspective. According to Michel de Certeau, the political lives in the 'tales of the unrecognized' immanent in everyday practices, their enthusiasm to fit these 'ethnological particularities' into an 'empty space' of theory (1984, Part-II). Now the challenge is in giving birth to these 'unrecongnized' tales that are entangled with different materialist chains of production in a space where the corporate capital is trying to establish its absolute hegemony. Only then can one retrieve this space of 'outside' without falling into the trap of neo-*Orientalism*, nativism and ethnicization. Hence we have to look for a new aperture and try for an option to reposition the 'difference' question in a radically disaggregated terrain of class focused analyses. Could there be a politics of outside which the prevalent consensus for capitalist growth has entirely made invisible? What are the constitutive elements of that post-Orientalist political that survives as an 'outside' in the midst of an aggressive pursuance of developmentalism?

Rethinking the Postcolonial Utopia and 'World of the Third'

"Class is an adjective, not a noun"
-Resnick and Wolff (*Knowledge and Class*)

Benita Parry in several articles and chapters including a seminal book titled *Postcolonial Studies: A Materialist Critique* (2004) has repeatedly drawn our attention to this purported failure of postcolonial theory and its complete turning away from the new realities of neoliberal global capital. She strongly contends that the contemporary socio-political plexus requires a 'recuperation of liberation theory as a revolutionary project for overcoming both colonialist social institution and archaic indigenous forms' (ibid: 9). By drawing upon Resnik and Wolf, Chakrabarti and Dhar have defined these 'new realities' as part of a global circuit of capital that has permeated all imaginable spaces of human sociality and has created for itself a constitutive outside, its 'Other' which is repressed and then occluded (2011). This domain of the other is what Fanon explored in *The Wretched of the Earth*, this is the same 'Other' that appears and reappears as 'gravel' in the 'Utopian footwear' of the neoliberal-state nexus (Chakrabarti and Dhar 2012: 107). According to Parry, 'What I have attempted to suggest is that post-colonial studies is in sore need of a different theoretical paradigm if it is to participate in the critique of globalization.' (Parry 2012: 355). She then further elaborates in a different work how after the institutionalization of postcolonial theory (Parry 2004) in the 1980s, it has distanced itself from any 'material impulse to colonialism, its appropriation of physical resources, exploitation of human labour and institutional repression' (Parry 2004: 3). Therefore the class analysis is unconsciously treated as a misnomer in the burgeoning field of postcolonial studies that arguably spends more attention in representing what Sumit Sarkar derides as 'rhetorical absolutism' and 'fragmented fetishism' (1998: 93). The following quote from Neil Lazarus further reinforces this point-

> It is, therefore, important to insist, in opposition to this emphasis, that whatever else it might have and, indeed, did *involve* – all the way from the systematic annihilation of whole communities to the cultivation of aesthetic tastes and preferences- colonialism as an historical process

> involved the forced integration of hitherto uncapitalised societies, or societies in which the capitalist mode of production was not hegemonic, into a capitalist world system. (Lazarus 2011: 11).

Now, the question is how to define this 'capitalist world system', while not sacrificing the main proposition that economy in Indian context is always a mix of 'differential forces' and these forces are in turn linked to community and other cultural configurations. Lazarus and other betray one way of articulating the major points of Wallerstein and how the dependency theory can be rethought in the contemporary situation of 'uneven and combined development'. Benita Parry's concept of 'Peripheral modernity' also shows how modernity in the periphery is derived from the capitalist logic of uneven development in the periphery and how that logic has given birth to specific forms of accumulation which is reflected in the cultural sphere of representation. Although there has been an attempt on their part to describe the predatory and exclusionary strategy of Capital that almost structures all spheres of reciprocation, what lacks in their discussion is how the cultural difference question is critical in refashioning a new resistant political. They in fact completely undermine any possibility of an 'outside' in the postcolonial scenario where the 'passive revolution' model is still operative and the Capital is yet to acquire a hegemonic role. Moreover, the point is that the concept of 'uneven and combined' development does not much problematise the hegemony of postcolonial Capital and how elements of non-Capital or something that Partha Chatterjee defines as non-corporate capital based on subsistence necessities is clashing with it. In fact in critiquing the logic of capital as the all-embracing force, the so-called 'materialist turn' in the postcolonial theory is also falling short of realizing how a space of 'outside' is foreclosed, how the hegemony of capital is based not on ensuring consensus for its exploitative logic, but by invisibilizing all spaces, language or expressions that do not fit its language-logic-experience-ethos.

The point that Kalyan Sanyal makes at the very beginning of his magnum opus, *Rethinking the Postcolonial Development*, is still immensely relevant to understand what we mean by Capital. In

Sanyal's words,

> The tendency to subsume under the term 'capitalist development' all developmental possibilities of a market economy, lodging—actually and potentially—different forms of production, derives from a social representation that sees capitalism as the dominant form of the economy. In this representation, capitalism's dominance overshadows other possible, existing forms of production that are always already present, thus pushing the heterogeneity that inheres in the economy to the background. The view of capitalism as hegemonic system informs not only the prevalent description of the advanced Western economies but also the description of the economy of the third world. (Sanyal 2007: 4).

Following the publication of *Knowledge and Class* by Resnik and Wolff in 1987 and the *The End of Capitalism* by Gibson-Graham in 1996, the politics of class has been understood as the class process comprising performance, appropriation, distribution and the receipt of surplus labour. Gibson-Graham on the other hand brings in the concept of 'Other' of capital, its disaggregated manifestations and the centric logic that reduces anything outside of capitalocentricity as redundant, the call of the 'primordial' 'backward' past. In post-development studies, in works of Escobar in particular these themes of the 'outside', its cultural specificities and the otherness have drawn substantial attention. What all these respective and immensely significant contributions have made clear is that there could be a possibility of a dialogue between postcolonial theory and a class-focused analysis of capital in contemporary times. The point that this paper wishes to reiterate is when we are talking about a possibility of a materialist turn of the postcolonial canon, it would be more significant and perhaps more productive if we can resurrect the political potenza of the project by re-engaging with this space of 'outside'. In fact in order to cultivate any subject of counter hegemonic potential, the given logic of the capital has to be tampered and contested. This position of an 'outside' can only offer any form of subjectivity which is not interpellated, therefore not hegemonized in the logic of capital. It is in the context of this 'Outside', that Chakrabarti, Dhar and Cullenberg introduced the notion of 'World of the Third' in distinction from the 'third world' framework. What distinguishes them from Lazarus and Timothy Brenan's discussion of 'uneven and combined development' is their problematization of the third world dynamic, their understanding of two different notions of 'outside', one which the capital has produced (the lacking other) to later incorporate in its goal of profit maximization and the second 'outside' which is foreclosed, therefore a constitutive exterior force that makes the constituted inside possible. This is what they call 'hegemony' of the global capital that within its centric matrix defines all realities as either pre-capital, post-capital, anti-capital and non-capital. In each of these explanations, capital is the constant referent which in turn differentially renders all temporal and spatial markers in relation to its overarching presence. In Chakrabarti, Dhar and Cullenberg's words,

> If a particular reality as a hegemonic system is produced through foreclosure, would not the perspective or perhaps the standpoint of the foreclosed particular, if made to bear upon the said reality, reality posing as the universal, inaugurate in turn a counter-hegemonic moment? (2012: 34).

Moreover

> if foreclosure defines and gives life to the hegemonic, then the return of the foreclosed puts to risk the hegemonic; it announces in turn the counter-hegemonic. The return of the foreclosed helps carve out the contours of the *expanded communism*...This standpoint gives meaning to what is already in the making as part of the production of forms of life. Such forms of life are counter-hegemonic because they are anachronistic to global capitalism (ibid.).

Therefore in rethinking Marxism in a renewed and disaggregated language of class processes and the surplus labour, they have quite succinctly built up a whole new cartography of political that has radicalized the space of "outside". Their interventions have proved why and how 'outside' can be re-thought as a political category, a space of new immanent possibilities which can jeopardize the dominant perspective. In radicalizing this space of 'outside', they have also paved the way for rethinking the postcolonial question in dialogue with the neo-colonial economies. Unlike what Parry, Timothy Brenan, Neil Lazarus and the entire Warwick collective is suggesting, we can envisage the revival of political in postcolonial theory by retaining the 'outside' space as 'an outside...not the outside' (Chakrabarti, Dhar and Cullenberg 2016: 277).

Conclusion

Let us return to the debate between Vivek Chibber and Partha Chatterjee and the way it relates to the postcolonial theory-Marxism interface to help formulate the avowed agenda of re-politicizing the postcolonial framework for imagining new paradigms of transformative politics in South Asia. Though several issues were raised and deliberated in that agonistic Chibber-Chatterjee encounter, there is however one fundamental line of contention that can sum up Chibber's objection to postcolonial theory. Chibber is convinced that we need to return to the Universalist standpoints for an adequate estimation of the capital and the 'revival of an international and democratic left' (2013: 78). For that he makes a common enemy in the postcolonial theory by calling it 'cobwebs' which he believes has to be cleared by 'a relative diminution of culturalism as the reigning framework of scholarship' (2011: 385). He accords a range of abusive, sometimes bloated rhetoric on the Subaltern Studies collective to elaborate his points. This particular line can give a precise sense to his quite extensive and provocative arguments:

> It is not that postcolonial studies is an assemblage of theories while Marxism was not – in fact, Marxism always comprised an eclectic range of theories, much as does the former. The difference is that Marxism always sought internal coherence and systematicity, while postcolonial studies resists any compulsion to bring together and assess its various stands (2013: 3).

These 'various stands' of postcolonial theory includes gender studies, area studies, social practices, critical anthropology so on and so forth. Undoubtedly this is sometimes a mind boggling menu for any critical effort to offer a coherent pattern of theory. Therefore, while agreeing with Chibber's basic presumption that we need a turn away from the 'culturalist' framework to revive a counter-hegemonic project, we need to however find it within the very scope of postcolonial theoretical repertoire, it's critical and what Robert Young calls the 'political perceptions and agenda' (1998) that can emerge from the discussion of possibilities of 'difference' and spaces of 'outside'. The point is that a great deal depends on how we look at the question of 'difference'. The perspectival question can turn the same apparently bland critical project into one of profound political potenza. The problem with the Chibberian hypothesis is that he wants to decimate the body which has a disease in one of its parts. Instead of curing the disease–the fact that postcolonial theory deserted its erstwhile emancipatory agenda for cultural representation of the 'Other', Chibber is arguing for a complete abrogation of the body. Such attempts are ultimately bound to be counterproductive as it ignores all fault-lines that can exist in any Universalist agenda. We need to rather continue this dual-pronged strategy of critiquing any essential portrayal of the 'other' in the postcolonial studies while keep on prodding to conceptualize and identify spaces of 'outside' that limit any hegemonic capitalocentricity.

There are therefore two responses emanating from this alleged crisis in the postcolonial theoretical bedrock. We can divide them in two standpoints of internal and external critique. If the internal critique (Parry, Lazarus, Brenan) is one of critical engagement to facilitate a materialist turn in the whole project, the external intervention (Gudavarthy 2016) can be seen as one of rejection and repudiation. The challenge therefore lies in how to work through these two propositions that are either directly or in tangent relating to the postcolonial theory-Marxism debate in the South Asian context. Could there be an alternative entry point, any third position that can negotiate both? Here I want to argue that this 'the third position' can be found in the works of Sanyal, Chakravarti, Dhar and Cullenberg. This is the position that both retain the necessary critique from the materialist perspective and also engenders a discussion of 'outside' which is both present and absent in the circuit of global capital. Present because it always contradicts, interdicts and resists that dominant capitalist dynamic; absent because it has been discursively foreclosed to establish the hegemony of the capital. This foreclosed space of the 'outside' therefore acts like a spectre, 'the return of the repressed', the return of those forms of life that survive in the shadowed world of abjection and depravity. To imagine any resistant political subjectivity from the global south, from areas where expansion of capital has been most brutal, we have to redraw this critical geographic space of the 'outside', the actors who inhabit this pace and the actions that can redefine the contours of postcolonial theory. This is where we have to weave a new 'cobweb' of postcolonial political which is not subjugated in the politics of universalism, not decimated in the capitalocentricity; rather on the contrary goes beyond the smokescreen of the so-called radicalism and enshrines a new domain of the emerging 'other', the spectral other.

REFERENCES

Ahmed, Aijaz. 1997. *In Theory: Classes, Nations, Literatures*. New Delhi: Oxford.

Certeau, Michael de. 1984. *The Practice of Everyday Life*. Translated by Steven Rendall. Berkeley: University of California Press.

Chakrabarti, Anjan and Anup Dhar. 2012. 'Gravel in the Shoe: National*ism* and World of the Third'. *Rethinking Marxism*, 24:1, 106-123.

Chakrabarti, Anjan, Anup Dhar and Byasdeb Dasgupta. 2015. *The Indian Economy in Transition: Globalization, Capitalism and Development*. Delhi: Cambridge University Press.

Chakrabarti, Anjan, Anup Dhar and Stephen Cullenberg. 2012. *World of the Third and Global Capitalism*. New Delhi: Worldview.

Chakrabarti, Anjan, Anup Dhar and Stephen Cullenberg. 2016. '(Un)doing Marxism from the Outside', *Rethinking Marxism,* Vol. 28, No. 2, 276-294.

Chatterjee, Partha. 2004. *The Politics of the Governed: Reflection on Popular Politics in Most of the World*. Ranikhet: Permanent Black.

Chibber, Vivek. 2013. *Postcolonial Theory and the Spectre of Capital*. Londn: Verso.

Chibber, Vivek. 2011. 'On the Decline of Class Analysis in South Asian Studies'. *Critical Asian Studies*, 38: 4, 357-387.

Chibber, Vivek. 2013. 'Capitalism, Class and Universalism: Escaping the Cul-de-sac of Postcolonial Theory' in Leo Panitch, Greg Albo and Vivek Chibber (eds). *Registering Class 50 Years: Socialist Register 1964-2014,* pp. 63-80. New Delhi: LeftWord.

Dabashi, Hamid. 2012. *The Arab Spring: The End of Postcolonialism*. London: Zed Books.

Dhar, Anup. 2016. 'Swaraj in Ideas: from 'Third World' to 'World of the Thirds'. Unpublished Working Paper.

Escobar, Arturo. 1995. *Encountering Development: The Making and Unmaking of The Third World*. New Jersey: Princeton University Press.

Fanon, Frantz. 1963. *The Wretched of the Earth*. London: Penguin Books.

Gopal, Priyamvada. 2016. 'Redressing Anti-Imperial Amnesia', *Race & Class*, Vol. 57(3): 18-30.

Gudavarthy, Ajay. 2013. *Politics of Post-Civil Society: Contemporary History of Political Movements in India*. New Delhi: Sage.

Gudavarthy, Ajay. 2016. 'Brahmanism, Liberalism and Postcolonial Theory', *Economic and Political Weekly*, Vol. LI, No. 24.

Guha, Ranajit (ed). 1982. *Subaltern Studies I: Writings on South Asian History and Society*. New Delhi: Oxford.

Herring, Ronald J. and Rina Agarwala (eds). 2008. *Whatever Happened to Class? Reflections from South Asia*. Delhi: Danish Books.

Lazarus, Neil. 2004. 'The Fetish of "the West" in Postcolonial Theory' in Crystal Bartolovich and Neil Lazarus (eds). *Marxism, Modernity and Postcolonial Studies*. UK: Cambridge University Press.

Lazarus: Neil. 2011. 'What Postcolonial Theory Doesn't Say', *Race & Class*, Vol. 53(1): 3-27.

Loomba, Ania and Jed Esty (eds). 2006. *Postcolonial Studies and Beyond*. Durham: Duke University Press.

Munshi, Indra (ed). 2012. *The Adivasi Question: Issues of Land, Forest and Livelihood*. New Delhi: Orient Blackswan and EPW.

Parry, Benita. 2004. *Postcolonial Studies: A Materialist Critique*. London: Routledge.

Parry, Benita. 2012. 'What is Left in Postcolonial Studies?', *New Literary History*, 43 (341-358).

Purakayastha, Anindya. 2014. 'Postcolonial Agonistic Demo-Crazy: Artivism and Mestiza Pluralism as the Dissensual Politics of the Governed', *Parallax*, 20(2): 49-60.

Rahnema, Majid and Victoria Bawtree (eds). 1997. *The Post-Development Reader*. Dhaka: University Press LTD.

Ray, Raka and Mary Fainsod Katzenstein (eds). 2005. *Social Movements in India: Poverty, Power and Politics*. New Delhi: Oxford.

Roy, Arundhati. 2005. *An Ordinary Person's Guide to Empire*. New Delhi: Penguin.

Sanyal, Kalyan. 2007. *Rethinking Capitalist Development*. New Delhi: Routledge.

Sarkar, Sumit. 1997. *Writing Social History*. New Delhi: Oxford.

Sarkar, Sumit. 2014. *Modern Times: India 1880s-1950s*. Ranikhet: Permanent Black.

Sen, Asok, 1987. 'Subaltern Studies: Capital, Class and Community' in Ranajit Guha (ed). *Suabaltern Studies I: Writings on South Asian History and Society*. New Delhi: Oxford.

Watson, Mathew C. 2013. 'The Poverty of Postcolonial Theory?' *Postcolonial Studies*, 16(2): 230-232.

Young, Robert J.C. 'Editorials', 1998, *Intervention* 1(1): 4.

6

State, Class and People's Struggles: Trajectory of the Left in Bangladesh—Crisis and New Formation

Anu Muhammad

Introduction

The 'left politics', as I understand, is an ideological position and activism that opposes any form of discrimination and hegemony, and that works for revolutionary transformation of the society for emancipation of humanity in harmony with nature.

Let us keep in mind the fact that there is not 'one' left, and the left is not a homogeneous body, there are many lefts under 'the left' broad category. Accepting Marxian ideology as the guideline of thinking and praxis is formally accepted by most of the left, but reading Marxism varies widely among different strands. There are differences among various strands, sometimes very fundamental. Moreover, there are also left as ideological activists—as writers, and social and political activists, academic, many of them remain outside party politics. So understanding the left requires recognition of its many strands and inclusion of activities and thoughts of individuals and groups as well.

Like elsewhere, there are different strands of political parties and groups within the left identity in Bangladesh, from underground to parliamentary, from the line of arms struggle to electoral path. Every party/group has its own strategy and tactics, therefore has differences with others. Within electoral and parliamentary groups there are differences in the relationships with the ruling parties, as some parties, known as left, have become partners of the ruling party that is pushing neoliberal development for the country. Within non-parliamentary groups, there are strategic lines of people's war to people's uprising. Therefore generalization about the left without considering these decisive differences would be highly misleading.

In different phases of history, in many socio-political urgencies, we find that the left, except some masked and opportunists, whether as a party, or as a group and also as individuals played their crucial role. Despite their failure in determining its course, the left raised many issues in the public sphere, formulated vision, disseminated ideas, organized struggles and suffered government repression the most. This is true for Bangladesh, also true for many other countries.

In this chapter I have made an attempt to write an historical overview of ups and downs, success and crisis, contributions and decline of the left in Bangladesh in the context of the state and class, its connections with socio-economic changes, globalization and neoliberal economic reforms, and the role of the intelligentsia. Also I have tried to locate new formations in the time of the left's general crisis.

Historical Overview: British Colonial Rule to Pakistan

Left politics in Bangladesh has historical links with British colonial India (up to 1947) and Pakistan (from 1947 to 1971). Armed insurgence against the British imperialism (so-called 'terrorist movement') created the fertile ground of revolutionary communist entry in undivided Bengal of undivided (or British) India. The nature of organization, spirit, personal devotion and practice in *Jugantar*, *Anushilon* during the 1920s and 1930s had an enduring influence on the communist movement in Bangladesh. On the other hand, the Russian October Revolution in 1917 had inspired the educated radical youth to study Marxism and to form the Communist Party (CP). Soviet revolutionary enthusiasm added strength to the anti-British anti-feudal left movement. During the 1930s and 40s the peasant movement against landlords, the Tebhaga movement being one of them, could connect rural peasants with revolutionary spirit and spread widely.

However, inability of the CP to deal with two factors, global alliances in the Second World War and rising communal conflicts, affected the growth of the anti-imperialist and anti-feudal people's movement adversely. As the Soviet Union became an ally of Britain (and the US) in the war against the Germany-led alliance, that put CPI in a difficult and confusing situation to push its strategic anti-imperialistic struggle at home where the British Raj was supposed to be the principal enemy. Secondly, when the anti-feudal peasant movement, known as the Tebhaga movement, spread into rural areas in the mid-40s and later, Hindu Muslim communal tension was also rising then. In the rising tide of the Tebhaga movement, communal issues could grab the social attention since most of the landlords were Hindu while most of the peasants were Muslim. In this setting, as the CP could not keep itself active and vigilant enough, the Tebhaga peasant movement gradually lost its spirit and in many places capitalized by communal politics.

The partition of India with unprecedented communal violence, specially in Bengal and Punjab, and its long lasting distrust and hatred between communities shaped politics in later years too. Communal riots and increasing hatred between communities resulted in mass migration in both directions. In East Bengal (present Bangladesh) not only were most of the zamindars Hindu, but most of the educated middle class were also from Hindu families. Therefore in the mass migration many of them including teachers, lawyers, writers and singers left East Bengal for India. Most of the CP organizers were from Hindu families. Many of them had to leave their roots.

In line with the partition of India, the Communist Party of India was also divided at the Kolkata Conference held in 1949 into two, i.e. Communist Party of India (CPI) and Communist Party of Pakistan (CPP). The same conference also rejected the P.C. Joshi line as 'pro-Nehru and the pro-Congress of soft opposition by the CPI' and endorsed the Randive line that called for an all out struggle against 'fake independence'. The CPP also followed this line only to face huge repression in Pakistan. The newly formed CPP did not have a strong base in East Bengal. Pakistan was then primarily an agricultural country, the eastern part (present Bangladesh) had a limited industrial base at that time, and trade unions were almost non-existent. Only organized workers could be found in the railways with 13,000 workers and tea plantations with 27,000 worker (Ali, 2015).

In East Pakistan, despite an all out attack on communists, the party activists and intellectuals played a decisive role in building the first ever challenge to the Pakistan state by mobilizing people to assert the right of the mother language. This language movement was not limited to urban areas, rural people also joined in different ways. Since it was not only about rights to speak in the mother tongue, it was more of a demonstration of huge public discontent against regional and ethnic discrimination, bad governance and repressive measures by the Pakistan government. Therefore agitated peasants and workers joined students to express their solidarity.[1]

In most of the Pakistan period, the Communist Party remained banned and many organizers were repeatedly thrown into jail. Nevertheless the party continued to work from underground and in several disguises. They also worked within the Awami League.

A faction of leaders and workers of the ruling Muslim League under the leadership of Maulana Bhasani left the party in 1949 to form the Awami Muslim League as a protest against autocratic rule. Later the name was changed to the Awami League in 1953, with Maulana Bhasani as its President, where Sheikh Mujibur Rahman later became Secretary. The 1954 general election brought an end to the Muslim League rule in Pakistan and opened up new possibilities of democratic governance. But in 1956, governor's rule was imposed on the then East Pakistan by the West Pakistan-based ruling elites, that manifested their unwillingness to accept democratic institutions and practices.

During this period, the United States emerged as the leading imperial power and it was trying to get a stronghold in Asia to fight the increasing Soviet and Chinese influence. As India became a staunch ally of the USSR, the USA found a firm foothold in Pakistan to counter that. The Suhrawardi-Mujib faction in the Awami League

(AL) was determined to go with the Pak-US military pact SEATO and CENTO. In 1957 the National Awami Party (NAP) was born under the leadership of Maulana Bhasani to protest endorsement of the US strategic design by the (AL) leadership. Till the Moscow-Peking divide, NAP under his leadership could work as an open platform of the left in both wings of Pakistan. After the division, NAP was also divided.

The leadership of a Maulana (Islamic religious leader) and his wide acceptance by the left was significant for the radical movement in a society where the left and communists had always been attacked and marginalized as atheists. When a Maulana was in the forefront of the left movement, the same tactic could not always work for the anti-people forces. Maulana Bhasani was branded as 'red Maulana' by many.[2]

The major student, peasant and workers' organizations in the then East Pakistan were actually linked to the Communist Party (CP). During the 1960s, they had played a key role in mobilizing people against imperialism, landlords, military dictatorship and the big capitalist regime, that culminated in the 1969 mass uprising and brought the Ayub rule to an end. However, growth of the left faced severe setbacks after division of the international communist movement and consequent disintegration. That put them in total disarray after its peak in the 1969 mass uprising. Breakdown of the left was intensified by internal conflicts under the shadow of the ideological divide between the Moscow and Peking (Beijing) line and later more divisions took place because of further differences on strategy and tactics among the pro-Peking leadership. The major pro-Peking groups created a disaster in mass organizations when they assumed the Charu Mazumdar line uncritically and withdrew from all mass organizations in 1970. In fact, that was the beginning of the fall of the left in Bangladesh.

In the setting of regional and ethnic discrimination, the nationalist movement under the leadership of Sheikh Mujib spread rapidly to contain people's discontent. Disintegration of the left helped the AL to become the main opposition of Pakistan autocratic rule. In the process, Sheikh Mujibur Rahman emerged as the most popular leader. Complete electoral victory of the AL in 1970 gave him absolute authority.

The State, Ruling Class and the Left After Independence

After independence, Sheikh Mujib with his party Awami League assumed power with unparalleled authority and popularity in Bangladesh. But, because of its class position, the ruling party could not use its enormous popularity to take the country to the direction as aspirations consolidated during the war of liberation. On the contrary, groups connected with the party used the strength to grab money, power and resources as a quick path to become new rich. People of Bangladesh, in fact, started experiencing defeat in many ways since their victory against Pakistan.

After independence, there was virtually no opposition except some left groups, open and underground. Nevertheless the ruling party leaders were intolerant to any opposition, they did not allow fair electoral process at the national level, in trade unions, professional organizations and also in student unions. Therefore we witnessed different forms of rigging, manipulation including armed attacks to capture voting centres and seizing ballot boxes.

The left during the Mujib period was sharply divided on the question of collaboration with the regime. The pro-Moscow faction preferred to maintain the alliance with Mujib in the line of the 'non-capitalist path to socialism' strategy prescribed by the Soviet Union. In the end the pro-Moscow Communist Party of Bangladesh (CPB) and allies joined one party BAKSAL floated by Sheikh Mujib after dissolving their parties. On the other hand, pro-Peking factions fell into a chaotic situation since 1970. In 1971, these groups fell into an anarchic situation, while a few leaders obeyed the Chinese position to remain soft on Pakistan while many others joined the liberation war on their own without any organized and disciplined guidelines. Their situation deteriorated after independence when they almost repeated the Randive line along with the Charu line.

In 1973, a new party Jatiya Samajtantrik Dal (JSD) was born by splitting the ruling party itself, with an objective to establish 'scientific socialism' in the country. The leadership included former student leaders of the AL. They also faced severe government repression. Many of them were killed. The role of the newly formed special paramilitary forces Rakkhi Bahini, along with police created a terror during that period, that force was used mainly for violent oppression of the dissenting left.[3] Ruling party organs were also used to spread fear and using muscles against any dissident voices and activism. Therefore thousands of left or dissenting people were killed by the state forces or party goons, while more than 1 million people were killed by famine during the same period (Musa, 1980).

The years of violence and anarchy, uncertainty and repression ended badly first with the declaration of emergency (December 1974), then to establish one party state with Sheikh Mujib as lifelong president (January 1975) and then by killing of Sheikh Mujib and his family members by some army officers (August 1975). Martial Law came back within four years of independence.

After many bloody clashes and dramatic events, the then army chief General Ziaur Rahman could grab state power and at a convenient moment became the President of the country. A new party was born to give Zia a platform, Bangladesh Nationalist Party (BNP). Religion-based political parties had been banned in the 1972 constitution, that was withdrawn after the military takeover in 1975. In the process Jamaat-e-Islami Bangladesh, main accused for collaborating with the Pakistan army in war crimes, returned to the political scene by the late 70s during Zia's rule.

President Zia was also killed by a section of the military on May 30, 1981. After a year of staged drama army chief General Hussein M. Ershad declared martial law again on March 24, 1982. First protest against martial law came from the students of the left leaning small organizations. They chanted slogans against military rule, pasted posters and organized demonstrations when these were completely banned and highly risky. Leading activists of these protests were arrested and sentenced to 14 years in jail in summary court.

Nevertheless young activists from the left continued organizing protests against military rule. Small initiatives and informal discussions culminated in a programme to gherao the Shikkha Bhaban on January 11, 1983. Within a month, a bigger demonstration on February 14, 1983 shook the regime. In this way, the student movement effectively influenced national politics to develop an anti-military rule movement. That resulted in formation of two alliances, one is the Awami League-led 15 party alliance and another one is the BNP-led 7 party alliance. Different left parties did not form their own alliance but were divided themselves into these alliances.

This phase of martial law, direct or disguised, continued till 1990. That was the period of the expanding repressive machine of the state, polluting politics, instutionalizing corruption, rise of communal politics, formation of the new super rich class, beginning of the structural adjustment programme and further erosion of the old left. The left of different strands could not cope with the fast moving political events and economic restructuring. Moreover, the fall of the Soviet Union and global renewed campaign against the socialist project acted as the final blow for many. A significant portion of the left became inactive or joined right wing politics.

Since the downfall of the autocratic military regime in 1990, 'elected' governments have been ruling the country. But the fact remains that elections have always been a matter of muscle and money power, the parliament was never allowed to function as a body of people's representatives, the 'elected' body was never allowed to formulate, not even discuss the crucial policies that determined the fate of the country. The left presence in these forums has been almost negligible.

Neoliberal Development and Decline of Workers' Power

The policies and programmes aimed for bringing everything into the reach of private business, turning every activity for profit, and opening everything for corporate interests are collectively known as neoliberal economic policy. Economic reforms in this model resulted in many changes in the economy and in social composition. Big public enterprises were dismantled; land of large mills was replaced by export processing zones, shopping malls and real estate. Export oriented garments factories became the mainstay of manufacturing.[4] Permanent industrial jobs were replaced by a temporary, part-time outsourced insecure work system. Remittances sent by migrant

State, Politics and Other Factors (1972-2015)

State and Policies	*Political Activism*	*Corresponding Scenario*
1972: New constitution with four principles: Democracy, Socialism, Secularism and Nationalism. 1972-73: : Bangladesh became a member of WB, IMF, and ADB. 1973-74: Bangladesh became member of the OIC. : General amnesty to the collaborators of the Pakistan army without specific war crime charges. : Rehabilitation of collaborators, bureaucrats, army officers, at different levels. : Rakkhi Bahini, a new paramilitary force was formed.	1972-73: Major parties Awami League (AL) and CPB, NAP (Muzaffar), NAP (Bhasani). The first three parties formed an alliance. January 1, 1973: Matiul and Kader, two student union activists were killed by police firing on anti-imperialist demonstration. 1973: Jatiya Samajtantrik Dal (JSD) was formed, became a major challenge for the ruling party. : Repression on opposition, many were killed and disappeared.	1973-74: Erosion of the high popularity of Sheikh Mujib and credibility of the Awami League government. : World Bank-IMF began their 'development' operations. : Price rise, fall in the production index. : Flood.
1974: Emergency declared.		1974: Large-scale famine, more than 1 million died.
1975 January: One party rule. August: Killing of President Sheikh Mujib and his family members. Martial law. : Secularism as a state principle was removed. : Prohibition of religion-based politics was removed. : General Zia assumed power following a series of bloody confrontations and 'sepoy' revolution.		1975: World Bank appreciated one party state, then bloody military coup, followed by Zia rule. : Relationship with the West improved further.
1978: President Zia formed BNP. : The leader of Jamaat and top war criminal Golam Azam was permitted to enter Bangladesh.	1979: Ruling party student, peasant and workers' branches were formed with direct guidance from administration and intelligence agency.	1976-8: Privatization process went further.

1981: President Zia was killed. 1982: Martial Law declared by Chief of Army HM Ershad. 1982-90: Use of religion in business and politics increased more than ever. 1986: Ershad formed his party Jatiya Party. 1987: Repression on mass uprising. : Emergency declared. : Scimitar deal for Haripur oil field	1983-84: student resistance against military rule and strong workers' movement. 1980s: Formation of student alliances in different phases to fight military rule. : Two alliances against military rule. : Workers' broad unity (SKOP), peasants broad unity (17 peasant and workers' unity) where left parties played key role.	1982: Martial law. 1983-84: strong workers' movement 1982-89: Structural Adjustment Programmes. Plundering of state resources, crime, accumulation of 'black money' went to the top. Deindustrialization. : Stagnation in productive sectors. Rise in unemployment. : Domination of WB-IMF- increased. : A new big propertied class, little related with productive activities, became visible.
1988: Parliamentary election held amid boycott by all parties, voters almost nil. : Islam was declared state-religion in that parliament.	1987-88: Countrywide strong mass movement. Peasant mobilization.	Flood Action Plan proposed by WB.
1990: December. Resignation of military ruler after the 8-year long public protest.	1990: Unprecedented unity of political parties and other organizations against military rule	1990: Countrywide anti-autocratic movement intensified.
1991: BNP won election, formed government with support from Jamaat. 1991: Golam Azam appeared publicly as Amir of Jamaat.	1991: Independent 'task forces for development' were formed.	1992: People's tribunal against war criminals, movement intensified. Communal tension and attack following demolition of Babri mosque.
1992: Privatization of education and healthcare intensified, Private University Bill passed, flourished quickly as profit making sector. 1993-94: Fatwa against women, writers, scientists intensified.	1992: Nationwide war crime trial movement began. : People's court was set with Jahanara Imam in the chair.	1993-94: GATT agreement. 5000 factories closed. 1 lakh workers were retrenched. 1993: Government started privatizing oil gas blocks by signing production sharing contracts (PSCs) with international oil companies.

		1994...marketization and globalization of economy intensified.
1994-95: Alliance between Awami League and Jamaat.		
1996...Awami League in power.		1996...Old policies continued
1997...Use of religion in power increased. Alliance between BNP and Jamaat. 1999: Terrorist attacks on rallies, religious places, and cultural programmes' festivals began.	National committee against privatization of energy and attempt to export gas was formed. Left parties and individuals took the lead.	1997... More PSCs signed. Privatization continued. Magurchara blowout in UNOCAL gas field caused huge losses to Bangladesh.
2001..2006. BNP, in alliance with Jamaat and Islamic Oikyo Jote, in power. : Secret agreements with the US on 'anti-terrorist' measures. : Terrorist attacks continued. : State-sponsored killing in the name of anti-terrorist measures increased.	2003: Long march and other mobilizations against bad deals on natural resources. 2006: Mass uprising against disastrous foreign contracts and plunder in Phulbari. Killing of protesters by paramilitary force. Protests spread. Phulbari agreement signed between the government and the people. 2006: Garment workers agitation, collapse of Dhaka city	2001... Closure of big public sector enterprises. More privatization of banks, utility services. 2005: Tangratila blowout.
2007-2008: Army-backed interim government in power. Government put many corrupt politicians and businessmen in jail. But repression, blackmailing and ransom spread.	Student, garment workers, jute workers' agitation.	Environment of fear. Further policy reforms and agreements to transfer public institutions to private ownership.
2008 December: General election. Awami League with alliance came to power. 2009-present: Trial of war criminals. : Extrajudicial killing and disappearance continued. 2014: Opposition crushed and one-sided election	2010...: Sundarban movement against coal-fired power plant. 2013: Shahbag movement to support and to ensure war criminals trial. : Youth and left activists active in Sundarban and Shahbag movement.	: Privatization of common property, grabbing of land, forest, river increased. Construction boom.

workers appeared as the lifeline of the economy. Energy resources and power were systematically privatized. Electricity became a costly commodity and costs for the productive sector increased. Moreover energy security was threatened because of wrong policies and corruption. Land grabbing, occupying public spaces by private business, and deforestation created an environmental disaster and uprooted many.[5]

Neoliberal reforms were initiated in Bangladesh, as elsewhere, in the name of curbing corruption, improving efficiency and transparency, increasing decent employment and reducing poverty. But as we found these reforms, instead, increased the scope and legality of corruption, criminality, resource-grabbing, commissions from bad deals, gangsterism and loss of secure jobs. This process of capital accumulation is in many ways similar to what Marx wrote about regarding the process of primitive capital accumulation in Europe, wherein old and new elites appropriated common resources and turned them into private property. This is the process which Harvey calls "accumulation by dispossession" (Harvey, 2011: 40-57).

Migration from agriculture to non-agriculture within rural areas and to semi-urban or urban areas has increased only to find temporary low wage jobs in the informal sector, small industries, transport and services. Desperate attempts by many unemployed youth to find jobs overseas have created human trafficking. It is evident that NGO credit operations helped non-farm activities to grow in the rural areas, like small trade, small money-lending, small-scale handicrafts and rickshaw-vans. But many studies revealed the limits of microfinance as a tool of poverty reduction. This has rather shown the face of, what I call, 'neoliberalism for the poor'. It is true that, BRAC and Grameen Bank have their own spectacular success stories. But that success is found not in poverty alleviation, but rather in corporate expansion and the establishment of a new form of financial industry. (Muhammad, 2009)

The neoliberal policy guided reforms that had shaped all the government's actions since the early 1980s played as an instrument of class hegemony. These reforms were intended to dismantle old industries, not only to expand rule of private capital, but it was also aimed at breaking workers' stronghold in public enterprises. The process reached its peak in 2002 with the closure of Adamjee Jute Mills, the largest jute industry of the world. The demise of this enterprise was arranged in the name of 'Jute Sector Development' with a US$ 250 million loan from the World Bank.[6]

The reform process created a large pool of labour: disorganized, scattered, unable to assert its rights, and forced to accept low wages. This has become, in fact, a global pattern employment in the neoliberal model: no stable secure jobs but only part time, contract or outsourced jobs, and expanding informal sector. No regular jobs, no trade unions, no organized workers' power. I agree that, 'added to the huge numbers of the unemployed is the 'precariat', the growing segment of the working population in jobs that are temporary, low-wage, and without benefits or protection. Conditions that were once associated with the informal sector in the developing world are now becoming truly global.' (Panitch et al., 2012)

Despite regimented control over labour, Bangladesh has witnessed outbursts of non-trade unionized workers several times in the last decade. In 2006, garment workers, who were deprived of trade union rights, demonstrated their strength and for the first time seized Dhaka city, repeated in later years. That, however, could not progress to transform spontaneous angry workers into a political force.

Left and Intelligentsia: Structural Adjustment of Economists

During the martial law period in the 1960s, studying Marxian literature was highly risky, even carrying revolutionary/left books/ magazines could be a cause of arrest. The Communist Party (later parties) remained underground, in educational institutions radical discussions were rarely possible, teachers were highly monitored even on their class lectures if they were listed as left, i.e. dangerous. There are evidences of forceful retirement of professors, beating of university professors by ruling party goons, even killing in protest rallies. Despite restrictions, regimentation and torture there were a number of left leaning active writers, artists and academics, some of whom also were members of the underground party.

These intellectuals made an influential contribution to literature, research and a cultural new beginning during Pakistan's rule. Their intellectual contribution was crucial to create counter hegemony in social consciousness to fight communalism, ethnic and regional discrimination, imperialism, to build a vision of socialism and to fight for independence. Although the AL could establish its authority over the people's struggle after 1969, left influence remained strong in the liberation war and eventually it influenced the constitution to accommodate principles of equality. However, many of these intellectuals were killed in 1971 by the Pakistan army or its collaborators.

After independence, restrictions on Marxian/leftist study were gone, the country endorsed socialism as one of the four principles, but at the same time we experienced a gradual fall of intellectual activities specially since the late 80s. One can argue that the shape of the middle class has some reasons behind this. This section of the society had been traditionally the main source of left activists. The expansion of the middle class is an important phenomenon in the last few decades. Affluence among a section of this middle class is mostly an outcome of privatization of social services, foreign-aided projects and expansion of the service sector. Options before the middle class to keep its status, and to find the ladder for graduating to the higher income group are linked with the dominant mode of accumulation. Beneficiaries of privatization of education and healthcare belong to a section of teachers and physicians. Career plans of the youth rely mostly on the commercialized service sector or other corporate capital. Therefore it is not surprising to find that the middle class, in general, becomes friendlier to grabbers, corrupt and rent seekers; also supportive to neoliberal functioning of the state.

Among academia, Marxian theories and exercises had a strong place till the mid-80s. In economics structural changes including land reform, public rights for education and healthcare, equality got much attention and preferred by many for discussion and research. Gradual shifting of the economists' from studying development issues in a comprehensive way to studies in a compartmental way can be explained by their increasing dependence on the funded projects by 'donor' agencies'. Rehman Sobhan, senior economist of the country, rightly pointed out that, 'we should have no illusions that any significant run down in technical assistance programming which finance these consultancies would have significant repercussions on the livelihood of many economists.... economists have never been so busy in aid-financed research and where their standards of living have become closely interlinked with the aid regime.' The reduction of the economists to a level of technician has also effects on teaching in economics and therefore 'perpetuating the same trend for generations to come and reproduction of the same species' (Muhammad, 2007). Needless to say, class analysis and the question of exploitation and investigating the causes of poverty became almost redundant in the economic writings of many since the late 1980s.[7]

Effectively neoliberal ideology is now dominant at the policy level as well as among academia. Hegemony of this line of thinking amongst academics specially economists make grabbing, occupation and destruction easy and 'raional'. In Bangladesh while foreign corporate investment in the energy sector has become a permanent curse for the economy, it has been hailed as a great success of economic policies; closure of manufacturing units are highly scored as successful reform; withdrawal of state responsibility from public education/health and through people to the rule of market added credentials to the government. In this approach privatization of common property, grabbing of natural resources appear as progress, destruction of wetland, forest or cropland in favour of profitable business are seen as development, dismantling of public institutions are considred as economic reforms.

With the strong wave of neoliberalism in the world, 'Marxist intellectual culture has undergone a decline across much of the world since the 1980s.' What Chibber described specifically about the United States and India, that is also true for Bangladesh, 'the past two decades have been a time of a rightward political drift, based on a balance of political power that has tilted massively towards dominant classes.' (Chibber, 2006: 357–387)

New Formation

However, that is not the end of the story. After the fall of the Soviet Union the world was given a promise to reach the free world, democracy, peace and end of war. The real world moved in the opposite direction. Global monopoly capitalism that reached the permanent arms economy opened a new front of war by attacking Iraq in 1991, eventually with the new American century project, 'war on terror' gave opportunities for eternal war and armament building. Neoliberal policies and globalization of finance capital strengthened the power of capital and brought distress to the global people and destruction of global nature on an unprecedented scale. All reactionary forces including racist, communal and sexist forces got new life in many parts of the world. People in every corner of the globe are now facing challenges to look for renewal of left ideology to build up resistance on a global scale. Therefore, we witness multiple forms of organization to resist this world (dis)order.

In Latin America we witnessed a wave of change that rejected the chain of global capitalism, in many countries in Asia and Europe there have been growing discontent and huge protests against neoliberal economic reforms and against war. Occupy movements in many parts of the USA and elsewhere also demonstrated discontent and resistance at this stage. Theories of organization and movement are evolving everywhere. Resistance and enquiry are still living activities of human beings. Reorganization of the left and experiments to restructure the movement have been ongoing.[8] That is also happening in Bangladesh.

In Bangladesh, democratic institutions and practices are far from real, left agenda and politics have become insignificant in power struggles, governance becomes a zamindari system that overrules any institutional and legal process in the country. Therefore space for healthy growth of political and cultural activism is still a dream, and a matter of continuous struggles. Nevertheless, there are sparks of protest against increasing repressive and anti-people role of the state. That gives birth of the new formation in every section of society. Among students, workers and women we find anger, sudden outbursts and a new form of alliance.

Under the banners such as 'general students' unity', 'nipironer biruddhe amra' (we are against oppression), 'nipiron o boishomya birodhi chatrasomaj' (students against oppression and discrimination), 'dhorshon protirodh moncho' (rape resistance platform), 'sundarboner rokkha committee' (Committee to save Sundarban), 'sramik adhikar rokkha moncho' (platform for workers' rights), 'samanadhikar amader nuntomo dabi' (equal rights our minimum demand), sampradayikotar biruddhe ama (we are against communalism), etc., these alliances are a few of many new attempts to fight dominant rule.

An example. In 1998 a new alliance was formed by the general students, mostly females, in Jahangirnagar University (JU) to protest sexual harassment and rape in the campus. Accused rapists and sexual harassers were ruling party leaders. Therefore, no single student organization could dare to wage a movement against them. Actually non-party or general female students made the breakthrough. Their participation was so great that the ruling party student organization tried their best to threaten and terrorize them but failed. Left student organizations had been consistent participants in the movement but the main force came from non-party general students.

In the following years, several movements with similar forms were born in different campuses on different issues. These movements such as movement against sexual harassment at Dhaka University (DU) (1998-99), movement against ruling party violence and terrorism in JU (2000) and police atrocity in the female dormitory in DU (2002), etc. have made a significant impact on student body politic. Movements against rising fees according to the World Bank's 20-year strategy paper have also been seen in various campuses in the following decades by alliance of general students, where left organizations had an active role (Muhammad, 2016).

Another area of political significance has been the natural resource and environment protection movement. The movement has actually been challenging the dominant development paradigm: neoliberal reforms, bad deals in favour of MNCs, corruption and privatization of public property.[9] This is in a way providing a left agenda without rhetoric and with concrete issues. A different organizational form with definite demands and programmes also deserve attention. It has not been a party-centric movement; although many left parties have been an active part of the larger alliance. It has created space for non-party individuals and other social groups to become important components of the alliance. This alliance called the 'National Committee to Protect Oil Gas Mineral Resources Port and Power' was established in 1998 to protest bad deals with multinational companies, against the Magurchara blowout by the US company Occidental, and against the gas export attempt by multinationals.

This alliance developed and gained nationwide attention and support through different movements and a few successes . The form of this alliance has been a new experience, and its mass support created theoretical and academic interest too. This 'party plus alliance' is qualitatively different from the 'non-party alliance' for social movement or any type of NGOized mobilization. The alliance, National Committee, through its people's movement, academic discourses and theoretical challenges to the dominant development paradigm created a new culture of unity and inclusion of different sections of people and raised expectations beyond its declared objectives.

All these alliances do not belong to any single left party but left activists are the vital force of these formations. These formations do not have any permanent organizational structure but they have proven the ability to attract larger participation and become a source of hope for the society in general.

I do not think that these formations are equipped adequately, theoretically and organizationally, to fight the power of the state and the global capital to go forward for a desired revolutionary social transformation. But I would like to insist that this is the phase of rebirth of revolutionary politics, phase of new creativity, ideas to accommodate struggles for emancipation from different dimensions of class, gender, colour, caste, environment and culture. In the last one hundred years since the Russian Revolution people around the world used to look at Moscow and later also Peking as their lighthouse. These do not exist any more, now everywhere left politics needs to stand on their own, to concretize their vision to connect with their people and to build their struggles in a rooted and globalized manner.

Perhaps many sparks around the world, many attempts to organize people to go beyond capitalist autocracy, many initiatives to go into critical review of theory and praxis to go forward will be able to add to a creative beginning, to bring a new growth of left politics in Bangladesh and elsewhere.

NOTES

1. For detailed research on people's lives, livelihood and discontent in the post-partition East Bengal and its links to countrywide mobilization in language movement, see three-volume scholarly works by Marxist thinker Badruddin Umar (Umar, 1995).
2. For discussion on Maulana Bhasani's life and works see (Moksud, 1994), (Kabir, 2012).
3. Among all of them, the Siraj Sikder led faction appeared as a threat to the government. He was arrested on January 1, 1975 and was killed in police custody the following day. He was such a threat for the government that after killing him, Sheikh Mujib in an expression of relief and victory observed in the parliament, 'where is Siraj Sikder?'
4. Despite its high growth, incidents like the Rana Plaza collapse exposed the vulnerability of the sector. For an analysis of the sector, its global chain and vulnerability see (Muhammad, 2015b). A more recent incident in Tampaco on September 10, 2016 shows that things have not changed much. http://www.dhakatri bune.com/bangladesh/2016/09/10/23-killed-in-tongi-factory-boiler-blast/.
5. Neoliberal reforms in Bangladesh and its multiple dimensions were discussed further (Muhammad, 2015a).
6. For details of the jute sector destroying project of the World Bank, see Muhammad, 2002.
7. Jean Dreze correctly pointed out that, "Exploitation' does not belong to the standard vocabulary of mainstream economics. It is quite possible to complete a PhD in a leading economics department without having heard about the notion' (Dreze, 2002).
8. A good collection of articles analysing this phenomenon is available in Panitch, 2013.
9. For a detailed discussion on the Resource Curse model see Muhammad, 2014.

REFERENCES

Ali, Kamran Asdar, 2015: *Surkh Salam: Communist Politics and Class Activism in Pakistan*, Oxford University Press.

Chibber, Vivek, 2006. "On the Decline of Class Analysis in South Asian Studies, *Critical Asian Studies* 38:4, 357–387.

Dreze, Jean, 2002. "On Research and Action", *Economic and Political Weekly*, March 2.

Harvey, David, 2011. *The Enigma of Capital and Crises of Capitalism,* Profile Books, New York.

Kabir, Nurul, 2012. *The Red Moulana*, Samhai, Dhaka.

Moksud, Syed Abul, 1994. *Moulana Abdul Hamid Khan Bhasani*, Bangla Academy, Dhaka.

Muhammad, Anu, 2002. "Closure of Adamjee Jute Mills: Victory of Anti-Industrial Development Project?" *Economic and Political Weekly,* September 21-27.

Muhammad, Anu, 2007. "Ideology in Economics and Neoliberal Reforms", *Jahangirnagar Economic Review,* June.

Muhammad, Anu, 2009. "Grameen and Microcredit: A Tale of Corporate Success", *Economic and Political Weekly,* August 29.

Muhammad, Anu, 2014. "Natural Resources and Energy Security, Challenging the 'Resource-Curse' Model in Bangladesh," *Economic and Political Weekly*, January 25.

Muhammad, Anu, 2015a. "Bangladesh: A Model of Neo-Liberalism", *Monthly Review*, March.

Muhammad, Anu, 2015b. "Workers' Lives, Walmart's Pocket: Garments' Global Chain, from Savar to New York", *Economic and Political Weekly*, June 20.

Muhammad, Anu, 2016. "Student Politics in Post-1971 Bangladesh" in *University of Dhaka, Making Unmaking Remaking*, ed. by Imtiaz Ahmed, Prothoma Prokashan.

Musa, Ahmed, 1980. *Itihaser Kathgorai Awami League*. Dhaka.

Panitch, Leo, Greg Albo and Vivek Chibber, 2012: "The Crisis and The Left", *Socialist Registrar 2012*.

Panitch, Leo, Greg Albo and Vivek Chibber, 2013: "The Question of Strategy", *Socialist Registrar 2013*.

Umar, Badruddin, 1995. *Bhasha Andolon o totkaleen Rajniti* (Language Movement and Contemporary Politics), 3 Vols. Second edition, Jatiyo Grantha Prokashan, Dhaka.

7

South Asia After Bangladesh: Some Aspects of the National Question in India

Salimullah Khan

'We are not a nation, so much as a world.'

—Herman Melville (in Eisenhower 1965: 485).

'In the colonies the economic substructure is also a superstructure. The cause is the consequence; you are rich because you are white, you are white because you are rich. This is why Marxist analysis should always be slightly stretched every time we have to do with the colonial problem.'

–Frantz Fanon (Fanon 1990: 31).

South Asia, to use a neologism for a subcontinent containing many nations and nationalities, contains more 'competing nationalist sensitivities' today and without any clear vision for an imminent resolution. India that was once known as 'a people of no-nation' is no longer there, nor can it be said to constitute a nation united against a foreign imperialism any longer (Thompson 1991: 16). In 1947 India gained her freedom but 'lost her unity', as Abul Kalam Azad once said so ruefully. The inheritance of the lands ruled by a British bureaucracy was divided into two patrimonies, India and Pakistan.

However, contrary to legends, neither Pakistan nor India became nation-states, in the sense of 'one state for one nation.' Pakistan broke up in time but India remained in place, even annexing certain smaller states to its body politic. Pakistan shows conclusively that not all is well with theories of nation-states known to liberal ideologies. The 1970-71 experience of Bangladesh raised other questions, not limited to Pakistan, all the same. 'Leaving aside the numerous claims to nationhood by various linguistic, tribal and ethnic groups,' as P.C. Mathur, an Indian ideologue, expressed it once, 'the formation of (and break-up of) Pakistan have demonstrated the impossibility of effecting a perfectly harmonious adjustment between nationhood and statehood.' 'Pakistan,' he added, 'was not a perfect "One-Nation-One-State" either in theory or in practice and nor is Bangladesh expected to conform to this criterion while India seems to defy analysis in terms of these categories' (Mathur 1977: 442). Writing in 1977-78 our theorist, perhaps in view of the fact that India defies analysis, warned us that 'there is a real danger' of the 'two-nation theory', so-called, being replaced by 'one-nation-one-state' theory, 'as far as India is concerned.'

'Leaving aside the political postulates of the 'Akhand-Bharat' school, the weakening of Pakistan, which provided a sort of 'third party insurance' to Indian Muslims,' the Indian theorist feared, 'is bound to lead to growing pressures for internal purification of the Indian nation-state in terms of Indianization or even Hinduization.' 'The Indian record of inter-communal coexistence during the last 25 years has been quite impressive,' this writer admitted, 'but there is no gainsaying the fact that the existence of a powerful Pakistan "externalized" the issue of Hindu-Muslim discord and turned it into an Indo-Pak issue with the result that Pakistan and Pakistani Muslims rather than Indian Muslims became the primary target of attack of Hindu communalists. The break-up of the Pak military apparatus has provided an excellent opportunity to Hindu communalists to implement their theory of one-nation-one-state within the boundaries of India (Mathur 1977: 442-43). The second objective, as far as the experience ever since Bangladesh shows, seems to have found favour with the communalists.

But the event of Bangladesh contains other prospects too. Whether they will be cultivated is another story though. It represents a return of the repressed, a return to longer term historical trends of state formation in the age-old subcontinent, a civilization of many nations. Bangladesh shows the day, as Ahmad Sofa, active participant in the cause of Bangladesh and a pivotal political theorist, argued repeatedly that the coming of Bangladesh happens to be just such a harbinger (Sofa 2008-12).

There is no denying the fact that India passes today 'through a deep crisis, if not the deepest ever'. 'Social tension,' as a concerned Indian put it at the turn of the century, 'has perhaps never been more severe in our entire history. Communal relations have reached the nadir—reflected glaringly among other things in the emergence of Muslim ghettos in the major cities, something that even the British, despite their policy of 'divide and rule', could not achieve. Caste wars in some parts have become endemic; revolt against established authorities is the order of the day everywhere; insurgency and violent secessionist movements are a common feature of our national life; law and order situation is out of control practically everywhere. As a result, no other democratic country has committed the might of its armed forces to quell internal disturbances or ensure domestic peace as often as India has done in the last few decades (Tripathi 2000: 937).

I. India: A Nation in the Making?

In the epilogue to *India Wins Freedom,* Abul Kalam Azad makes a characteristic observation. 'In fact the more I think about it the more I am convinced,' Azad writes, 'that the creation of Pakistan has solved no problem.' 'One may argue,' notes India's statesman-savant, 'that the relations between Hindus and Muslims had become so estranged in India that there was no alternative to partition. This view was held by most of the supporters of the Muslim League and after partition, many of the Congress leaders have held similar views. Whenever I discussed the question with Jawaharlal Nehru or Sardar Patel after partition this is the argument they gave in support of their decision.' Azad was not convinced of the wisdom of the decision. 'If however we think over the matter coolly,' he reasoned, 'we will find that their analysis is not correct. I am convinced that the scheme I had framed on the occasion of the Cabinet Mission and which the Mission had largely accepted was a far better solution from every point of view. If we had remained steadfast and refused to accept partition, I am confident that a safer and more glorious future could have awaited us'(Azad 1988: 247).

From the point of view of defenders of Pakistan either the action was not a wise or correct one at all. Azad articulates their difficulty: 'Mr. Jinnah and his followers did not seem to realize that geography was against them. Indian Muslims were distributed in a way which made it impossible to form a separate state in a consolidated area. The Muslim majority areas were in the north-west and north-east. These two regions have no point of physical contact. People in these two areas are completely different from one another in every respect except religion.' The sage Azad tunes his argument a trifle finer: 'It is one of the greatest frauds on the people to suggest that religious affinity can unite areas which are geographically, economically, linguistically and culturally different. It is true that Islam sought to establish a society which transcends racial, linguistic, economic and political frontiers. History has however proved that after the first few decades, or at the most after the first century, Islam was not able to unite all the Muslim countries on the basis of Islam alone'(Azad 1988: 248).

On the strength of this historical foundation alone, Abul Kalam Azad goes on to predict fledgling Pakistan's imminent demise. 'No one can hope that East and West Pakistan will compose all their differences and form one nation. Even within West Pakistan the three provinces of Sind, Punjab and the Frontier have internal incompatibility and are working for separate aims and interests,' Azad does not hesitate to predict with ten years of Pakistan's coming into being. 'Some people hold,' Azad goes on adding, 'that what has happened was inevitable. Others equally strongly believe that what has happened is wrong and could have been avoided. We cannot say today which reading is correct. History alone will decide whether we had acted wisely and correctly (Azad 1988: 248).

This paper takes Maulana Azad's observation rather seriously. How do we account for the observed difference, until now in any case, between Pakistan and India's resolution of the national question? The Empire's endgame yielded two successor states of imperial proportions, India and Pakistan. Azad predicted Pakistan's breakup, of the second of the two, quite astrologically. And Bangladesh proved him right. Whatever happened to India, primus inter duo? How did she escape her neighbour's destiny? Does the instance of Bangladesh, a nation state of course, then can be said to negate the 'two-nation theory', that much maligned daughter attributed often to Mohammad Ali Jinnah? A casual negation of that 'two-nation' theory, as seen in this instance, does not necessarily re-affirm the other, one-nation approach, however.

Bangladesh may, on the contrary, help the historian remember, repeat and work through the archives for a retrieval of the repressed. What has been repressed, namely the national question, may return with a vengeance even. The anxiety is manifest in much of the literature on nation building, on both right and left flanks of the upper class and bourgeoisie in India. Fortunately, there are still a few voices around not yet hushed, if dimmed. Since when has India become a nation with a centre in Hindustan and regions around? Not even ever since 1947. Take, for instance, this incidence: in 1960 a conference of state education ministers recommended formation of a committee on national integration. The mandate of the committee, justly named "the Committee on Emotional Integration", was in earnest to "study the role of education in strengthening and promoting the process of emotional integration in national life..." 'The mandate,' as Mathew Pandian rightly comments, 'is thus a confession that the Indian nation was not yet and it had to be invented' (Pandian 2009: 65).

How does this Indian nation to be invented would look like in its time? The path to integration, as the *Report of the Committee on Emotional Integration* stressed, lies through combating a host of differences in identities, namely identities based on regions, languages, castes and religions, among other things, these being the chief threats to the young Indian nation. 'Nationhood,' as the Committee was insisting, 'has a strong psychological basis and depends on the people concerned having had similar experiences and, what is no less important, interpreting them in the same way. If political and other events convey different meanings to different groups, they will continue to be a source of dissension and disintegration...'

In combating these demons of difference two tactics of national integration were recommended. The first tactic appealed to a putative uniform 'Hindu memory' in bridging the gap between the north and the south. It was, as it turns out, one job too many. In integrating the Hindus across two sides of the Vindhyas it not only reduces the south to the bottom end but perforce excludes non-Hindus out of the pantheon as well. To wit: 'One may recall the beautiful legend of Agastya, still the patron saint of the south, who crossed the Vindhyas from the north and never returned. Who does not know that though the Upanishads were uttered first in the forest *asrams* of the north, Vedic philosophy owes so much to the creative and critical exposition of it by Shankaracharya from Kerala? Ayodhya, Madura and Vrindavan in the north are places sacred to the memory of Rama and Krishna, but Rama's journey across the south to Ceylon is deeply enshrined in Hindu memory, and pilgrim places like Kanchi and Rameswaram have equal claim to reverence' (Pandian 2009: 66).

Advocates of north-south unity had no better tale to tell than this puree of myth and history in their repertoire. But it is at the same time a tale of hierarchy and exclusion, as Pandian argues so forcefully. That dissenters from south India would take with a grain of salt is only understandable. 'The Dravidian argument,' as Selig Harrison has mentioned in his old book, 'is based on the very substance of Hindu mythology, and the *Ramayana*, so proudly hailed as a force for synthesis, became the basic text cited to establish Aryan iniquity. In Dravidian propaganda the southward march of Rama to the lair of King Ravana, abductor of Sita, is nothing less than the allegorical story of the triumphal Aryan progress over the original Dravidian inhabitants of India. To many non-Brahmin Tamils, the legions of monkeys Rama encounters in the southern jungles to be none other than the Dravidians. Thus the epic is a racial insult before half told' (Pandian 2009: 66).

A second tactic was called for in order to address unmistakable linguistic differences prevailing in India's regions and also to inaugurate a right lingual hierarchy in place, i.e. to contain possible 'sources of dissonance and disintegration' across regions of India, if not to deracinate them all. 'The question,' in the Committee's formulation, 'still remains as to which Indian language, both for the sake of national pride and national sentiment, should be taught in all the schools of the Indian union as a common means of communication and as a common ground for the sharing of ideas, a language that is of the land.' The answer, 'Hindi', is as good as predestined. In case one reasons why here it is: 'Hindi is spoken by large sections of our people and a number of other languages spoken in India are closely allied to Hindi, as Hindi is allied to them; and therefore, adoption of Hindi as the common language of India would greatly facilitate the growth of a common medium of communication binding the whole country together.' If the language question were to be so simple, India would perhaps have no national question to worry about. But the anxiety is evident: 'The crux of the problem is to make learning of Hindi in non-Hindi areas practicable.' The rule of majority in settling for a national language apparently does not suffice in India. It also calls for a rule of alliances, i.e. affinities among languages, again an alliance based on the primacy of Hindi. What is to be done about languages not allied to Hindi? One can then make an appeal to 'Hindu memory'.

Two tactics of national integration in India, namely *Hindu* as national memory and *Hindi* as national language, between themselves contain a contradiction best described by the Freudian notion of 'over-determination'. We will return to this proposition later in this paper.

II. Is there a National Question in India?

'There was no basis for the emergence of nationalities before the British conquests,' Irfan Habib, the well-known Aligarh historian, once argued, 'because there was no trace of any emerging bourgeoisie.' Habib's is a stance that may be taken as typical of what goes by the moniker Marxism in South Asia, our part of the world. 'And quite predictably,' he was impelled also to add, 'we find no trace of national consciousness in whatever is preserved in the regional literatures of the period' (Habib 1975: 18). Habib was nonetheless inclined to argue at the same time that there was evidence of a nascent pan-Indian national consciousness long before the British intrusion, leaving only the task of making 'loyalty to India supreme over all other territorial loyalties in the popular consciousness' to the lived experience of British rule (Habib 1975: 16).

'There is no doubt,' writes Habib, 'that there has been a consciousness of India as a country down the centuries. Partly, this is due to geography—the Himalayas and the western and eastern ranges separating it from the rest of the world. Partly, the Brahmanical culture with Sanskrit as the lingua franca, has given it unity in the eyes of the upper strata of society. Fourteenth-century poets like Amir Khusrau and Isami sang of the glories of Hindustan, of its riches, its beauty and culture. Their descriptions leave us no doubt that they meant by Hindustan the entire subcontinent of India' (Habib 1975: 16).

As Amir Khusrau and others had already noted, a host of languages were spoken throughout the length and breadth of India by the fourteenth century. It is also well known that devotional songs were sung extensively in languages like Bengali, Awadhi, Braj, Panjabi, Marathi and others in the fifteenth and sixteenth centuries. Habib however designates all these as 'regional' languages and these linguistic facts do not convince him to agree with an older generation of writers who found evidence of emergent nationalities in them. He would find the argument that the Indian economy before the British conquest contained any 'germs' of bourgeois development 'questionable', because such a view betrays confusing commodity production which developed to some extent then with capitalist production. Merchant capital grows and flourishes, Habib claimed, on the basis of pre-capitalist modes of production without bringing in any 'change' in the mode of production.

'The pace of technological development in pre-British India,' writes Irfan Habib, 'was extremely slow and of no comparison to what was taking place in Europe between the sixteenth and eighteenth centuries. The manufactory regarded by Marx as representing the last stage before the crucial shift to 'machinofacture' (factory system), had not been developed in Mughal India. Above all, there was little or no market in the countryside for the products of the towns, which flourished in a parasitical manner upon the distribution of the agricultural surplus, obtained principally in the form of the land revenue by the ruling class. There was, therefore, neither a bourgeoisie, nor any urge to demarcate separate regions as domestic markets' (Habib 1975: 17-18).

Since an economic basis for the creation of nationalities was thus 'utterly lacking before the British conquests', Irfan Habib would discount 'the existence of regional languages and development of some of them into literary languages' altogether as a fact. That fact, he says, 'does not in itself signify the emergence of nationalities.' 'One would then have to date,' according to Habib's rhetoric, 'the rise of the Tamil nationality to the Sangam Age. Similarly, should the emergence of Persian as a literary language about AD 1000 be taken to mean that Persia was then becoming a nation?' In our good old historian's universe such a thing is a dire contradiction in terms, an unthinkable monstrosity that is.

'The emergence of nationalities in India,' for Irfan Habib, 'is thus a phenomenon subsequent to British conquests and one that accompanied the rise of the Indian bourgeoisie, for which the British rule created the necessary preconditions.' This little presupposition, however, confronts our historian with small contradiction. Historians know very well that it was not in Bengal that the Indian bourgeoisie or whatever you call it first developed despite a rule of property for Bengal introduced before anywhere else in South Asia. Thus, citing old Stalin, our historian tries to save appearances. 'Stalin said of the early phase of the development of the bourgeoisie in India,' as Habib writes, 'that "in the case of India too, it will be found that nationalities till now lying dormant, would come to life with the further course of bourgeois development"'(Habib 1975: 18).

Irfan Habib is eventually obliged to admit the phenomenon he chose to call 'the consciousness of Bengal as a nationality' in the early part of the nineteenth century which cannot explain or rather explain away without contradicting himself. He thus re-invokes an argument he had initially to regret in the name of Marx. 'Just as bourgeois ideology, once formed on the basis of development of bourgeois society in one part of the globe,' Habib now asserts, 'may anticipate bourgeois development in another; so too in India, it is quite possible that in a case like Bengal, the consciousness of Bengal as a nationality was the result initially of the implementation of modes of thought from Europe during the earlier part of the nineteenth century.' 'For India as a whole,' , 'it would be true to say that the loyalties to regional languages and cultures developed largely with the growth of the bourgeoisie in India during and after the second half of the nineteenth century'(Habib 1975: 18-19).

How did one of India's many 'regional' languages, Hindi or Hindustani if you like, become 'national' eventually? Irfan Habib, not unlike a host of nationalists, resorts to an assertion instead. 'The freedom movement,' for him, 'played a dual role in relation to the emergence of such regional consciousness. Inasmuch as it relied upon mass support, it could not but give great impetus to the politicization of the content of literatures in regional languages, and it thus laid the foundation of nationality-consciousness. On the other hand, by invoking the greater loyalty to the Indian motherland in a united struggle against the British rule, it subjugated the urge of the peoples of the various regions for developing into separate nationalities' (Habib 1975: 18)

Habib attributes the emergent phenomenon of an Indian 'nation' to the 'big' bourgeoisie's account and pins sundry 'nationality-slogans (linguistic states, regional reservations, preference for "sons of the soil")' to the cause of 'the rising medium and smaller bourgeoisie'. He doubts if this smaller bourgeoisie have not seen so many 'protective walls for themselves' in such claims in the name of their nationalities. 'The big bourgeoisie, on the other hand,' Irfan Habib writes 'can operate best with a highly centralized apparatus controlling the whole of India. This may explain the official opposition so long offered to the redrawing of the boundaries of British-Indian provinces on linguistic lines.'

Interestingly, as Habib finds out by 1975, 'conflicts between the big bourgeoisie and the other sections of the bourgeoisie have not in the main assumed 'national' forms in India. Even today not only is the nationality-consciousness extremely uneven in different regions; but the nationalities themselves have not generally fully developed' (Habib 1975: 19). Such a lukewarm admission that certain nationalities also exist on the sidelines of an Indian nation gets lost in the climes of a corollary which finds no overlap between the big bourgeoisie and national oppression that obtains in India. 'The emerging nationalities in India,' as Habib plainly puts it, 'had no common oppressor-nationality within India, either before 1947 or after' (Habib 1975: 19). It is undoubtedly a remarkable opinion.

Achin Vanaik, a most unlikely admirer for one, would more than agree with Irfan Habib on the question. Rejecting any characterization of India as a multinational state or entity, Vanaik rather vociferously argued that what faces the bourgeoisie in India is not a 'national question' of the Marxist provenance; what confronts them is rather the problem of 'nation-building' or rather, to express it in bourgeois liberal terms, 'the problem of national integration', in the face of various regional movements and pressures (Vanaik 1988: 2279, 2283). 'Such regional pulls are on the rise, not on the decline,' admits Vanaik. 'Regionalism,' for him, gets partly resolved into 'the dialectic of centralization and decentralization between the centre and the states, the devolution of power'. Through issues of linguistic (rational) reorganization of states to the irrational desire of imposing Hindi as the 'official language', all would appear to be mere mundane problems of national integration in this view.

Vanaik has, on the one hand, claimed that 'India is very much a nation-state which in the Marxist sense has "solved" its "National Question". On the other hand, he also argues that the Indian nation did not have a national question to solve to begin with. 'In fact sub-national identities [i.e., non-hegemonic nations or nationalities] are often of as recent vintage as the national identities they are supposed to oppose. In the Indian case they can sometimes post-date the emergence of a national identity and be linked to the problems thrown up by the nation state's attempt to promote national integration. That is, they are linked explicitly to the post-independence phase of capitalist development.' Vanaik is not in favour of seeing them as historically growing identities, but at best as some competing 'imagined communities' of sorts. 'National identity,' Vanaik thinks, 'did not substitute for them but grew alongside.' This, in his view, suggests no necessary opposition between subaltern nationalities and the hegemonic nation. On the contrary, it also reveals that processes of the subaltern nations' identity formation and those of the hegemonic formation are 'largely distinct and separate' (Vanaik 1988: 2282).

Vanaik denies a national (or 'nationality') question in India only to bring it right back in two forms. One form, of a wider dispensation, he encounters in those 'regional' movements or struggles which seek to gain 'a more decisive say in the Centre, more local say through greater federalism and regional autonomy, or greater access to centrally organised (and sometimes, state organised) distribution of resources.' The other, better known as 'separatism', he sees as posing the issue of complete independence. As 'the guiding principle of consistent political democracy and the struggle for socialism' Vanaik would admit that a 'right to self-determination' for an oppressed nation/nationality' holds in India too but he nevertheless denies that an oppressor nationality in India exists but for the fact of a nondescript '*Indian* nationality' and that 'great Indian chauvinism' to condemn. He thus finds it all the more difficult to justify causes of Naga and Sikkimese self-determination because their 'national question' is allegedly not perceived of as a collective 'state of mind striving after a political fact' but as an entity 'discovered' as a result of 'a peopled territory fulfilling a formal set of criteria as to what constitutes a nationality or nation.' Vanaik is, to be fair, critical of the CPI/CPM endorsing 'though critically, the denial of Naga independence and the annexation of Sikkim.'

Other cases, for example the question of Khalistan, he finds even more problematic. He would compare it to Pakistan or worse. 'So there is no justification,' Vanaik writes, 'for describing Khalistan as a nationalist movement or sentiment. But even if it were to reach such a stage it does not follow that communists would have to support its right to self-determination, a commitment that is contingent on an assessment of the movement's democratic credentials, i.e., its aims, methods, motivations, the social forces behind it, and overall historical evaluation of the oppressed character of the community represented by the movement.' Thus, in his opinion, 'though it was legitimate to talk of a Muslim nationalism (in the sense of a political movement) before partition, it was not legitimate to support the formation of an intrinsically undemocratic confessional state (as the CPI did) based on the false principle that Muslims qua Muslims were an oppressed community, let alone a nationality' (Vanaik 1988: 2282).

'The nationalist struggle in Nagaland,' Vanaik assures us by the late 1980s, 'is a low-intensity insurgency whose protagonists are unable to translate wide sympathy from a war-wearied Naga population into a qualitatively higher level of mass or even guerrilla struggle.' 'In addition,' as he then put it further, 'the Indian government's carrot and stick policy of pouring in development funds, consolidating a Naga elite and carrying out sustained and brutal repression has been largely successful in reducing the political aspirations of more and more Nagas from independence to autonomy and centre-sponsored development within the Indian union.'

India's national question thus got solved, Vanaik concludes. 'The central problem' that remained in his view for 'the Indian state and the ruling coalition' was 'regionalism' or sundry demands for decentralization. 'The general factors behind the growth of tendencies towards greater decentralisation and regionalism,' according to this sage journalist, 'are the cultural and linguistic diversity of India; the inevitable unevenness of capitalist economic development; the growing strength of the agrarian bourgeoisie and the "intermediate classes", i.e., the rural and urban petty bourgeoisie; and such political features as the growing electoral strength of opposition parties along with the deinstitutionalisation/decline of the Congress' (Vanaik 1988: 2283).

III. Bangladesh: Return of the Repressed?

Given his avowed admiration of Benedict Anderson's thesis that 'nation/nationality' is an 'imagined community', i.e., one among other 'imagined communities', it hardly surprises anyone that Vanaik would see the coming of Bangladesh as no more than an aberration or an exception. 'In over forty years,' he in fact writes, 'the solitary example of a completely successful secessionist struggle and the subsequent creation of a new nation-state has been Bangladesh. By its very exceptionalism it serves as a salutary reminder that the post-war nation states, even where they seem most fragile, e.g. in Africa or South and West Asia, have powerful underlying sources of cohesion and durability which are all too often grossly underestimated' (Vanaik 1988: 2282).

What lesson, if any, does Bangladesh have for the resolution of the national question in India? Bangladesh in 1971, we will argue, earmarks a return of what was repressed in 1947. It represents the rational or democratic kernel of the mystical or undemocratic chaff of Pakistan. Even if the contention that Muslims qua Muslims were an oppressed community, let alone a nationality, in colonial India were false, it was not because India was already one nation. It was on account of the fact that Muslims of Bengal and Muslims of Punjab, between themselves, did not form one nationality. What was repressed in 1947 was the multinational identity of India in the whirlwind of two-nation politics. What appears to be an exception is in fact a return of the repressed. To argue that a chain usually breaks at its weakest link is not to plead exception.

How does Bangladesh make a nation? 'The nation in Bangladesh is a nation,' as Abdur Razzaq, a leading theorist in Dhaka once argued, 'because it intends to be a nation and nothing else.' Razzaq worked it out somewhat afield by the end of the new nation's first decade: 'Enumeration of all that is peculiar to itself or all that it shares with a lot of other people, dead cargo or live heritage, would not explain or explain away the nation. The unbending pride, the shared identity with 80 million people [this was the estimated size of the population in 1980] in weal and woe, the insistence on being a Bengali and nothing else, this is what makes the nation.' If sentiment carried our author a little off his ground one hopes one would understand. 'Patriotism, a wise Greek has observed,' notes Abdur Razzaq, 'is the act of falling in love with one's own country, its mountains and rivers, with whatever else God or nature has endowed it, including, of course, its people.'

'A man falls in love with a woman or a woman does fall in love with a man not because she or he is the most perfect specimen of her or his kind and he or she does fall in love and thereby begins the greatest adventure in life.' What does this sentimental insistence on nationality entail at bottom? 'It does not take a great deal of learning,' according to Bangladesh's premier theorist, 'to know the greatness of heritage coming from Assyria, Chaldea, Egypt or Greece or Rome or Arabia or Iran or the more recent contributions of Red Russia, the nature and significance of which is being so hotly debated in Moscow and Peking, echoed all over the world, at Dacca ['Dhaka' as it gets written today] too. This nation of ours has nothing to offer comparable to all this or any of these. Yet, what holds us together, makes of us a nation, is the exclusive passion of each to identify himself with this nation and nothing else' (Razzaq 1981: 4).

It would be rash to shrug it all off as pure hogwash. It is true that Abdur Razzaq is not explicit about a driving force behind his nation yet, I would argue, his intervention deserves at least a second thought. It is a kind of morale that can stand on its head. Recounting the tale in 1980, Razzaq traces origins of his nation within a certain span of the near past, and certainly not in a distant millennium. 'Nearly 75 years ago the Bengali-speaking people of the British Indian Empire, at least the vocal and vociferous section of it,' writes Razzaq, 'vowed to unsettle a settled fact and to a large extent succeeded in unsettling it. The Bengali-speaking people were to live together ever after, presumably happily too. In 35 years time a vocal and vociferous section of the Bengali-speaking people, albeit a minority section of the Bengali-speaking people, would have nothing to do with a future in which it did not have the right to lose itself in the great identity of an Indian nation' (Razzaq 1981: 2).

'I do not know,' he adds, 'how well it has succeeded in its renunciatory task: of course there has always been a strand of thought developed in the subcontinent which has glorified in losing itself in a greater identity. But the majority of the Bengali-speaking people, not altogether willing to go it alone, outside India and Pakistan, eventually opted to merge itself in the new nation state of Pakistan, but not without reservation. The reservation resulted in the Language Movement, the end product of which is the new nation state of Bangladesh' (Razzaq 1981: 2).

Somewhere in his exposé, Abdur Razzaq returns to the 'language question' only to underscore the difference between Bengali as its stands in Bangladesh and its predicament in West Bengal, India. 'The most abiding product of the genius of a people, its language,' comments our savant supposed to know his metier, 'is neither the product of labour in isolation nor [a thing] unshared by other people. The language of our nation is also the language of a part of the great nation in India—Surendra Nath Banerjee's nation in the making. With us it is the language of a nation, a national language. With our neighbours across the border in West Bengal it is a regional language, a very important one but not a national language.'

'The literature in West Bengal, a more sophisticated, a maturer literature,' Abdur Razzaq takes note, 'bears no sign which would prepare us for a language movement there. Bricks and mortar are there, but there seems to be no design which could result in an architecture.' What is amiss in the wonder that was the great literature of West Bengal? 'Erudition of a Jadunath [Sarkar] speaking of the lonely furrow of Bengal away from the mainstream of Indian life and civilization,' notices Abdur Razzaq, 'does not seem to have a hearer, not in West Bengal.' 'West Bengal,' he wails, 'is a victim, perhaps a willing victim of the siren call of Indian civilization' (Razzaq 1981: 3-4).

These paeans for an 'imagined community,' reminiscent of an old timer's own words, can hardly be dismissed off as a tale told by an idiot even if it is full of sound and fury. 'Bengal,' as Sir Jadunath Sarkar once put it, 'had been despised and thrown into a corner in the Vedic age as the land of birds (and not of men), in the epic age as outside the regions hallowed by the feet of the wandering Pandav brothers, and in Mughal times as "a hell well stocked with bread." But now under the impact of the British civilisation it became a path-finder and a light-bringer to the rest of India. If Periclean Athens was the school of Hellas, "the eye of Greece, mother of arts and eloquence," that was Bengal to the rest of India under British rule, but with a borrowed light, which it had made its own with marvellous cunning.'

If Bengal's swansong, in old Jadunath's shrill voice sounds too nostalgic the hearer is hardly to be blamed. 'In this new Bengal originated every good and great thing of the modern world that was passed on to other provinces of India. From Bengal went forth the English-educated teachers and the Europe-inspired thought that helped to modernise Bihar and Orissa, Hindustan and Deccan. New literary types, reform of the language, social reconstruction, political aspirations, religious movements and even changes in manners that originated in Bengal, passed like ripples from a central eddy, across provincial barriers to the furthest corners of India.'

If history would repeat itself, must it be as an irony this time over? Listen then to this sage reflection, c. 1948: 'Finally after less than two centuries of rule the British have left Bengal free, and better fitted to keep that freedom in the modern world than the Romans had made Britain when they abandoned their imperial dominion over the white island, more permanently civilized than the Hellenistic world on the dissolution of Alexander's empire, and more peaceful and progressive than the American colonies of Spain when they shook themselves free of European rule.' Bengal in Jadunath's imaginary, has at the end of the day become a *nation* (his italics), thanks again to Great Britain. 'Has not Bengal, unknown to herself,' wonders Sir Jadunath, 'been working through the ages to reach this consummation?' Her storied past, as narrated in these pages,' as the historian reflects, 'shows how the diverse limbs of the country and warring tribes and sects of the people fused into one by the silent working of time and a common political life till at the end of the Muslim period a Bengali *people* had become a reality.'

But the Bengali people had not yet become a Bengali *nation*, according to Jadunath, 'for the pre-requisites of a nation were then wanting.' The missing link was as if awaiting the coming of the British: 'Two centuries of British rule and the neighbouring example of British society have now ground down large sections of the Bengali people to that uniformity of life and thought which alone can create a nation. It is for the future to perfect this good work,' (Sarkar 1976: 497-99), as far as the historian's calling goes.

IV. Contradictions and Overdeterminations

Freud's discovery of the unconscious was predicated upon encountering some of its symptoms, dreams for example. These symptoms or formations of the unconscious have been attributed to a plurality of determining factors. This plurality itself, in turn, may be taken in more than one sense. For instance, in one of his earlier works, *Studies in Hysteria*, Freud attributes hysterical symptoms to a constitutional predisposition as well as to a number of traumatic events. As a useful handbook of psychoanalytic terms puts it; 'One of these factors on its own is not enough to produce or to sustain the symptom, and this is why the cathartic method of treatment, although it does not attack the constitutional causes of the hysteria, is nonetheless able to get rid of the symptom through the recollection and abreaction of the trauma.' A second sense of over-determination refers to 'a multiplicity of unconscious elements which may be organized in different meaningful sequences, each having its own specific coherence at a particular level of interpretation'. At another instance Freud takes it in the sense of multiplicity of elements in a chain of association: 'The chain of associations which links the symptom to the "pathogenic nucleus" is here said to constitute a ramifying system of lines and more particularly...a converging one' (Laplanche and Pontalis 1973: 292).

Overdetermination as revealed in Freud's own clinical practice, appears to be a consequence of the work of condensation. It is expressed not only on the level of isolated elements of the dream, a dream as a whole may be overdetermined. 'The achievements of condensation,' as Freud says, 'can be quite extraordinary. It is sometimes possible by its help to combine two quite different latent trains of thought into one manifest dream, so that one can arrive at what appears to be a sufficient interpretation of a dream and yet in doing so can fail to notice a possible 'over-interpretation'. Over-determination, it should be noted, does not imply independence or parallelism of different meanings of a single phenomenon' (Laplanche and Pontalis 1973: 292).

Jacques Lacan emphasizes the fact that overdetermination is a trait common to all unconscious formations and is 'constituted by a double meaning (symbol of a conflict long dead over and above its function in a *no less symbolic* present conflict).' If we would only follow, in the wake of Freud, 'the ascending ramification of the symbolic lineage in the text of the patient's free associations in order to map it out at the points where its verbal forms intersect with the nodal points of its structure then it is already quite clear that the symptom resolves itself entirely in an analysis of language, because the symptom is itself structured like a language, because it is from language that speech must be delivered (Lacan 1977: 59). Freud shows, with regard to hysterical symptoms, that this develops only where fulfilment of two opposing wishes, each arising from a different psychical system, are able to converge in a single expression.'

Louis Althusser once undertook to account for the Russian Revolution as an instance of overdetermination. 'How was this revolution possible in Russia, why was it victorious over there?' The French philosopher so asked only to paraphrase Lenin's answer in a brand new Freudian formulation: 'It was *possible* in Russia for a reason that went beyond Russia: because with the unleashing of imperialist war humanity entered into an *objectively revolutionary* situation' (Althusser 2005: 95).

Althusser's road to Freud, it is widely known, had been paved with Lacanian bricks. Overdetermination, according to Lacan, is a trait common to all unconscious formations, best illustrated by hysterical symptoms, slips of the tongue, and dreams. Lacan always insisted in the name of Freud, with regard to symptoms, whether neurotic or not, there must be a 'minimum of over-determination constituted by a double meaning (symbol of a conflict long dead over and above its function in a *no less symbolic* present conflict)'. Thus in the text of the patient's free association the lineage of the symbol is ramified in an ascending order so that verbal forms of the text intersect with nodal points of the symbolic structure. It's raison d'être being that 'the symbol resolves itself entirely in an analysis of language, because the symptom is itself structured like a language, because it is from language that speech must be delivered (Lacan 1977: 59; emphases in the original).

Being 'structured like a language', we will argue, is not far from as being overdetermined. It means that processes constituted by the dual axes of metonymy and metaphor, of displacement and substitution, are by definition processes of elision and layering of meaning. As a commentator put it in brief, 'just as a word cannot be reduced to a signal, a symptom cannot be the unambiguous sign of a single unconscious content' (Laplanche and Pontalis 1973: 293).

I propose to advance the hypothesis that the national question as such in South Asia can in fact be better addressed if we take into account certain processes of overdetermination in the analysis of modes and relations of production, not excluding formations of states and cultures. As in Freudian interpretation of dreams, in the analyses of national formations too, lack of one definitive determination is of fundamental importance. One may yet argue that analysis of historical experience can render this problematic more determinate. A prologue to any analysis whatsoever of 'the politically and analytically intractable national question' in India must remain wedded to a consideration of the historical course of development of India's high bourgeoisie.

According to some of the best accounts available Indian merchant communities, who would form the core of the high bourgeoisie, passed its formative era before India's subjection to British rule in which they were able to find a symbiosis throughout that fateful era. In the colonial era, they found themselves in the service of British imperialism not simply in India but also in other colonial and semi-colonial possessions. This high bourgeoisie, as is well known, insisted on a unitary Indian state at the end of the colonial rule. For this bourgeoisie, who were already operating on a pan-Indian scale, and even beyond in the Pax Britannica, the interest was not just some regional bazaar but the All-India market, even when it was in its mercantile formation.

In the phase of its transition to industrial capital, under the tutelage of British capital, there surfaced no new reason to compromise the accent on a pan-Indian nation. 'It was not out of small capitals serving local markets,' as the sage commentator, DN, puts it, 'that the big capitals arose. Thus it was not necessary for them to identify with local sub-nationalisms. Along with aspiring to the all-India market went the necessity of pan-Indian nationalism' (DN 1989: 456).

An ideology of building a pan-Indian nation was framed contemporaneously, working itself out in an overdetermination. Indian nationalism swallowed a dose more of Hindu nationalism. Along with this came the decision to promote Hindi as the national language of India. That non-Hindi big bourgeois groups, such as Gujarati Banias, lent their support to Hindi for a national language of India is an interesting fact though 'obviously in the interests of fashioning an all-India market, based on pan-Indian nationalism'. It is more interesting, perhaps, to note that "some upper caste groups, which were not big bourgeoisies in the all-India markets, like the Tamil Brahmins, also supported Hindi as *the* national language.'

For India's high bourgeoisie, defined here as those merchant-bankers and industrialists of pan-Indian orientation who did not advance their demands on the basis of a regional market, nation building was committed to 'Hindu memory' as the basis of the Indian nation and the 'Hindi' as *the* national language of India. It is in the wake of this nation-building policy nurtured by the high bourgeoisie that the national question in India came up-front. Given the use of caste discrimination by the high bourgeoisie as barriers to entry against outsiders and outliers in both state and civil society, 'the Muslim bourgeois elements sought to gain an area where their community's numerical majority would enable them to use the state machinery for capitalist accumulation.'

'Over a series of demands and counter-demands what finally emerged,' as DN reminds in the interest of historical truth, 'was that, while the Muslim League was willing to settle for a federation in which the Muslim–majority states would have full (as full as possible in the imperialist world) economic and political power, the Congress, representing the Indian big bourgeoisie, was not willing for such a federal scheme. The Congress insisted on the right to fashion a constitution as it wished, on the basis of its majority, i.e., a Hindu majority.' As everyone knows the Indian National Congress, true to its commitment, preferred partition of India to a federation. Hardly anyone would notice the act of repression though. 'A federation, with major economic and political powers (other than foreign and military affairs) in the hands of the provincial governments would have helped the growth of not just a bourgeoisie from the Muslims, but also other competing, regional bourgeoisies. This the Indian big bourgeoisie was determined to prevent. Birla, for instance, was clear that partition was preferable to federation' (DN 1989: 456).

India, accordingly, India turned out to be a voluntary union one fine morning in place of a 'voluntary federation' as promised. Thus, not unlike the erstwhile Union of Soviet Republics in the wake of the Romanov Empire, the Unions of India and Pakistan came to succeed the British Empire, with perhaps a difference. The steel frame (the army and the civil service) was partitioned as the basis of building two imperial states, with the addition of Hindi and Urdu as signifiers of the two nationalisms, Hindu and Muslim.

In retrospect, after Bangladesh, it appears this primary repression of historical nations killed two birds at the same shot. First, the 'two-nation' theory, a dignity it hardly deserves, was pushed forward as a charter of political demands, a justification rather for a section of Britain's Indian Empire. Articulating such a demand, if worth a community's salt, as a national credo permitted shoving all followers of one creed off to the procrustean bed of a single nation.

Jinnah, and other Muslim leaders, as is now widely accepted, did not mean to plead partition of India in the beginning. They meant the 'two-nations' theory to come into operation only when British rule came to an end. 'In other words, it was not intended to be a demand for National Self-Determination or for independent Nation-Statehood but was a pre-emptive strategy to counter-back the options of the Indian political leadership which was carrying on the struggle for freedom from British rule' (Mathur 1977: 435).

An analysis of the actual course of events, c. 1940-1947, leaves no doubt indeed that to Muhammad Ali Jinnah and his admirers it was no more than 'a convenient political formula' imagined to be acceptable to India's British masters. The Lahore Resolution of 1940, which provided for more states than one with a Muslim majority in British India, must have brought to closure the old debate on Pakistan. It was never meant to be a nation-state, neither in the opening bids nor during the endgame of old Pakistan's.

Pakistan's endgame in 1971 all the same tells the same old story all over again. The Pakistani elite perhaps never ever believed in the fantasy that Punjabis and Bengalis would form one nation. 'Faced with a mounting sense of distrust and discontent in East Pakistan, the Pakistani ruling elite placed very little premium on the religious identities of East Pakistanis and banked mainly on their armed forces to maintain the integrity of Pakistan.' Anyone who is forced to take recourse to a military solution to the problem of national integration must be taken for one who has lost faith in the efficacy of any theory whatsoever as an integrative force.

For India it proved easy to teach her neighbour perhaps a lesson or two on how not to build a nation, it seems a trifle harder to learn as much from her. The national crisis that India faces today is all apparent but is this altogether an unprecedented event? India resisted the crisis rather successfully, compared especially to Pakistan. It is perhaps too early to ask if India's resilience may prove 'too weak against a continuing string of divisive policies and actions' (Tripathi 2000: 937).

Before I conclude this rather inconclusive paper let me recall what an old orientalist once said on the national question in ancient India. As Sylvain Levy of Collège de France once put it in a luminous lecture, delivered a little less than a hundred years ago (incidentally on August 15, 1922) at the Calcutta University, 'India is not a unity in the ethnological sense. There is not a people [on earth] that reveals so clearly as India [such an] extraordinary diversity of origin. India is not a unity in the linguistic sense [either]; the languages of India are even more numerous than races. And yet India is not a mere geographical expression devoid of human value, determined only by the nature of the ground, by elevations and depressions' (Levy 1922: 373).

'No one can dispute,' added Levy who knew what he was raving about, 'the existence of an Indian civilization, characterized by the predominance of one ideal, of one doctrine, of one language, of one literature and of one social class.' 'From the Himalaya to Ceylon,' the occidental savant added, 'cultured minds and simple souls alike believe in the same transcendental law—the "Dharma" bound up with eternal transmigration —"Samsara" and the inevitable recompense of acts from existence to existence—"Karman." Religions and philosophies agree in preaching the nothingness of the individual and the vanity, the illusion of things. Sanskrit, the language of the gods, has enjoyed a prestige for two or three millenniums. Vyäsa, Välmiki, Kälidäsa are unanimously held to be models of taste, of poesy and of style. The Brahmin is everywhere venerated as a sort of divinity on earth. But India is a proof of the fact that a civilisation is not enough to form a nation. A comparison with the great peoples of classic antiquity will show only too clearly what is wanting in India' (Levy 1922: 373).

Sylvain Levy nonetheless lost no time to insert a caveat. 'And when I speak of "India",' he quips, "it is of ancient India that I mean to speak; I must refuse resolutely to take any part in the controversies and the passions of the present moment' (Levy 1922: 373). It has been the burden of this paper to suggest that despite all the controversies and passions of the last hundred years, with the warts and all of anti-colonial struggles, India has not become a nation by 1947. Neither has it become one since then, Pakistan too has not proven an exception. Only Bangladesh, if any, has come anywhere near the measure of the 'great peoples' of the classical Greek world.

As the Constitution of India, that well crafted document puts it, India is a 'Union of States,' having features of both a federation and a union with a systematic flexibility that has allowed it to becoming a three-tiered polity with a single citizenship, and with the capacity to be either unitary or federal, according to the requirements of time and circumstances. As a well known Indian statesman reminds us today, the point was well-taken by B.R. Ambedkar whose charge it was to chair the Drafting Committee of the Constituent Assembly of India. 'The Drafting Committee,' as Ambedkar in fact noted, 'wanted it to be clear that though India was to be a federation, the federation was not the result of an agreement by the states to join in a federation,' adding that 'the federation is a Union because it is indestructible. Though the country and the people may be divided into different states for convenience of administration, the country is one integral whole, its people a single people living under a single imperium derived from a single source' (Ansari 2016: 11-12).

Does it matter, really, if we call a rose or an imperium by any other name whatsoever? India remains a nation in the making in the thick of it all, elevations and depressions not forgotten.

REFERENCES

Althusser, Louis. 2005. *For Marx*, trans. Ben Brewster, reprint. London: Verso.

Ansari, M. Hamid. 2016. *Citizen and Society: Selected Writings*. New Delhi: Rupa.

Azad, Maulana Abul Kalam. 1988. *India Wins Freedom*, the complete version. Hydrabad: Orient Longman.

DN, 1989. 'Indian Big Bourgeoisie and the National Question: The Formative Phase,' *Economic and Political Weekly*, 24(9), March 4.

Eisenhower, Dwight D. 1965. *The White House Years: Waging Peace 1956-1961*. Garden City, NY: Doubleday.

Fanon, Frantz. 1990. *The Wretched of the Earth*, trans. C. Farrington, reprint. 1990. London: Penguin Books.

Habib, Irfan. 1975. 'Emergence of Nationalities,' *Social Scientist*, 4(1): 14-20, August.

Lacan, Jacques. 1977. *Écrits: A Selection*, trans. Alan Sheridan. New York: W.W. Norton.

Laplanche, J. and J.-B. Pontalis. 1973. *The Language of Psycho-Analysis*, trans. Donald Nicholson-Smith. New York: W.W. Norton.

Levy, Sylvain. 1922. 'Ancient India,' *The Calcutta Review*, New Series, 4(3), September: 367-380. http://www.southasiaarchive.com/Content/sarf.120137/211241/002 (accessed on December 30, 2014 at 04.47:17).

Mathur, P.C. 1977. 'Theories of Nation-Building in the Indian Sub-Continent: A Political Analysis with Special Reference to the Emergence of the State of Bangladesh,' *The Indian Journal of Political Science*, 38(4): 435-443, October-December.

Pandian, M.S.S. 2009. 'Nation Impossible,' *Economic and Political Weekly*, 44(10): 65-69, March 7-13.

Razzaq, Abdur. 1981. *Bangladesh: State of the Nation*. Dacca: University of Dacca.

Sarkar, Jadunath. 1976. 'Chapter XXVI: The End of Muslim Rule,' in Jadunath Sarkar (ed.), *The History of Bengal: Vol. II (Muslim Period: 1200-1757)*, 3rd imp. pp. 481-499. Dacca: University of Dacca.

Sofa, Ahmed. 2008-2012. *Ahmed Sofa Racanabali*, in Bengali, Vols. I-IX, Nurul Anwar (ed.), Dhaka: Khan Brothers.

Thompson, E.P. 1991. 'Introduction', in Rabindranath Tagore, *Nationalism*, reprint, pp. 1-16, Calcutta: Rupa.

Tripathi, Dwijendra. 2000. 'Crisis of Indian Polity: A Historical Perspective,' *Economic and Political Weekly*, 35(11): 937-946, March 11-17.

Vanaik, Achin. 1988. 'Is There a Nationality Question in India?' *Economic and Political Weekly*, 23(44): 2278-2289, October 29-November 4.

8

Radical Route to Neoconservative Resolution in Nepal

Shubhanga Pandey

Less than quarter of a century after the fall of the Soviet Union, Nepal joined the modest list of nations where a revolution from the left had seen success. When the Maoists began their guerrilla insurgency in 1996, Nepal appeared to be firmly on its way to the Fukuyaman "end of history," with a newfound halo of parliamentary democracy, a liberalized economy, and a constitutionally constrained monarch.

Things did not go as planned. By 2005—the year Nepal's King Gyanendra Shah suspended parliament and took direct control of the government—nearly thirteen thousand lives had been lost to civil war. The royal coup also had the effect of alienating parliamentary parties, who were till then allied with the king in the conflict against the rebels.

With the king's suspension of democratic government, these parties—led by the two major rivals of electoral politics, the liberal Nepali Congress (NC) and the Communist Party of Nepal–Unified Marxist-Leninist (UML)—found the opportunity to align with the Maoists and mount a common front against the authoritarian rule. The parliamentary parties would begin a popular movement demanding the reinstatement of the parliament while the Maoists continued their armed conflict with the state forces.

A year later, in April 2006, the king was forced to finally restore the parliament, which effectively ended his regime; in less than a month, the reinstated parliament passed laws that formally curtailed the already defanged monarchy's powers. In November that year, the Maoists and the parliamentary forces signed a Comprehensive Peace Treaty, finally ending the decade-long war and paving the way for constituent assembly elections in April 2008, where the Maoists (presently the United Communist Party of Nepal-Maoist, or UCPN-M) emerged as the largest party. By May 2008, Nepal was a republic.

Nepalis, it seemed, were to finally have a constitution, one written for the people and by the people.

At least, that is how it was supposed to be.

But when Nepal's constitution-writing body finally promulgated the constitution on September 20, 2015, the country was deep in a crisis. Despite extending the deadline of the first constituent assembly more than once, it was suspended in May 2012. The primary reason behind the aborted assembly's failure to produce a draft of the constitution was disagreements over what was the most contentious fulcrum for political polarization in Nepal: federalism.

The particulars of the disagreements were in whether the new states would be created on the basis of ethnic, linguistic, and geographic considerations, or if they would be purely administrative divisions. On one side of the divide were the Maoists (UCPN-M) and the parties built on the platform of ethnic identity post-2006, who wanted to carve out states where minority ethnic and linguistic groups would have a demographic advantage. On the other side were the Congress, UML and other parties of the old parliamentary fold, many of whom were either critical or actively opposed to the very idea of federalism.

After a year of impasse, another constituent assembly was elected in 2013, this time making the Congress and the UML the leading parties, who went on to form a coalition government. For months, the polarization over questions of federalism endured. But in June 2015, when the country was still reeling from devastating spring earthquakes, the ruling coalition and the largest opposition, the UCPN-M (along with a small ethnic party) agreed on the fundamentals of a new draft of the constitution. This move effectively ended the Maoists' alliance with other dissident parties that advocated for a more radical form of federalism.

As the unnatural troika of former rivals pushed through the country's constitution, the prospects of political resolution appeared increasingly dim. The constitution was promulgated while the southern belt of the country, known as Madhes (or Tarai), was up in flames following the release of the draft of the document in early August. Large protests broke out across its cities and towns, in particular disputing the proposed borders for carving out new federal states, which failed to both address the historic marginalization of ethnic minorities and ensure inclusive representation—borders that will in effect perpetuate the control of the ruling elite. The protests were to continue for the next six months.

The government, created from the same constitution-writing body, was brutal in its response. In the first month or so, demonstrations were met with harsh repressions and several towns were put under frequent curfews. The national army had been deployed in some areas and police presence was permanent. In the process, over forty-five people have died and hundreds injured.

According to one Human Rights Watch report, there was "abundant evidence in several cases of serious crimes by police against protesters and bystanders, including disproportionate use of force and extrajudicial killings." The report also noted "criminal attacks on defenceless police by protesters." One person was shot dead by the police less than an hour before the president announced the promulgation of the new constitution of the young republic.

The shutdown of transport and businesses across many towns in Madhes assumed new proportions after the release of the constitution. Following it, the groups leading the protests in southern Nepal decided to shift strategy and start blocking the flow of goods at key customs ports around the border with India. It was a significant decision, as Nepal heavily depends on imports from India (and from other countries via India), including petrol, diesel, and cooking gas. It was a clear move to increase the pressure on the capital, as the mere street demonstrations were appearing to have a diminishing effect.

Crucially, the Indian state also imposed trade restrictions on their side of the border. Although the Indian government officially denied that it had imposed a blockade, it was clear that they had been constricting the flow of goods, particularly of petroleum products. With that, the crisis that was once concentrated in the south now gripped most of the country. This was one of those unfortunate paradoxes of international politics, where the legitimate claims of the oppressed can be undermined by the support — real or perceived — of a regional hegemon. And unsurprisignly, it gave the ruling sections of the two countries an opportunity to articulate their agendas.

India's Prime Minister Narendra Modi found a perfect tool to expand his authoritarian methods beyond the Indian nation state and clarify the nature of an Indian hegemony which treats Nepal as a client state. For the ruling elite of Nepal, primarily composed of hill-caste men, it once again gave them the chance to amplify a nationalist rhetoric and undermine the Madhes movement by projecting Indian intervention as the root problem. Meanwhile, the Madhesi cause, and by extension, other forms of ethnic politics, receded into the background.

What explains this sudden chaos in Nepal? Why such objections to a constitution prepared by a democratically-elected body, headed by parties that call themselves socialist or communist and made explicit promises of secularism, federalism, and inclusion? And what has become of a politics that seemed remarkably revolutionary not long ago?

A History of Hegemony

The oldest nation-state in South Asia, Nepal's origins lie in the campaign of successive military conquests by the rulers of Gorkha — a minor kingdom from the central hills of Nepal from which the word "Gurkha" comes. Led by the upper caste men from the hilly regions, the Bahuns and Chettris, the Gorkhali empire's expansionist zeal was halted by the Chinese empire in the north and the British empire (in the form of the East India Company) in the south, giving Nepal its present territorial dimensions.

In the process, the young empire brought a wide range of nationalities under its control: the indigenous people or "Janajatis" of hills and mountains; the Newars of Kathmandu Valley; and the

Tharus and Madhesis of the southern plains, among others. The diversity of ethnic identities, and the regions they have historically inhabited, are essential in understanding the country, especially given the clichéd and misleading portrayal of Nepal as a "Himalayan" nation, even as half of the population lives in the southern plains which is geographically the continuation of northern India.

For nearly two hundred years, the state operated as a feudal-military state, with ruling elite extracting surplus from the largely agricultural workforce. Hegemony came in all forms. A strict legal code called Muluki Ain came into effect in 1854, where all the people were categorized based on an improvised Hindu caste division system. Those ethnic groups outside the Hindu caste–fold were placed even lower in this institutionalized hierarchy. A policy mandating only Nepali language—one used by the hill Bahuns and Chhetris—was enforced, and teaching and publishing in other languages was punishable. The political economy of the country was highly centralized, with the royalty and a handful of military, priestly, and merchant clans holding the reins of administration.

Democratic reforms began in 1951 with the overthrow of the authoritarian and oligarchic rule of a prominent military clan, the Ranas, who had for the previous century reduced the monarchy to a minor force. But within a decade, the king, who controlled the military and had the support from the landed aristocracy, suspended the parliament and banned all forms of party-political activities. For the next thirty years of what was called the "Panchayat" regime, all political activity was driven underground and the country saw a wide range of pro-democracy activism where the current crop of leadership came of age—from covert memberships of student unions to a failed revolution inspired by the left-wing Naxalites of neighbouring West Bengal.

In the spring of 1990, following the success of a popular movement forged by a coalition of the bourgeois liberal Congress and leftist forces (largely comprising of what has been today reduced to a reactionary UML, with its deep ties to NGOs and private businesses), Nepal had a new constitution in place, one that was in perfect congruence with the ideas of liberal democracy.

Yet its shortcomings soon revealed itself. The constitution's liberalism functioned in ways that benefited the emerging urban middle class (largely from the hill uppercaste), who had supported the popular movement as they thought the partyless panchayat had suppressed their natural economic and political potentials. Politically, the grip of those from the hill uppercaste on the state machinery saw little challenge. In fact, under the universalizing grammar of liberalism, the problem of underrepresentation of the remaining 85 per cent could not even be framed adequately.

As a result, politics based on ethnic identity were almost driven out of the mainstream party politics, leaving it to find a place in NGO activism, or more explosively, a few years later, in the Maoist insurgency. The economy took a similarly reactionary trajectory. The country had already started flirting with neoliberal policies, and under the Congress—the party that had led the movement and was the biggest beneficiary of the parliamentary system in the early years—Nepal saw the full range of economic liberalization: the necessary legislative changes to fuel foreign investment and privatization of state-owned industries.

It is this post-1990 liberal utopia, in addition to the long history of marginalization, that needs to be taken into account in understanding the question of identity federalism. Within less than six years, a split faction of a radical left party, the Communist Party of Nepal-Maoist (CPN-M), declared a "People's War." Their demands were largely of the economic-nationalist and anti-imperialist fold. Secularism, republicanism, and autonomy for ethnic nationalities were also mentioned—demands that were to not only dominate but almost completely replace the economic slogans.

This was an ideological novelty of sorts: no communist party in Nepal had till then advocated that caste and ethnic identity be a central pillar for mobilization. With their leadership and support coming mostly from the rural petty bourgeoisie, hill Bahuns, and Chhetris, this was not unusual. But the Maoists, following Lenin's formulation of the nationalities question, identified ethnic grievances and eventually made them one of their most explicit causes, naming as many as nine regions that deserved regional autonomy. It was this demand for autonomy that allowed their insurgency to expand beyond their traditional base in the remote hills of western Nepal. Given the centrality ethnic autonomy took in both the formulation of their rhetoric as well as their organizational forms, their armed rebellion gave what could have become purely an ethnic conflict a fuller and broader political face.

While the popular movement of 2006 is often credited with ending monarchy in the country, it is sometimes ignored that the principal energy behind the insurgency and the culminating popular movement came from the need to radically transform the nature of the Nepali state. This meant framing a new constitution that ensured creation of federal provinces (based on ethnic and geographical realities), proportional forms of representations in legislature and state institutions, and institutionalization of secularism — transformations, that if set in motion, would fundamentally begin to alter the political economy of Nepal.

Among these, it was the first two changes that posed the greatest threat to the ruling elite. The manner in which new states would be created in the as yet centralized Nepal — and what that would mean for its ethnic nationalities — defined the central contradiction in the country, since it opened the possibility of disturbing the ethnic hegemony of hill upper caste and class: whereas all hues of politics in Nepal, whether it be from the right, centre or even Left, had theretofore largely been the preserve of the Bahuns and Chettris. And in the early days of 2007, protests in Madhes and the state's violent reaction to it showed that the contradiction was just below the surface.

Radical Departures

The southern region of Nepal is mostly populated by Madhesi and Tharu people (although many from the hills migrated here starting in the mid-twentieth century) who share ethnic and kinship ties with people across the border in India. Its inhabitants have historically been marginalized, especially vis-à-vis economic and civic rights, by the state in a manner that could be termed internal colonization.

The region was also at the forefront of popular movements that explicitly demanded that federal states be divided recognizing ethnic, linguistic, and historical continuities. And so when the country's interim parliament (before to the first constituent assembly) adopted a new interim constitution that did not guarantee federal restructuring of the country, widespread demonstrations filled the streets of Madhes.

The government had to eventually reconcile with the demands: the interim constitution was amended to explicitly commit to federalism and proportionate representation in the electoral system. Not just the Madhesis, but the indigenous people (Janajatis), Dalits, women, and other religious and ethnic minorities were to be included in state bodies in proportion to their population. In addition, there would be forms of affirmative action in place. But the new constitution largely ignored these demands. This also explains why it is the Madhes where the agitations denouncing the constitution written by the troika are most intense.

This departure from the revolutionary spirit of 2006 was not sudden. Following the failure of the first constituent assembly after it could not agree on the issue of federalism, the Maoists and the Madhes-based parties, who dominated the assembly, faced severe popular criticism. This was compounded by the increasing strength of establishment forces (the bureaucracy, the army, the police, and the judiciary), until it was reflected in the electoral arithmetic of the second constituent assembly elections in 2013.

Apart from the resurgence of the two parties that ran the country in post-1990, liberal Nepal, there was also palpable growth in support for royalist groups. The UCPN-M, now a faction smaller than before, lost 149 seats. The showing was even poorer for Madhesi and Janajati parties. After much horse-trading, the top two parties, Congress and UML — the two rival forces of Nepal's electoral politics — came together to form a coalition government. It was a clear right-wing resurgence, with those who represented dominant caste and class at the helm again.

The opposition bloc, consisting of the Maoists, and the Madhesi and Janajati parties, was numerically insignificant. The ruling coalition had over 60 per cent of the total seats; 66 per cent was needed for writing the constitution as per their wish. Given this, the opposition, led by the UCPN-M, had to resort to ground mobilization.

Starting in February, the opposition coalition began rounds of demonstrations around the country, including bringing the capital of Kathmandu to a halt. Their central demand was "consensus" in constitution writing: a euphemism suggesting that the ruling NC-UML alliance could muster enough numbers to ram through the document, and so it was in the streets — not the floor of the Assembly — where the opposition parties had any traction. But by August, with the once-radical UCPN Maoists hastily aligning forces with the conservative block, represented by the NC and UML, to finalize the constitution, the critical agenda of identity-based federalism was compromised and the counterrevolution complete.

Why the UCPN-M chose to take this road and abandon its radical stance is a question whose answers are still coming. But their deradicalization was not unusual or unforeseeable. Many party members spent almost a decade in the legislature, an ideal incubation time for becoming professional politicians. They, along with thousands of local-level party workers, were to eventually act as rent-seeking agents in a political economy where its rival parties had been ahead of the game by at least another decade. Inevitably, this led to clearer ideological drift resulting in the rampant factionalism; since their entry into electoral politics, they have been split into three other "Maoist" parties with relatively small bases of support.

Nepal's Neoconservative Moment

All hues of reformist politics are premised on the idea that economic and social inequalities can be reduced through democratic methods, without necessarily resorting to revolutionary tactics. Economically, the aim is to get more essential goods and services out of the commodity market and into a public sector; socially, the marginalized and oppressed social groups are to be given greater share and ability to exercise power. However, as was clear from the decade of parliamentary democracy from 1990 into the 2000s, even these aims found minimal success in a centralized Nepal.

It was because this form of democracy was built on a legislature formed on the basis of first-past-the-post elections, in a state where the hill upper castes monopolized much political and economic surplus. Representation of minorities was reduced to tokenism. The result was that the very problems the progressives wanted a solution to became more intractable. By contrast, many on the left hoped that the creation of federal states based on ethnic and linguistic identities would, to begin with, enable a space for challenging the hill-caste hegemony.

This is not to undermine the role of class-based formations in the political struggles of the left, but precisely to underscore the need for a larger solidarity that tries to align interests with the realities of caste, gender, and ethnicities. Those in the left who profess a federal politics of identity do need to acknowledge an issue in the long run: that an identity politics — especially one formed around ethnic-linguistic nationalism — can degenerate into petty-bourgeois nationalism if not complemented by a grounding in pro-labour, feminist, pro-queer, and anti-imperialist ambitions. The question of how such a movement is forged is still being grappled with. But in Nepal, no political solution to this question could begin without the formation of federal states that considered ethnic identities, or subnationalisms, as a major criterion.

Meanwhile, a surprising development in late 2017 indicated that Nepal's regression into a conservative polity was near complete, spurred, ironically, by the merger of two 'communist' parties. Two months before the first ever national elections that were held under the new constitution, the UML and Maoist Centre (UCPN-M had seen more mergers and splits) forged a pre-poll alliance and committed to form a unified 'communist' party after the elections. This creation of a self-described 'Left Alliance' was unexpected, largely because the UML and Maoist Centre had always been political rivals that, along the NC, were competing with each other for votes in every election.

Despite its name, however, there was little that was 'left' or progressive about this union. UML, which was Nepal's biggest nominally communist party, was a seasoned parliamentary force that had abandoned issues associated with communist, or even social democratic or liberal, forces: scepticism of free markets and foreign investment, redistributive economic policy, state-guaranteed public goods and services, and a base made up of working-class groups and social-justice movements. Instead, the party transformed itself into a nationalist, right-wing force, both socially (as the party of hill-caste chauvinism) and economically (as promoter of extractive 'development' and foreign capital). The merger with the Maoists, who had seen large-scale deradicalization among its ranks and in its political aims, was therefore more of an absorption of the former radicals into a new neoconservative force.

To be clear, the descriptor 'neoconservative' here is used in its original formulation: as someone of the liberal or left persuasion who had been, in the words of neoconservative essayist Irving Kristol, "mugged by reality." The word went on to develop connotations of foreign policy misadventure and imperialism, due to the advocacy for the 2003 Iraq War by neoconservative policy think tank and journalists. But the original definition is useful, since it captures tendencies not always possible to describe in the traditional left-right political spectrum. In the Nepali context, this neoconservative block is distinguished from the Nepali Congress and some royalist parties in its explicit, high-pitched use of populist rhetoric to push majoritarian nationalism. They successfully distinguish themselves from the NC, the party of the bourgeoisie, who are portrayed as soft on India and when it comes to geopolitics, and from other traditional conservatives, such as the royalist parties, who are irrelevant in the new republican political space. With the patina of 'communism', this new force is able to project itself as the party of development and large-scale infrastructure projects. At the same time, they are able to marshall cultural and religious elements of the high-caste hill Hindus as symbols of strong, anti-imperial, independent Nepal— a function previously performed by the monarchy.

The UML-MC coalition went on to record an overwhelming victory in the landmark national elections, winning nearly two-thirds of the seats. The main reason behind this was the premiership of the UML leader Khadga Prasad Oli during the period of Madhesi protests and blockade which was also enforced from the Indian side. Oli's ability to withstand both the domestic pressure, even after the deaths of scores of protesters, and international pressure, despite the blockade and bad press, won his party favours across the political and demographic spectrum in Nepal—with the key exception of the Madhesis. UML saw its fortunes rise also because Oli signed a transit treaty with China during the blockade, which at least symbolically decreased Nepal's reliance on trade with India. With the successful completion of this election, along with municipal and state elections earlier that year, the Nepali state, and the conservative defenders of the Nepali constitution, have therefore assumed ideological hegemony.

For many centrists and conservatives in Nepal, the absorption of an already depleted Maoist party into the larger UML was welcome news after decades of militant politics by the Maoists. But the deal was encouraging for many long-time leftists, too, who saw it as an opportunity to finally have a decisive, albeit only notional, leftist government. With this, the trade unions and professional groups that are generally assumed to be the forces of resistance, have also been transformed into essentially petty-bourgeois defenders of the conservative state. At the same time, the disadvantaged groups for whom this the last decade of transformation was purportedly carried out, have either been politically coopted or ghettoized. Therefore, with the opposition to the new government likely to come from the right rather than the liberals or the left, Nepal can expect conservative forces to dominate the centre of national politics for the foreseeable future.

Early signs appear to validate this. Affirmative action, which generated much debate during the constitution writing and was advocated by all minority groups, eventually became a part of the constitution. But despite some positive aspects (reservation for women and Dalit women in local government) the provision has at best seen limited success, and at worst appears to be cynically used to justify the status quo. Women's quota in municipal elections, for instance, has either been reduced to tokenism or been explicitly used to justify nominating too few female candidates for higher offices. Most absurdly, the constitution also provides reservations for the hill-caste community, who have been the dominant political, linguistic and social group since the beginning of the nation state, in all state bodies. This is akin to having affirmative action for white Anglo-Saxons in the US.

Increasingly, organized civil society, and dissenting groups in general, are also facing pressures. In a highly unusual move, the prime minister's office has centralized a number of other government departments, including the one that oversees the NGOs and INGOs. The Nepal government is formulating a National Integrity Policy, which aims to tighten regulations on non-profits, and will enable the use of army, police and intelligence services in monitoring their work to see if they are meeting the government's standards. Also, according to one news report, "The proposal has provisions for deporting foreigners working in Nepal if they are found involved in working against the national interest and government policies or involved in religious conversion." One senior office bearer told the media in April 2018, "NGOs should function to meet the government's objectives rather than working unilaterally based on its own strategy and agenda." As the Nepali state courts Indian and Chinese capital for rapid, and often unilaterally decided upon infrastructure projects, many see that such provisions will be used to silence organizations that disagree.

In Lieu of a Conclusion

Many critics have argued that the current constitution is an illiberal one. But its failure is a function of liberal ideology itself: it was supposed to reflect people's deepest radical desires, instead it has become a balance sheet of power arrangement. In the absence of an arrangement that in concrete ways addresses the continuation of historical marginalization of ethnic communities, as well as other social groups, there will be hardly any room for a truly left politics in Nepal.

Solidarities formed around these movements provide the most effective form of anti-capitalist politics in the present conditions, especially with the two largest "Communist" parties in the country showing few signs of any socialist politics and there being practically no trade union movement in the country. Only these radical interventions, which looked quite possible at the beginning of the decade, will ensure space for class-based politics.

9

Revisiting the Marxist Approach to Sex Work

Anuja Agrawal

Introduction

For several decades now, the feminist debate on sex work/prostitution has been extremely polarized. The main lines of this division are broadly between liberal and radical feminists. The liberal feminists focus on prostitution as 'sex work' and argue that in its voluntary form it should be treated as legitimate and hence decriminalized. Radical feminists, on the other hand, see prostitution as a gross instance of male domination and sexual violence against women and hence assert that it needs to be dispensed with. The signs of this polarization giving way to a common ground are not at all obvious and there are many further divisions and several complex alliances within these camps. It is however not the purpose of this paper to deal with these details of the broader scenario. What I seek to highlight here is that, not very long ago, feminist positions on the issue of sex work were categorized into three and not two groups: liberal, Marxist and radical. But this is no longer the case as, at some point, the Marxist position seems to have collapsed with radical feminism and the former is no longer very visible in the contentious debates on this issue.

This shift can, for instance, be illustrated by looking at two pieces written by Alison Jaggar, a prominent feminist writer from the US. Jaggar wrote two papers on prostitution in 1980 and 1997 respectively. While she counted the Marxist approach as one of the major approaches in her earlier piece, in her second piece, she did not treat it as one among the 'contemporary' approaches and her very brief account of this position was somewhat dismissive of its potential as a viable mode of thinking about prostitution questions. It appears that by the mid-90s, Marxism had ceased to be a relevant position on the issue of sex work.

Why did this happen? Does this mean that Marxism has little to offer by way of illuminating the very fraught issue of sex work? Or is there something that can be salvaged from this theoretical framework? Are there new directions in which the same may be developed? In this paper, I wish to argue that the dominant feminist approaches to the prostitution question that occupy much of the discursive space are often one-sided and inadequate to theoretically grasp the complexity of the empirical contexts in which sex work takes a material form. A reworked Marxist approach on the other hand provides a desirable alternative to these polarized positions as it is able to accommodate, make sense of and provide a complex understanding of many different empirical facts that get clubbed under the category of sex work/prostitution.

Starting with the classical positions, this paper will provide a brief overview of the trajectory of Marxist thought on the question of sex work/prostitution. It will also draw critical attention to the more recent renewal of interest in the insights which such thinking can offer as well as provide a brief assessment of the relevance of such renewed thinking for the Indian context. The paper is divided into two parts. The first part outlines the classical Marxist position on sex work and also discusses the possible reasons for waning of this position; the second part critically considers some of the elements of a reworked position on sex work and considers the same in light of the varying contexts of sex work in the Indian context. This is a very brief foray into a much broader terrain and draws upon my ongoing research in this area.

I

Before we inquire into the factors which lead to the marginalization of the Marxist approach to the question of sex work, we need to consider what this position was. The answer to this question is not easy to provide as neither Marx and Engels nor other Marxist and Socialist writers paid any direct and persistent attention to this issue and some were even very dismissive of the same. In her summary of the Marxist position on prostitution, Jaggar (1980) refers primarily to the works of Marx and Engels (here I will not recount her philosophical rendering of this position) and it would seem that there was very little by way of advance in these positions over almost a century. However one can also refer to some of the contemporaries of Marx and Engels such as August Bebel (1879) as well as the writings of Marxists such as Clara Zetkin, Alexandra Kollontai and Emma Goldman among others, who all together roughly wrote from the second half of the nineteenth century almost up to around the Second World War. This broadening of the field will allow for a somewhat more general perspective when we are trying to formulate the elements of what may be considered the classical Marxist position on prostitution.

One may begin such an exercise by pointing out that there are numerous strands of ideas about prostitution in this body of work. In what follows, I shall briefly summarize some of these strands. In the first place, it is not at all surprising to find that most of these Marxist and Socialist writers treat prostitution as a part and parcel of historically changing conditions and not as rooted in or deriving from nature or biology. It is thus treated as an institution which is invariably found in class-based societies and hence one which, it is suggested, would and should cease to exist in a truly communist and socialist society. Engels (1884) also located prostitution within the changing context of relations between the sexes, which were seen as undifferentiated to begin with (group marriage) and subsequently became differentiated (marriage, hetaerism, prostitution). But such shifts were also seen as linked to the changing materialist foundation of society.

It is in this vein that Alexandra Kollontai (1977), who is foremost among those who dealt with women's issues in the communist movement, sought to place prostitution within the historical materialist framework, however, cursorily. She thus saw it as a 'legal complement' to family relations in the ancient world and as 'something natural and lawful' in the middle ages when prostitutes had guilds and guaranteed the chastity of the daughters of propertied citizens thereby serving the interest of this class. But despite its presence in earlier class-based societies, most writers see prostitution as assuming unprecedented proportions only in a capitalist society owing to the exploitative character of this economy (see Bebel 1879; Goldman 1910; Lenin 1913). For Bebel, for example, 'prostitution is fostered by the industrial crises that have become inevitable in bourgeois society, and [which] to hundreds of thousands of families mean bitter need and desperate poverty' (see Bebel 1879). What I wish to emphasize here is that despite this attempt to place prostitution within a historical materialist frame of reference, no very detailed attempt to discern the specific forms taken by prostitution in these different conditions was forthcoming in this sort of theorization. The same has been attempted in some of the recent writings on the subject as we will see in the later part of this paper.

Apart from the above historical outline, a second line of Marxist ideas on this issue draws attention to the similarities between prostitution and marriage. In an oft-quoted statement, Engels distinguished a married woman from a prostitute only in so far as 'she does not let out her body on piece-work as a wage-worker, but sells it once and for all into slavery'. Thus if prostitution is an economic exchange, so is marriage. By drawing attention to the economic basis of all sexual relations in a bourgeois society, Engels laid the foundation for a critical understanding of a whole range of relations in which men and women are implicated in such a society. This can be treated as a radical insight of Marxist and socialist literature, although one which is no longer very popular. At present the similarities and commonalities between marriage and prostitution are more likely to be provided as a justification for prostitution and as a reminder of the hypocrisy of the critics of prostitution but not as a criticism of the institution of marriage itself. Moreover, if we refer to Trotsky's writings about the post-revolutionary Soviet Union, a critical economic interpretation of marriage was increasingly diluted while the same cannot be said about the stance towards prostitution (see Trotsky 1937).

A third and most important aspect of Marxist thinking on prostitution is whether and to what extent it was treated as a form of labour. It is possible to suggest that Marxist writings draw a strong connection between prostitution and wage labour. However, in most contexts this connection is a metaphorical one as prostitution emerges largely as a paradigm of the degrading relations that are characteristic of a capitalist system. Thus Marx famously said "Prostitution is only a specific expression of the general prostitution of the labourer" (Marx 1844). But such statements do not necessarily illuminate the specific character of the prostitution exchange. The above cited Engels' statement in which he treats the prostitute as someone who lets 'out her body on piece-work as a wage-worker' draws a closer analogy between wage work and the act of prostitution. But such statements also do little more than establishing that women's bodies are very much a part of the process of commodification and exchange in class-based societies.

The question which arises at this point is whether prostitution can be entirely subsumed as a form of wage labour. Insofar as wage labour is a capitalist relation of production but prostitution exists in pre-capitalist class societies as well, the former cannot be an adequate framework to address the specific character of prostitution exchanges in varying contexts. We will see later how other ideas such as slavery and feudal relations of work have also been drawn into an understanding of sex work. Attention will also be drawn to the limitations of the concept of wage labour in understanding the relations of sex work.

What is however more critical to point out here is that while Marx and Engels seem to have drawn a very close connection between wage labour and prostitution, other Marxist writers such as Alexandra Kollontai and even Lenin did not treat the latter as a form of labour. Rather it was treated as an escape from labour and women were seen as 'labour deserters' if they were engaged in prostitution. In a 1921 speech, Kollontai wrote: '... what after all is a professional prostitute? She is a person whose energy is not used for the collective; a person who lives off others, by taking from the rations of others... From the point of view of the national economy the *professional prostitute is a labour deserter*' (Kollontai 1879, emphasis added).

Similar suggestions and arguments are apparent in the approach to prostitution adopted in the Soviet Union in the early as well as later years. Elizabeth Waters' work on the Soviet approach to prostitution with 'perestroika' or opening up of the Soviet economy shows that much the same approach had survived for well over 70 years (Waters 1989). Increasingly prostitution was seen as an anachronism in the Stalinist Soviet Union and even its existence was not acknowledged. However, in the post-perestroika period its existence was not denied but the ideas that prostitutes are the 'unlabouring types' (ibid. 7) who 'shirk honest toil, ... abandon regular state' employment or take on a light-weight job just for the record, [and] even then frequently pay... someone else to do it for them' (ibid. 8-9), appear to be very much in the same spirit as can be discerned from Kollontai's 1921 speech.

Thus the classical position, which equates prostitution with forms of marriage and work in which women exchange sexual favours for economic considerations in their dependent relations with men, does not treat such sexual relations as the domain of 'work' and 'labour'.[1] Such an approach would seem to be in dramatic opposition to the contemporary positions that urge us to speak of 'sex work' and 'sex workers' and even speak of sex work as a form of 'commodification'. They also seem to be at odds with the earlier writings of Marx and Engels which saw prostitution as akin to wage labour and wage labour as akin to prostitution. It is obvious that this way of thinking about prostitution which came to dominate the Marxist thinking at least in some quarters is considerably out of sync with the by now generally accepted positions in feminist thought.

What one may therefore say here is that while classical Marxist thought was foremost in theorizing the question of labour in a capitalist economy, it somehow lagged behind in its recognition of specifically gendered forms of work in which women engage, both in unpaid as well as paid contexts. Thus the marginality of the Marxist theorization of the issue of prostitution, which is increasingly seen as a form of sexual labour, may partly be understood as a consequence of this approach which characterized some of the explicit Marxist thinking on the issue in the early twentieth century.

Indeed, the deficiencies in the Marxist understanding of women's work did become one of the key issues in feminist debates in the 1970s and 80s. Than Dam Truong (1990), a Vietnamse scholar and Luise White (1990) who did a historical study of prostitution in colonial Nairobi were among the early attempts which departed from classical Marxism in casting prostitution as a form of sexual labour. But the feminist critiques of Marxism predominantly focused on domestic work and also the unpaid dimension of women's work, particularly in terms of the capitalist appropriation of such unpaid labour. They did not give similar attention to the contexts in which women did get paid for a host of activities which had however not always been considered work.

Indeed the greatly increased visibility of paid (as opposed to unpaid) domestic work both within and across international boundaries has been accompanied by a visible increase in sex work, reproductive work, care work and even emotional work. That is to say, a large array of activities in which mostly women routinely engaged have increasingly become part of market exchanges (see Delphy and Leonard 1992, Hochschild 1983; Ehrenreich and Hochschild 2004, for example). In the meantime, anthropologists and sociologists have also paid attention to activities such as status work (Papanek 1979) and kin work (di Leonardo 1987) and in doing so have also significantly broadened the notion of women's unpaid labour. The focus on unpaid labour can considerably complicate the idea that married women or women engaged in prostitution are simply 'labour shirkers', even though it is not sufficient to grasp the complexities of issues which emerge in contexts in which the hitherto unpaid activities enter the domain of paid work. But it is obvious that understanding of women's work has greatly expanded in terms of its paid as well as unpaid aspects owing to both Marxist and feminist theorizations.

Here one can suggest that sex work was one of the earliest to enter the domain of paid labour although it now belongs to a large and heterogeneous category of what may be seen as gendered reproductive and care work which includes domestic work, surrogacy, child care and elderly care, emotional work, etc.[2] Although each of these have their own distinctive features and carry vastly variable social and economic valuation, it is increasingly difficult to ignore the gender and class dimensions of such work which is also often deeply embedded in local and global inequalities.[3]

II

As pointed out earlier, in more recent times, some scholars have attempted to revive a Marxist approach to sex work and in a distinct departure from the conventional Marxist approach, they have made a direct use of the Marxist categories to examine the economic forms taken by prostitution.[4] I will now turn to a discussion of some of the insights we can derive from this work and argue that we need to give more thought to such approaches to the problem of prostitution.

One of the features of these approaches is that sex work is now treated as a form of labour. Even more importantly, an attempt is made to recast the specificity and variety of prostitution relations. Thus unlike Alexandra Kollontai who neither traced the *specifically* slave-like, feudal or capitalist relations in sex-work nor entertained the possibility of simultaneous co-existence of these different modes within one historical epoch, Marjoelin van der Veen (2000; 2001; 2002), who has argued for what she calls a 'class-based' analysis of prostitution, does both. She suggests that prostitution may be carried on under relations of slavery, it may be carried out under relations akin to feudalism and of course it may be subject to capitalist relations. She also discusses the individual and communal forms of such work. This approach takes into account both, the specific form of relations of prostitution, and not simply the larger historical configuration of which they are a part, and also the possibility that slave like relations or feudal relations of production can and do co-exist in a predominantly capitalist system. I will primarily focus on some aspects of her framework in the rest of this paper as an example of how Marxist categories can be usefully applied to an analysis of sex work.[5] In this discussion, I would like to interweave some of my own ideas on how Marxist concepts can be fruitfully applied to contexts of sex work and yield understandings which are otherwise not easily available within the existing frameworks. I will also draw on the insights of others who have written on sex work in India in doing so.

I suggest that van der Veen's approach draws our attention to the specificity of what we may call, following Marxist vocabulary, *relations of sex work* as a subset of the overarching relations of production in a society. Although the distinction between slavery, feudal and capitalist forms may be too close to the Marxist stages of historical materialism, and there may well be scope for a further elaboration and refinement of these categories, it serves as a useful way of distinguishing different conditions in which sex work occurs or rather it provides us a framework to examine the different modes of profiting via trading in sexual services.

Thus for instance van der Veen argues that 'if the prostitute is kidnapped or sold and becomes the property of another (an agent, pimp, madame, or trafficker) for an extended period of time, the relationship could be characterized as one of slavery. The slave owner may have the prostitute work in a slave class process in which the slave owner sets the terms of the work, appropriates and distributes all of the surplus labor, and spends an amount just large enough to cover the slave's subsistence' (2000: 126).

It may be possible to suggest that instances which would exemplify such a form of prostitution abound all over the world as well as South Asia. We frequently come across stories of abject servitude and conditions of slavery in the sex trade as also in many other trades. However, liberal feminist critics argue that it is such a picture of prostitution which over-determines our understanding of the trade and also characterize certain political positions such as radical feminism who have persistently used the idea of 'sexual slavery' as the paradigm to characterize the relations of sex work (See Barry 1979, for instance). Some of the state discourses on prostitution are also framed within this model of prostitution. The change in the legal definition of prostitution in India from the earlier one in the Suppression of Immoral Traffic Act 1956 (SITA) which defined it as 'the act of a female offering her body for promiscuous sexual intercourse...whether in money or in kind' to the later one in the Immoral Traffic Prevention Act 1986 (ITPA) which saw it as 'the sexual exploitation or abuse of persons for commercial purposes' can similarly be seen as moving in the direction of treating prostitution exclusively in terms of coercive exploitation.

Much of the discussion on 'trafficking of women' can also be seen as taking this form of prostitution as the dominant or only form and has been much critiqued in recent years by scholars who usefully distinguish trafficking from migration (see Agustin 2007, for instance). Liberal feminists have also rightly found the conflation of prostitution with trafficking problematic as it casts all women engaged in sex work as slaves even if the conditions in which they are engaging in such work are not slave like (see Murray 1998: 52). It is also suggested by some writers that slave like conditions in the sex industry are a consequence of social and political exclusion of those who are working in this industry (see Bindaman 1998, for instance).

While such critical perspectives have been very useful in problematizing the victimhood model of sex work, they run the risk of undermining and denying that sex work may indeed also be carried out in slave like conditions. The denial of existence of slavery like conditions in the sex trade almost entirely on the grounds that the construction of a sex worker as a slave is over-determined by the imperative of presenting oneself as such since an admission of one's volition in entering the trade would either run the risk of being seen as a crime or at least go entirely against the legitimate narrative of such an entry (see Joshi 2007; Blanchette et. al., 2013) seems as inadequate as the reduction of all sex work to slavery is. Another fact that is not clear from such accounts is how such conditions can altogether disappear, for instance with decrimnalization of sex work, when by their own admission slavery like conditions continue to persist in many other sectors of a capitalist society which are not necessarily criminalized. That the logic of profiteering as well as the necessity of criminalization of, for instance, child prostitution may continue to make space for slavery like conditions also need to be taken into account in such arguments.

Thus the usefulness of having a separate category of sex work under conditions of slavery, as suggested by van der Veen is that it allows us to recognize the possibility that such work may indeed be carried out in conditions of slavery without either conflating this with all conditions of sex work (like radical feminists) or denying such a possibility altogether (as in case of the liberal position in some variants). Moreover, it leaves open the question of the extent of such a condition in the sex trade and allows for the possibility that this is not a dominant form under all circumstances. It also invites us to examine the relation such practices have both with the legal regimes as well as with capitalist economy.

The same can be said about the category of feudal relations of sex work offered by van der Veen. Thus according to her, sex work can be said to be taking place under feudal relations when the sex worker is indebted and under some sort of obligation to an agent (or pimp) for a period of time. 'The bonds of obligation may be formed by familial or love commitments, debt obligations, or a status of illegality' (2000: 131). Again, such relations in sex work are extremely common, perhaps even more common than the relations of slavery as outlined above. The critics of the trafficking discourse have pointed out that one of the factors for the exploitation of the women who migrate for engaging in sex work is their being indebted to those who facilitate their migration and with whom they end up sharing a large portion of their income. Although this is a characteristic of a whole range of other contexts in which workers migrate for work and seek the intervention of agents to provide them access to work, the illegal character of sex work in many conditions is seen as exacerbating this situation considerably. Moreover, the extent of such indebtedness can border on debt bondage.

The Institute of Social Sciences' (hereinafter ISS) report *Trafficking in Women and Children in India* (2005) records many instances of such debt bondage. Thus the *Chukri* (*or Chokri*) system operative in West Bengal is described as one in which minor girls are 'bought' by brothel owners and almost all of their incomes are kept by brothel owners (see ISS 2005: 673). The illegal migrants from Bangladesh and Nepal are said to be most vulnerable in this respect. In another instance described from a Mumbai brothel where an account register was recovered following a raid, it appeared that women were paid less than ten per cent of what they earned and even police, pimps and the 'goonda' were paid more (ibid.: 560). Earlier studies of women of the low-caste Kolta community of the Jaunsar Bawar region of Uttarakhand working in brothels of Delhi have also shown that debt bondage led many women into the sex trade. In fact this is one of the few instances we know of in which the married women are engaged in prostitution with the complicity of their husbands. The reasons suggested for the prostitution of the Kolta women is the debt which the men incur in the process of acquiring wives in order to relieve themselves from which they send their young wives into urban brothels (see Mukherjee and Mukherjee 1982: 3; Gupta 1984; Gupta 1990). In such cases, though debt bondage may be the initial impetus behind entry into sex work, the sex worker may not be indebted to the brothel owner. Gupta (1990) has noted the use of feudal idioms among the Koltas whose women are sent to brothels under conditions referred to as *batai*, a clear analogy with sharecropping. Such systems of income sharing are also described in the ISS study which describes the 'Adhiya' or half share system in which the women give half their earnings to the brothel owner.[6]

It is very hard to decide which category such relations of sex work should be put in and perhaps it might be more suitable to categorize some of these as a form of slavery. The last two seem different from *Chukri* and the example from the Mumbai brothel which are characterized either by complete or partial bondage to a brothel owner. The conflation of slavery and debt bondage may in many contexts arise due to such conditions. The *adhiya* and the *batai* however seem more akin to a feudal system of income sharing. There is thus a strong case to be made for distinguishing *adhiya* and *batai* from *chukri* and the latter may be treated as akin to slavery as defined above. Here it may be pointed out that both *chukri* and *adhiya* may be operating within the same brothel. Indeed yet other systems which are more akin to a capitalist form may also coexist here as will be discussed below.

Furthermore, I would also argue that the category of feudal relations should be applied where the relation with the brothel owner cannot be severed easily. Otherwise it may not be very different from some form of a capitalist relation. The difficulties of moving from one brothel to another may not arise merely due to conditions of debt bondage and may also be a result of the importance of networks in becoming linked with particular brothels. Although the information on this score is not available in the above instances, it is vital for us to understand the nature of such relations.

I also wish to suggest that the category of feudal relations of sex work is itself complex and can include other variants. Thus prostitution in the Bedia community of which I have done a detailed study can be largely said to be structured by relations of obligation fostered within the family (See Agrawal 2008). These can be seen as feudal relations of sex work but they are different from *adhiya* and *batai*. Again, within the Bedia community, there are also other forms of earning, including those akin to *adhiya*, which thrive. The non-familial variants include working in brothels in which women have the status of' 'tenants' and hotels in which 'dancing women' function to attract male customers to whom they provide sexual services on an individual basis. In the former situation the division of earnings may take the feudal form akin to sharecropping: the earnings are divided into half between the owner and the tenant. But the latter may be a variant of the capitalist form. While we need not deny the affinity between the feudal and the family variant of prostitution, the Bedia case highlights how crucial it is to take into account the differences between the two. A lot more can be said about the form taken by feudal relations in sex work but the above should be indicative of both, the complexity as well as the usefulness of the category.

In discussing the capitalist relations of prostitution, van der Veen argues that:

> The activity of prostitution is often conducted within a capitalist class process. In this process a third party (an employer) buys the labor power of the sex worker (employee) and consumes it in the process of producing and selling a commodity to others (clients). The employer pays the employee a wage equal to only a portion of the total value the worker contributes to the enterprise and appropriates and distributes the surplus. Workers may be free to sell their labor power in exchange for a wage and free of feudal or slave obligations to work for any one

> particular person. But workers may also be subject to supervision and managerial control, may have little control over decision-making (e.g., regarding prices and earnings), may be vulnerable to speedups (attending to more clients in a shorter period of time) and an intensification of duties (e.g. offering more services to the employer or clients) (2000: 127-28).

In my understanding of forms of prostitution in India, it is hard to come by instances in which one can identify wage like payments to the sex-worker. Here I wish to argue that there is need to further explore conditions in which sex assumes a form of labour. In order to do so we need to think in terms of another concept which draws its inspiration from Marxist categories. Here I wish to draw attention to what I suggest we call 'means of sex work' or 'means of prostitution'. This concept is not so evident in van der Veen's otherwise useful class-based analysis of sex work. In using this concept, I wish to draw attention to the fact that any possibility of deriving income from prostitution rests on some sort of access to means of prostitution, or rather that there are a set of minimum conditions that are required to carry out this work in any given setting. Apart from the sex worker herself (or himself), this would include some means of access to clients (what is generally referred to as soliciting) and a place to entertain them. There may be additional paraphernalia which may add to the quality of the service but, I wish to argue that these two are the minimal which may be treated as the irreducible means of sex work. Thus, for one who has ownership of the two means of sex work, an access to a sex worker becomes imperative or rather a condition for a derivation of income. Such means of sex work could be owned by the sex worker herself or they may be owned and controlled by others. An owner/tenant may use the premises to carry out sex work themselves or employ/enslave/indebt others to carry it out thereby deriving profit in different degrees and forms. The form of relationship which is forged with the worker would in part give shape to the particular character of sex work being carried out.

It follows that it is the control over the means of prostitution which allows different categories of actors to derive different forms of income from sex work. Although much work on this remains to be done, it seems to me that the dominant capitalist form in which the income from prostitution is derived is through provision of access to clients and through provision of a place to carry out the sexual act. Sometimes the two may be combined and at other times the two may be separated. This way of looking at the issue of sex work becomes extremely relevant if we look at the increasing instances in which the so-called red light areas in many parts of the Indian subcontinent have been demolished or even become unviable economically due to rising real estate prices. Many of the very old red light districts in India are located on what has become prime property in course of time. In the last more than a decade several of these brothel areas have shut down, most often at the instance of an overzealous police machinery which suddenly takes on the mantle of being anti-sex trade while all along it had turned a blind eye to it. Thus in 2004 the red light area on Baina Beach in Goa was demolished and most recently the Ganga Jamuna red light district was shut down in Nagpur. Similar processes which see a direct involvement of the state apparatus have seen the almost complete disappearance of Kamathipura, a well known and established red light district of Mumbai. Svati Shah who has documented in detail the decline of Kamathipura argues perceptively that 'emptying brothels must ...be understood within the politics of urban land use in contemporary India. The closures of the brothels are part of a larger urban land grab occurring throughout India' (Shah 2014: 149). This draws a direct relationship between the changing forms of private property and operation of the sex trade.

Typically also the capitalist relations of sex work do not take the form of a wage relation but rather that of an owner and tenant or a middle-agent renting out the place to a worker for varying durations. The income is thus derived in the form of a 'commission' charged by a middleman and rent charged by the owner of a property. This may have superficial similarity with feudal relations in which there may be a similar sharing of income derived from prostitution between the worker and the agent to whom she is obligated. What is missing in a capitalist form is the element of obligatory relation to one particular owner of the means of sex work. The freedom of the sex worker under such conditions would consist of being able to move from one owner of means of sex work to another. Being without access to means of sex work would however mean being unable to carry out sex work or being able to carry it out only under very precarious conditions and finally of course carrying it out by sharing one's income with someone who has access to the means of sex work. The ISS report (2005) notes that tenancy and working part-time are two major patterns of engaging in sex work. In the former system, the women are for all practical purposes tenants who pay the rent as well as expenses for services such as electricity and maybe obliged to buy drinks etc., from the owners. On the other hand there are those who rent the premises for a very short time. These places are therefore almost like hotels which allow the sex trade to occur within their premises. However, within such premises other forms of the sex trade may also be carried out. Thus the women who are tenants may also get hold of a few girls who work under conditions of *chukri.* Once again one notices the co-existence of variant forms of sex work existing in close proximity.

In this context, it may be worth noting that van der Veen also refers to the category of 'independent sex worker':

> With independent commodity production, it appears that the producer of the commodity is determining the terms of the prostitute/client relation – what is provided, when, where, with whom, how, and at what price. For the prostitute, economic self-determination is associated with *control over one's sexuality*' (2000: 132, emphasis added).

However, it can be argued that the independence of the sex worker and her control over her sexuality do not merely derive from being able to decide 'what is provided, when, where, with whom, how, and at what price' (ibid.) as all of this may be very well the freedom that a worker may be able to exercise within a capitalist system. None of these preclude the possibility of another person or persons deriving profit from one's (sexual) labour. Following from the above, I wish to argue that the category of an independent sex worker can be conceptualized as a possibility of working in a manner where no one else derives any income from one's sex work. A control over the means of sex work, in this view, would be prior to control over one's sexuality. In this sense we could suggest that the independent sex worker could very well be a part of a capitalist system or any other society even though she has to be someone poised at a somewhat advantageous position within the system in which she commands a control over the means of her work. Moreover, there could be degrees of independence and lack of independence that is available to a sex worker, comparable to other categories of workers in a society.

In a broader sense, it may even be possible to argue that in the very first instance, the differential access to property brings forth a set of people for whom there is *nothing to sell except their sexual labour*, to use a Marxist phraseology. However, even if we do not wish to reduce all sex work as an outcome of such destitution, the above discussion would lead us to expect that a capitalist society is bound to offer very differential possibilities of deriving an income from prostitution and the ability to derive substantial income from prostitution would rest on either a sex worker having a very economically privileged position within the existing social order which enables her to directly own and control the means of sex work or of being one who is in control of such means and therefore only needs to somehow get hold of the workers themselves to realize the actual use of the means of sex work.

It is true that women in prostitution do sometimes seem to graduate from 'working' women to owners and controllers of means of sex work. The NGO Sangram even suggests referring to 'women in prostitution and sex work' as 'business women'. However, there is no data which would allow us to see this as a regular and even common occurrence. It is obvious that in either case the property relations are critical to the workings of the trade.

Conclusion

On the whole the argument which is being put forward here is that in order to make sense of the varieties of conditions under which sex work occurs, it is critical to take into consideration the nature of control that is exercised over the means of prostitution and then assess how the same are deployed in the derivation of income from prostitution. This conceptualization of conditions of sex work focuses our attention on the ownership and control of means of sex work. Therefore it is possible that while different forms of relations of prostitution prevail in contemporary societies, the overall framework of capitalist private property shapes the ownership pattern of the means of prostitution.

This perspective would also allow us to assess the role of the state in regulating sex work. In most parts of the world, the state is a major factor in determining patterns of control over means of sex work. This is particularly true in conditions where sex work is illegal and thus state intermediaries become critical in facilitating use of specific locations for sex work. This is what allows us to make sense of how criminalization of sex work leads to more exploitative relations for the sex worker who becomes dependent on those who are able to find ways of bypassing the state machinery. This indeed validates the critique of liberal feminists that criminalization of prostitution leads to greater exploitation of the sex worker. However, to this must be added that the structures which perpetuate differential access to private property are also implicated in the exploitation of the sex worker.

While brief illustrations have been provided above to show the usefulness of such an analysis, a far more detailed and rigorous formulation of the framework as well as its application in specific contexts may prove to be very insightful and also allow us to move out of the kind of impasse which has arisen in the polarized feminist debates.

NOTES

1. In fact domestic work that is largely performed by women was also treated as unproductive in classical Marxism as such work was not seen as contributing anything to the 'national economy', and was therefore not seen as a form of commodity production.
2. See Braverman (1974) for insights into mechanisms which accelerate this process of commodification of many activities which were formerly performed within the family. Particularly, see Chapter 13.
3. Sahni and Shankar (2013) demonstrate the deep linkages of sex work with many informal sectors of work in India.

4. Although some of the insights of the conventional positions, particularly those regarding the parallels between prostitution and marriage are not so evident in the recent discussions, due to the limited scope of this paper, I shall not dwell on the significance of the latter in this paper.
5. Prabha Kotiswaran (2012) has also referred to and used her analysis in her study of sex work in India and so have I in my study of the Bedias (Agrawal 2008).
6. Similar idioms have been noted as being used in the brothels of Calcutta (see Sleightholme and Sinha 1996: 11).

REFERENCES

Agrawal, Anuja 2008. *Chaste Wives and Prostitute Sisters: Patriarchy and Prostitution Among the Bedias of India*, Delhi: Routledge.

Agustin, Laura 2007. *Sex at the Margins: Migration, Labour Markets and the Rescue Industry,* London: Zed Books.

Barry, Kathleen 1979. *Female Sexual Slavery*, New Jersey: Prentice-Hall.

Bebel, August 1879 (1910). *Women and Socialism*, Socialist Literature: New York.

Bindaman, Jo 1998 'An International Perspective on Slavery in Sex Industry' in Kamala Kempadoo and Jo Doezema (eds), *Global Sex Workers: Rights, Resistance, and Redefinition*, New York and London: Routledge, pp. 65-68.

Blanchette, Thaddeus Gregory, Ana Paula Silva, Andressa Raylane Bento 2013. 'The Myth of Maria and the Imagining of Sexual Trafficking in Brazil', *Dialectical Anthropology* 37: 195–227.

Braverman, Harry 1974. *Labor and Monopoly Capital: The Degradation of Work in the Twentieth Century*, New York: Monthly Review Press.

Delphy, Christine, and Diana Leonard 1992. *Familiar Exploitation: A New Analysis of Marriage in Contemporary Western Societies*, Cambridge: Polity Press.

di Leonardo, Micaela 1987. 'The Female World of Cards and Holidays: Women, Families, and the Work of Kinship', *Signs* 12(3): 440-453.

Ehrenreich, B. and A.R. Hochschild 2004. *Global Woman: Nannies, Maids, and Sex Workers in the New Economy*, London: Granta Books.

Engels, Frederick 1884 (1948). *The Origin of the Family, Private Property and the State,* Moscow: Progress Publishers.

Goldman, Emma 1910. 'The Traffic in Women' in *Anarchism and Other Essays.* Second Revised Edition. New York & London: Mother Earth Publishing Association, pp. 183-200.

Gupta, Jayoti 1990. 'Class Relations, Family Structure and Bondage of Women' in Leela Dube and Rajni Palriwala (eds), *Structures and Strategies: Women, Work and Family*, New Delhi: Sage Publications, pp. 151-173.

Gupta, Robin 1984. 'From the Hills of Purola to the Brothels of Delhi', *Manushi*, 20: 28-33.

Hochschild, Arlie Russell 1983. *The Managed Heart: Commercialization of Human Feeling*, Berkeley, CA: University of California Press.

Institute of Social Sciences 2005. *Trafficking in Women and Children in India*, New Delhi: Orient Longman.

Jaggar, Alison M. 1980. 'Prostitution' in Alan Soble (ed.), *The Philosophy Sex: Contemporary Readings*, New Jersey: Rowman and Littlefield, pp. 348-68.

Jaggar, Alison M. 1997. 'Contemporary Western Feminist Perspectives on Prostitution', *Asian Journal of Women's Studies*, 3(2): 8-29.

Joshi, Sushma 2007. '"Cheli-Beti": Discourses of Trafficking and Constructions of Gender, Citizenship and Nation in Modern Nepal', *South Asia: Journal of South Asian Studies*, 24(1): 157 – 175.

Kollontai, Alexandra 1977 'Prostitution and Aays of Fighting It' in *Selected Writings of Alexandra Kollontai*, Tr. Alix Holt, London: Allison and Busby.

Kotiswaran, Prabha 2012. *Dangerous Sex, Invisible Labor: Sex Work and Law in India*, Delhi: Oxford University Press.

Lenin, V.I. July 13, 1913. 'Fifth International Congress Against Prostitution', *Rabochaya Pravda* No. 1, Source: *Lenin Collected Works*, Progress Publishers, 1977, Moscow, Vol. 19, pp. 260-261

Marx, Karl 1844. *The Economic and Philosophic Manuscripts of 1844*, Moscow: Progress Publishers.

Mukherjee, K.K. and Sutapa Mukherjee 1982. *Lowliest of the Low: Study on Socio-Economic Status of Kolta Women*, Ghaziabad: Gram Niyojan Kendra.

Murray, Alison 1998 'Debt Bondage and Trafficking: Don't Believe the Hype' in Kamala Kempadoo and Jo Doezema (eds), *Global Sex Workers: Rights, Resistance, and Redefinition*, New York and London: Routledge, pp. 51-64.

Papanek, Hanna 1979. 'Family Status Production: The "Work" and "Non-Work" of Women', *Signs,* 4(4).

Sahni, Rohini and V. Kalyan Shankar 2013. *Sex Work and its Linkages with Informal Labour Markets in India: Findings from the First Pan-India Survey of Female Sex Workers*, Brighton: Institute of Development Studies.

Shah, Svati 2014. *Street Corner Secrets: Sex, Work, and Migration in the City of Mumbai*. Durham: Duke University Press.

Sleightholme, Carolyn and Indrani Sinha 1996. *Guilty Without Trial: Women in the Sex Trade in Calcutta*, Calcutta: Stree Publications.

Trotsky, Leon 1937. *The Revolution Betrayed: What is the Soviet Union and Where is it Going?* New York: Doubleday.

van der Veen, Marjolein 2000. 'Beyond Slavery and Capitalism: Producing Class Difference in the Sex Industry' in J.K. Gibson-Graham, Stephen A. Resnick and Richard D. Wolff (eds), *Class and its Others*, Minneapolis/ London: University of Minnesota Press, pp. 121-141.

van der Veen, Marjolein 2001. 'Rethinking Commodification and Prostitution: An Effort at Peacemaking in the Battles Over Prostitution', *Rethinking Marxism*, 13(2): 30-51.

van der Veen, Marjolein 2002. *Rethinking Prostitution: Analyzing an Informal Sector Industry*, Ph.D. Thesis, University of Massachusetts at Amherst.

Waters, Elizabeth 1989. 'Restructuring the "Woman Question": Perestroika and Prostitution', *Feminist Review*, 33, pp. 3-19.

10

Marxism and Queer Theory: A Critical Analysis

Pushpesh Kumar

This essay begins by outlining the Marxist approach towards gender and sexually marginalized subjects. Despite Engel's concern with women's emancipation Marxist praxis mostly remained indifferent to issues of gender and sexual oppression. Against this backdrop, it is paradoxical that post-war American political culture suspected a close alliance and an overlap between communists and homosexuals promoting violence, loss of employment and an institutionalization of a climate of fear for the gays and lesbians. The origin of the first gay association in the US and its dissociation with communism have to be understood in this specific historical context. The climate of fear generated in post-war America limited the sexuality politics to influencing public opinion and very limited civil rights.

The next section of the paper charts out the articulation of the post-Stonewall gay movement which was radical and leftist in orientation yet less concerned with the issues of class and historical materialism. A cursory look at the *Gay Left* magazine published from Britain during this period validates this. The subsequent emergence of the Queer theory in the late 1980s and early 90s took a cultural and performative turn aimed at disrupting the heteronormative without concerning itself with questions of class and material inequality. Queer theory drifted more towards post-structuralism than Marxism. But a group of contemporary scholars located within queer theory have been trying to incorporate questions of class, political economy and historical materialism and are engaged in developing a thorough critique of mere 'cultural and performative' in queer theory to make the latter a transformatory tool of analysis and political action. The paper discusses in brief the works of Rosemary Hennessey and Kevin Flyod, the two contemporary American queer theorists to demonstrate how the Marxist concepts can enhance the emancipatory promises of queer theory.

Gender Non-Conformity, Sexual Pluralism and Marxism

The capitalist and neoliberal celebration of sexual diversity across the globe as a well-intended and emancipatory project is held problematic by those queer studies' scholars who either use a materialist approach to investigate sexuality (Hennessey 1995, 2000) or critically engage with queer emancipation as an unfinished project and foreground multiple marginalities within the discourse (see Duggan 2004; Namaste, 2000). Before outlining the Marxist position within contemporary queer theory it seems pertinent to implore how gender and sexual oppression/s drew Marxist concerns since its inception. Engels' groundbreaking ideas about 'subordination of women' received contradictory feminist responses. Feminism (re) claimed his thesis of women's oppression proposed in the *Origin of Family* while simultaneously finding it a contentious exposition of gendered oppression (see Sayers et al. 2009)[1]. Heidi Hartman's (1979) paper 'Unhappy Marriage of Marxism and Feminism' offers many stances of patriarchal privilege of socialist/Marxist men which precluded possibilities of incorporating gender and sexuality in revolutionaries' mobilizational agenda. She (ibid) writes:

> The left has been ambivalent about the women's movement, often viewing it as dangerous to the cause of socialist revolution...And of course, many left organizations benefit from labour of women...The working classes' struggle against capitalism should take precedence over any conflict between men and women. Sex conflict must not be allowed to interfere with class solidarity...presence of feminist issues in the academic left is declining as well. Day care is disappearing from left conferences...the pressure on radical women to abandon this silly stuff and become serious revolutionaries have increased. Our work seems

> like a 'waste of time' compared to inflation and employment. It is symptomatic of male dominance that our unemployment was never considered a crisis. It is not clear—from our sketch' from history or from male socialist— that the 'socialism' being struggled for is the same for both men and women.

The excerpt above encapsulates the patriarchy inherent in the socialist and Marxist praxis notwithstanding Fredrick Engels' provocative theory about women's subordination and their emancipation. Implicit in this masculine dominance of the socialist politics are also heterogender and heteronorm. This is evident in Zaretsky and Engels' (quoted in Hartman 1997) romanticization of preindustrial family and community- where men, women, adults and children worked together in family-centred enterprise and all participated in community life. In Zaretsky's human socialism the family would reunite and recreate that 'happy workshop' (ibid). Rosemary Hennessey (2000: 38), a materialist feminist and a Marxist scholar of queer theory mentions that both the work of Marx and most of the canon of Western Marxism has with rare exceptions dismissed or ignored sexuality, desire, and affect, and simply not seen heterosexuality as a normative institution. Engels died the year of Oscar Wilde's arrest, but the Labouchere Amendment[2] under which Wilde was accused was enacted a decade earlier as the Criminal Law Amendment Act of 1885 (ibid). In other words, both Marx and Engels could—and perhaps should—have known about these struggles, and especially about the law reform efforts in their native countries (ibid).

Alexandra Kollontai, a Marxist revolutionary and Bolshevik who extensively wrote on women's freedom envisaged a workers' state in which equality of economic relations had been intended to support, and in turn, be fostered, by a new communist sexual morality of free, open and equal relations of love and comradeship (Porter 2016; Ebert 2016). She was a pioneer among Marxists in suggesting that socialist debate and social theory need to address questions of sexuality and attend to the relationship between personal and political (Hennessey 2000: 42). Her isolation and lack of political support for advocating gender and sexual freedom shows how sexuality was cordoned off from socialist class struggle (ibid). After Lenin's death, Leon Trotsky, one of the central figures in the 1917 Revolution and the chief opponent of Stalin's bureaucracy, continued to maintain the importance of women's emancipation and the reorganization of the family to socialism (ibid). But he had little to say about (homo)sexuality. In the 1930s the Stalinist counter-revolution exiled and murdered Trotsky, gave priority to the reproductive family, and ultimately revoked most of the legal gains of the earlier revolutionary period (ibid). By 1934 homosexuality was once more a criminal offence in the USSR, abortions were illegal, prostitutes were arrested, and the maintenance of the family as an economic unit became a priority (ibid). The view that homosexuality was a decadent bourgeois deviation continued to dominate Marxist orthodoxy after the 1930s (Jeffery Weeks quoted in Hennessey 1995: 42).

Despite leftists' subordination of the gender question to class struggle and repression of non-heterosexual sexuality it seems paradoxically intriguing that the cold war sexual politics in the US suspected a close alliance between homosexuals and communists leading to the mass persecution of gay and lesbian subjects during the 1950s. In the perception of the US both the communists and homosexuals were considered to be allies because of their subversive attitudes and disrespect to moral principles.

The "Red Scare" "Lavender Scare": Communist and Pervert Combine

The 'Lavender Scare' refers to the persecution of gays and lesbians in the US from 1945 to circa 1969 (Wiley and Burke 2008) and Red Scare was the perceived threat posed by communists during this period in American history. Both Lavender (marginalized erotic subjects) and Red (communists) were thought as having overlapping concerns because of their subversive mode of existence[3]. During the Second World War, a kinship between the gays and lesbians in the military was formed and in the post-world war they were able to foster communities across the US (ibid). Though sodomy was forbidden in the military and punished harshly in the US, the Second World War made possible entry of gays and lesbians in the military as every warm body was needed to win the war and exclusion of this constituency at this juncture was not thought important (Chrislove 2012). Women were allowed to enlist in the Women's Army Corps (WAC) and every patriotic American was expected to join in the war effort in some way (ibid). This is not to say that gays and lesbians were well treated and allowed to be open in the military. But from 1939-45 they were policed much less and in many cases allowed to flourish within the confines of the military (ibid). After the Second World War ended, life returned to "normal" where women were forced from the job market in great numbers, men returned to civilian jobs and gay and lesbian witch-hunts resumed in the military, in greater force than ever (ibid). Without the urgent need for bodies, authorities made every effort to weed out as many homosexuals as possible (ibid).

David K. Johnson in his book *The Lavender Scare: The Cold War Persecution of Gays and Lesbians in the Federal Government* writes: 'Republican Members of the Congress began to express concern about homosexuals in the State Department in 1947, at the very onset with the cold war with the Soviet Union. With the rise of McCarthy in 1950, their concern became public and sparked a moral panic within both popular and political discourse. Gay men were attributed to have "unconventional morality" and were construed as vulnerable to blackmail. They could divulge the secrets of the American state to the enemy camp or the communists through blackmail and hence posed serious national security threats'. This view according to Johnson permeated 1950s' American political culture. Conservative periodicals seeking to embarrass the democratic administration delighted in raising the possibility that federal civil service, which had ballooned during the Roosevelt and Truman administration was brimming with homosexuals (ibid: 8). Johnson (ibid) further writes: 'Government security officials routinely characterized homosexuals as so gregarious that they were unable to keep secrets. Their great desire to talk, officials asserted, meant that they were quick to confess and name names. It was said that information passed through homosexual networks with astounding speed'. With the nation on moral alert because of the cold war, stable, monogamous, heterosexual marriages were seen as a key weapon in the arsenal against degeneracy and internal communist subversion (ibid: 14).

Johnson's 'Lavender Scare' also reflects upon the homophobic and anti-communist affirmations of McCarthy and the latter's conflation of gay with communists and vice versa. To McCarthy, homosexuals were "unusual individuals" who were active members of 'Communist Front Organizations' and Soviet agents. Homosexuality he asserted, was a psychological maladjustment that led people towards communism (ibid: 16). Majority of the newspapers reinforced this understanding and people feared both communist "cells" and homosexual "nets" within the federal government (ibid: 33). The Wherry-Hill investigations and Hoey Committee investigations of 1950 were instrumental in detecting 'perverts' in civil services and between 1945 to 1960 thousands of gays and lesbians lost their government jobs (Adkin 2016). An unknown number of gay men and lesbians stripped of their livelihoods, facing embarrassments and unemployment, took their own lives (Johnson, 2006: 158).

Separating Communist Influences: Gay Associations in the Wake of the Lavender Scare

David Johnson (2006) mentions that the Lavender Scare and suppression of gays created a rigid boundary between heterosexuality and homosexuality. He (ibid) writes that through labelling anyone with even one such encounter in their past as homosexual, the purges enforced a rigid homosexual/heterosexual divide and facilitated the demise of the older sexual system based on gender identity. Confronted with the possibility of being labelled, some abandoned same sex behaviour while others adopted the new identity and became part of the gay subculture (ibid: 169).

The purges played a pivotal role in the formation of an organized gay movement both at national and local levels (ibid). The first organization was formed in California in 1950 by Harry Hay and his friends which determined the direction and trajectory of gay protest till the 1970s. The organization was called Mattachine Society which believed in educating the society about non-heterosexual subjects and influencing and changing the naive public opinion. Due to the fear generated through the Lavender Scare the Mattachine Society could not adopt a confrontationist approach and decided to confine itself to the immediate concerns of the gay and lesbian community and limit itself to civil rights. It also felt the need to *dissociate itself from communism* (emphasis is mine) in view of the dominant perception of the latter as a major security threat to the nation. David Johnson (Ibid: 171) writes:

> Throughout the 1950s, the nascent movement articulated a sustained critique of the federal government's security program and its effects on gays and lesbians. Both of the movement's California-based publications, the *Mattachine Review* and *One*, ran frequent news items and critical essays concerning the government security system, suggesting it was a major concern of their readership, which by the end of the decade exceeded five thousand. Such articles refuted the alleged connection between homosexuality and communism, pointing out that the Communist Party also excluded homosexuals and the life of an average gay person was too stressful for political activities.

The above discussion suggests that the Lavender and Red Scares and the American establishment's suspicion of proximity between communists and sexual subverts created a very hostile environment for the latter. It simultaneously resulted in Gay Associations' distance from communism. The US suspicion of communists and homosexual proximity, however, was rather unreasonable given the fact that communists were not so accommodative of sexual freedom and gender non-conformism since the very start of the communist revolutionary parties. This is evident from the fact that initiatives to place gender and sexual freedom on the revolutionary agenda by veteran communist leaders like Alexandra Kollontai were not very successful. As discussed earlier, the revolutionaries did not react to the famous celebrity Oscar Wilde's trial and conviction even though this case entered wider public debate parallel to the Dreyfus Affair in France[4]. Considering this indifference and disengagement the conflation of communism and homosexuality during the cold war period in the US as overlapping subversions sounds more of a sophistry than constituting a sincere assessment; but this conflation had real and disastrous consequences for erotically marginal subjects. The ruthless suppression and witch hunt of homosexuals through the 'vice squad' continued for more than fifteen years in the US. 'Red Scare' created a great deal of frustration among the sexually disadvantaged groups as it imagined an alliance and solidarity with Marxism and communism. Moreover, the communist revolution never took the sexual revolution seriously.

Despite the state initiated suppression of homosexuals in the US during the 1950s which continued up to the late 1960s, sexual sub-cultures were simultaneously present and were flourishing in American urban city life. It is pertinent to discuss, albeit in brief that the capitalist state which suppressed homosexuals in the federal government through the 'vice squad' failed to erase the market mediated spaces of pubs, clubs, bars and bath houses opening up possibilities for 'sexual deviants.' The anonymity of city life allowed for individualism and the new 'communities' of hippies and bohemians.

John D'Emilio (1983), the eminent American historian of sexuality argues that capitalism displaced older rural-based community life but created new communities in city spaces making certain ways of organizing life possible while simultaneously institutionalizing class and material inequalities. But D'Emilio is aware of the limits of this market mediated freedom as he writes: 'The dialectics of the constant interplay between exploitation and some measure of autonomy—informs all of the history of those who have lived under capitalism. To Emilio, the dislocations of the Second World War severely disrupted traditional patterns of gender relations and sexuality, and temporarily created erotic situations conducive to homosexual expressions. Free from the traditional ties of family and community, many homoerotic men and women decided to act on their desire which formed the underpinnings of an urban subculture of gays and lesbians (ibid : 110). Describing the post–Second World War scenario, Emilio writes: 'And the gay subculture was not to be found just in the largest cities. Lesbian and gay male bars existed in places like Worcester, Massachusetts, and Buffalo, in New York;

in Columbia, South Carolina, and Des Moines, Iowa'. But every society needs structures for reproduction and childbearing so, ideologically capitalism drives people into heterosexual families (ibid: 111). Capitalism, however, also weakens the bonds that once kept families together so that their members experience growing instability in the place they have come to expect happiness and emotional security. D'Emilio proposes here the structures and programmes of social security with autonomy as he (ibid: 114) writes:

> We need community or worker controlled day care, housing where privacy and community co-exist, neighbourhood institutions—from medical clinics to performance centres–that enlarge the social unit where each of us has a secure place. As we create structures beyond nuclear family that provide a sense of belonging, the family will wane in significance. Less and less will it seem to make or break our emotional security. In this respect gay men and lesbians are well situated to play a special role. Already excluded from families...networks of support that do not depend upon the bonds...or the license of state, but that are freely chosen and nurtured...a society where autonomy and security do not preclude each other.

The New Left and Sexual Radicalism: Mapping the Trajectory of Left-Oriented Gay Organizations

This section deals with the left orientation of the post-Stonewall gay mobilization in the 1970s and analyses the trajectory of this new radicalism.

The Mattachine Society which came to prominence as the first gay organization, as mentioned earlier, believed in keeping itself away from communist influences in view of the perceived communist and gay alliance in the American establishment. The Society was growing in a climate of fear. The meetings and discussions which were held in private homes, were conducted in such a way that most of those attending had no idea who was in charge (see Marcuse 2002). Chuck Roland, one of the Mattachine leaders mentioned—'the only way we were ever going to get along in the society was by being nice, quite, polite little boys that our maiden aunts would have approved of. We were not going to get along...by flaunting our homosexuality... we could not do anything naughty like having picket signs or a parade. Only communists would do things like that' (ibid: 44). The Mattachine Society wanted their goals achieved through evolutionary and not revolutionary methods and public protest was not part of their programme (ibid). By the late 1950s gay organizations had reached beyond San Francisco, New York and Los Angeles to establish smaller chapters in a handful of cities around the country including Chicago, Philadelphia and Denver (ibid). With growing press coverage of the 'deviant life' and naming of gay organizations like Mattachine Society the newspapers helped publicize and heighten the sense of a community. In 1965 gay men and lesbians took to the streets.

To protest federal anti-gay policies demonstrations were staged in the nation's capital at the White House, Pentagon, Civil Service Commission and State Department (ibid: 74). There was a felt need to build coalitions which resulted resulted in the North American Conference of Homophile Organization which had begun to abandon gentle arts of persuasion and adopted a strategy of confrontation based on non-negotiable demand for equal rights (see ibid: 118). By 1968, the anti-war movement, the women's movement, the black and civil rights movement, the students' revolt and the politics of New Left had not only energized nearly fifty gay organizations across the country, but also inspired bitter internal battles over the direction of the homophile movement (ibid: 122). The Stonewall Inn riots of 1969 triggered the formation of new radical organizations across cities and universities which dismissed the old homophile movement as old fashioned 'accommodationists' paving the way for left-oriented formations such as 'Gay Liberation Front' in 1970 (ibid) which forged alliances with other revolutionary groups like Black Panthers. The other was the Gay Activist Alliance which represented a dissident group from the Gay Liberation Front.

Without getting into the details of these various confrontationist gay organizations in post-Stonewall America I wish to address the issue of the New Left and its impact on the gay movement of the 1970s to understand as to what extent Marxist philosophy and the question of class and political economy permeated the Gay Left.

Reflecting on the leftist and gay liberation alliance, Steve Valocchi

(2001) mentions that the organizational centralization of the Old Left prevented an extension of the collective identity of the 'oppressed' to the gay people. Homosexuality was considered a bourgeois deviation by the Communist Party and a public disclosure of homosexuality ensured expulsion from the party. Although the organization and ideology of the political left during the 1930s and 1940s did include concerns of building a collective identity and recognizing the existence of other groups (black and women) as subjects of oppression, its core political project was still an economic one (ibid). Organizational rigidity of the Stalinist left provided no space in which individuals with same sex desire could politicize these practices and identities (ibid). The decentralized organizational structure provided those involved in the New Left with greater autonomy in stretching the limits of collective identity (ibid). There was a partial rejection of the hierarchical mode of decision-making in the new left embedded in Students for a Democratic Society (SDS) premised on a participatory mode of decision-making (ibid). Derived from the notion of the beloved community from the early Civil Rights movement SDS not only embodied the instrumental politics that predominated the Old Left but also understood that "living differently" or expressive politics was as important as liberatory ideology (ibid). Capitalism, colonialism, racism and sexism became the conceptual tools to analyse American society. The idea that different groups based on different structures of oppression can pursue their own agenda while adhering to the revolutionary group prompted the Gay Liberation Front (GLF) to add the concept of heterosexism to the range of oppression (see ibid). GLF offered a vision of a new society in which sexual and gender roles would no longer exist (see Altman 1993; Kissack 1995). The Red Butterfly, GLF's cell of Marxist intellectuals, invoked the conclusion of Herbert Marcuse's 1966 'political preface' to Eros and Civilizations: In their articulation- '[T]he fight for Eros, the fight for life, is the political fight' (see Escoffier 2015). But there was no complete absence of homophobia in other groups. The Black Panthers still used the word faggots and debates occurred among the gay groups whether to mobilize funds for the Black Panthers or not (See Valocchi 2001).

This sense of alienation felt by several gay men and lesbian women led to the formation of the Gay Activist Alliance based on a narrowed understanding of minority identity with gay and lesbian issues forming the core agenda of the group.

In the autumn of 1975, a publication called *Gay Left* appeared in Britain, published by the collective also called Gay Left (ibid). Many members of the Gay Left Collective became influential writers and thinkers in the following decades. But the thinkers and writers in the gay collective drew upon the works of Marxist theorist Antonio Gramsci, psychoanalyst Sigmund Freud and philosopher Michel Foucault (ibid). This shows that many members of the Gay Left Collective became influential writers and thinkers in the following decades: Jeffery Weeks on *History of Sexuality*; Frank Mort on the *History of Health, Medicine and the Regulation of Sexuality*, Richard Dyer on *Film and Gay Culture*; Simon Watney on the *Impact of Media*; and Bob Cant on the *Integration of Sexual Politics in the Left* (ibid:3). Writers such as Mary Macintosh (in Great Britain), Dennis Altman in Australia, and Amber Hollibaugh (in the US)—all loosely affiliated with the British group made their own contributions to the gay left perspective (ibid). In the late 1970s, centres of gay left thinking emerged in North America. Most important among these centres were, The Body Politics in Toronto (whose writers and editors included James Steakley, John D'Emilio, Michael Lynch and Tom Waugh); *Gay Community News* in Boston (whose contributors included Michael Bronski, Urvashi Vaid, Sue Hyde, Amy Hoffman, and Ellen Harman); The San Francisco Lesbian and Gay History Project (whose participants included Amber Hollibaugh, Gayle Rubin, Allan Berube and Jeffery Escoffier; a series of study groups on sexuality in New York City (whose participants included John D'Emilio, Jonathan Ned Katz, Lissa Duggan and Nan Hunter (ibid: 4). Rosemary Hennessey (2000), the prominent Marxist queer scholar has noted that the persistent resurgence of cultural politics has been the defining discourse of the new left. She reiterates that by taking cultural categories as the starting point, both identity politics and cultural constructionism are quite compatible with the liberal centre's pluralist strategy for incorporating differences. Jeffery Escoffier

(2015), however, suggests that the gay left has addressed the relationship of homosexuality with capitalism, social class and economic forms of oppression. Gay left has long challenged the myth that the LGBTQ community is an economically privileged elite: Gay left writers have explored the ways by which that the economy has shaped the lives of GLBTQ people who come from all social classes and occupations.

The very first volume of the *Gay Left* journal begins with the Marxist critique of family and the sharp polarization of male-female roles in the family which serves the capitalist interest and bears implications in terms of suppression of women and also gender and sexual non-conforming individuals and groups. The second volume contains an essay on gay workers' movement which mentions that they were also involved in the trade union movement but found it difficult to raise the issue of gay workers. The third issue talks about incorporation of feminism and women in the Gay Left to make it fully democratic; another essay entitled 'Was Marx Anti Gay'? which deliberates upon the (in)compatibility of gay aspirations and Marxism and oppressions of the gay community in Russia and Cuba were also discussed. The fifth volume begins with an essay 'Why Marxism'? It says: 'Firstly as Marxists we reject reformism—the belief that all... socialist and gays goals desires can be attained within the confines of existing society. The major thrust of development of attitudes within capitalism has been the acceptance of homosexuality but only within the confines of patriarchal and familial framework.' The sixth volume includes an essay by Dannis Altman on 'The State Repression and Sexuality'. Other volumes carried articles on gay art, women's control over their own bodies, desire and pleasure, gay theatre, racism and sexism.

Rosemary Hennessey (2000) in her book *Profit and Pleasure* attempts to chart out the gay left's engagement with Marxism. To her, Gay liberation of the early 1970s was inspired by the Black Movement and Feminist Movement and like the new left there was general agreement in the gay liberation thinking that capitalism was oppressive. Many gay liberation manifestoes at least rhetorically drew connections between capitalism and repressive sexuality, racism and imperialism (ibid). But the gay liberation movement was not thoroughly influenced by Marxism or a united socialist front and as Hennessey points out, both the gay left in Britain and Gay Socialist action Project in New York linked gay oppression under capitalism to the role of family and subjection of women in the capitalist system of production. Both groups understood that sexuality is inextricably linked to gender and that gender ideology ultimately serves to reproduce the sexual division of labour (ibid: 48). They argued that because it is bound up with gendered division of labour sexual oppression probably would not be eliminated under capitalism (ibid). Hennessey therefore concludes that the gay Marxist left was inadequate in developing a Marxist theory of sexuality.

Queer Theory and Judith Butler: Performativity and Eclipse of Leftist Concerns

By the 1980s the founding principles of the gay Marxist Left had been dismantled or abandoned even by its chief promoters due to the refusal of socialist groups to meaningfully address sexuality. This alienated the pro-Marxist homosexual men with many among the latter redirecting their energies to work with autonomous groups (focusing on issues of sexually oppressed) and they focused more on a cultural rather than a historical materialism (Jeffery Weeks quoted in Hennessey 2000: 49).

Hennessey (ibid) writes that the rise of the right in the 1980s was a time of crisis for Marxism and political fragmentation on the left. It was also the decade when cultural studies began to flourish in the academia whose retreat from Marxism and rush to the Foucauldian approach virtually dominated the analysis of sexuality.

Queer theory according to Hennessey presented itself in the late 1980s as an emphatically post-Marxist critique of sexual identity politics—a denaturalization of the way sexuality was imagined. Queer theory is a significant departure from lesbian and gay studies as it is premised on the understanding that sexual and gender identities are considered as a cultural effect of repetitive performance of gender establishing an internal coherence of 'man' and 'woman' (see Butler 1997). Judith Butler claims that heteronormativity is absolutely central to the bourgeois ideology of expressive and coherent selfhood (Hennessey 2000: 50). If gender for Butler is not a mark of one's essential identity but rather the effect of repeated performances of cultural signs and conventions it constitutes a precarious fabrication and is always potentially at risk (ibid: 51).

In *Bodies that Matter* Butler talks about the materiality of body. Hennessey critiques Butler's materiality by asserting that materiality for Butler is simply a matter of *norms* (emphasis is mine). She (2000: 56) sums up Butler's arguments thus:

> Regulatory conventions function in a performative fashion to constitute sex and to materialize body's sex and sexual difference in the service of a heterosexual imperative. It is through the repetition and reiteration of already established norms that one "performs" a sexual identity. Norms regulate in part by exclusion...Butler argues that the exclusionary normative matrix by which sex is constructed requires simultaneous production of a domain of abject categories. Any identification with these abject is continually disavowed by the norms or laws of dominant culture...this threatening abject puts forward as the critical space of queer performative politics.

To Hennessey, Butler's emphasis on norms injects into poststructuralism's textualized understanding of identity as a signification, a social and historical analysis more attuned to workings of power in language. But understanding the materiality of social life as exclusively normative also limits social relations to the domains of culture and law (ibid). Hennessey gives the concluding remarks on Butler by making a distinction between Butler's materiality of body and the idea of body within historical materialism as she (ibid) writes:

> The emphasis on culture and law in Bulter's normative understanding of materiality is quite different from what materiality means in historical materialism...the differences between the two are important to consider. Historical materialism understands social life to be historically and materially produced through relations of labour through which people make what is needed to survive. But this process does not happen without the ways of making sense, normative practices (cultural ideology) and law (state organizations) that are part of material production of social life.

Despite Hennessey's critique of Butler, performativity and instability and the power of normative construction and language remain dominant threads within queer theory. In the recent editorial introduction of the Routledge *Queer Studies Reader* Donald E. Hall (2013: xvi) writes that queer studies constitutes the unmethodical critique of normative models of sex, gender and sexuality.

Marxism within Queer Theory

Rosemary Hennessey lists out a group of scholars within queer theory; she refers to these scholars as going against the grain (queer theory)[5]. These scholars are involved in groundbreaking works in understanding how sexual identity features in and is shaped by capitalism. The list includes—David Evans, Nicola Field, Kevin Flyod, Chrys Ingrahm and Donald Morton. Hennessey herself is listed in Kevin Flyod's (1998) writing as a Marxist thinker. The limit of space does not, however, allow her to engage with each of these thinkers' work. I try to reflect upon Hennessy and Flyod's Marxist understanding of the queer issue; the choice of thinkers emanate from my own familiarity with some of the important works of these two thinkers. 'Queer Visibility in Commodity Culture' appearing both in Hennessy's book *Profit and Pleasure* and as a separate research article in 1995 in the journal *Cultural Critique* provides a Marxist critique of 'queer visibility' in the contemporary US. To Hennessey, visibility of social identity in the late capitalist consumption is often a matter of commodification.

Here I take two instances from Hennessey's essay to illustrate how the queer politics of disrupting the heteronormative and articulating an indeterminate sexual identity through performative politics overlooks and confuses the social with 'mere cultural'. In Marxist understanding social is the domain of extraction and appropriation of surplus and human relations based on exploitation which cannot be simply transformed through playfulness and subversive performances or through the exotic and spectacular.

Hennessey (2000: 115) writes—'Chants like "We're Here" We're Queer, Get Used to it' and actions like Queer Bash Back, Queer Night Out and Queer Kiss-Ins and Mall Zaps which ushered in public reclaiming of queerness in the early 1990s were aimed at making visible those identities that the ubiquitous heteronormative culture would erase'. Queer visibility of such kind in late capitalism is often a matter of commodification that invariably depends on the lives and labour of others (ibid).

Hennessy first turns to Butler's essay "Performative Acts and Gender Constitution" which appeared in 1988 in *Theatre Journal.* The essay is about the subversiveness of gender parody. Gender parody in Butler's understanding exposes the fiction of gender identity. Butler claims that drag exposes the precarious fabrication of a coherent and an internal sexual identity by putting on display, the made up (in)congruity of sex, gender and desire. Hennessey (ibid: 125) reacts to this easy playfulness and subversion as she writes: 'For many lesbians and gays who have not had the social resources or mobility to insulate themselves from heteronormativity's insistence that sex equals gender, drag has not been so much playful subversion as a painful yearning for authenticity, occasionally with brutally violent results.[6]

Hennessey draws the illustration of Butler's reading of Livingston's American documentary of Harlem Balls *Paris is Burning* in Butler's book *Bodies That Matter* and provides a Marxist reading of the same. For Butler, Drag Balls[7] both de-naturalizes and reidealizes gender norms. Hennessey cites the example of Venus Extravaganza, an American transgender who was struggling to save money out of sex work for her sex reassignment surgery and dreaming of a rich lifestyle, who was killed by her client upon discovering that Venus had male genitalia. The murder of Venus is not a playful subversion of gender identity in Hennessey's understanding, it rather speaks of the vulnerabilities of a person of low class position and marginal racial background as she contrasts Venus with Willie Ninja[8] who made it as a gay man into the mainstream of celebrity glamour. Hennessey writes that Venus is ultimately treated the way most poor women of colour are treated in the United States.

From Butler's idea of drag as subversion Hennessey moves to the activism of Queer Nation[9] based in New York with local chapters stretching from coast to coast. This section is titled 'Queer

Nationalism: The Avant-Garde Goes Shopping'. The motto of queer nation is visibility and guaranteeing gays a safe public existence (ibid: 127). To this end, writes Hennessey, the queer nation reterritorialized various public spaces through an assortment of strategies like policing neighbourhood by pink panthers dressed in "Bash Back" T-Shirts or queer Nights Out and Kissing where groups of gay couples invaded straight bars or other public spaces (ibid: 129). In its most "postmodern moments" Queer Nation used hypersapces of commodity consumption as sites for political intervention. Tactics like producing 'Queer Bart Simpson' T-Shirts and re-writing the trademark—changing the "P" in GAP as "Y"—were meant to demonstrate that the commodity is the central means by which individuals tap into the collective experience of public desire and and disrupt the heterosexual presuppositions on which that desire rests (Berlant and Freeman quoted in Hannessey 2000: 128). Hennessey then mentions how the Queer Shopping Network of New York and the suburban Homosexual outreach programme of San Francisco stage Mall visibility actions. By parading into suburban shopping spaces dressed in full gay regalia, holding hands and handing out flyers, they inserted gay spectacle into the centre of straight consumption (Hennessey 2000).

Hennessey finds a resonance here between queer theory and the activism of Queer Nations. Based on Berlant and Freeman, she (ibid: 128) writes: 'Like queer theory, Queer Nation tended to focus exclusively on construction of meanings, on forging an oppositional practice that disrupts the *semiotic* boundaries between gays and straight...'.

Foregrounding a Marxist interpretation of queer visibility she (ibid: 128) demonstrates how social change through this visibility is reduced to cultural representation by infusing consumer space with a gay sensibility which may make 'queer-y' commodities, but by "making queer good by making goods queer" the commodity remains securely fetishised and when the commodity is fetishised the labour that has gone into its production is rendered invisible. She (ibid: 128) writes further—'Changing the Bart Simpson logo on a T-Shirt to queer Bart' may disrupt the normative conception of sexuality that infuses the circulation of commodities in consumer culture but it offers a limited view of social relations for commodities to rely on, and to this extent it reinforces its fetishisation.

In sum, without addressing the question of class, political economy, labour and production relations it would be difficult to conceive queer politics as anti-assimilationist and radically disruptive. Can we think of an anti-assimilationist queer politics without reflecting upon the drag queen, Venus Extravaganza's story who was trying to excel in a consumer culture as an unequal subject and earning money through sex work to undergo sex reassignment surgery? Did she have the privilege to enter consumerist spaces so comfortably and rewrite the meanings of heteronormative consumer products?

Kevin Flyod, Reification and Queer Politics

In this last section, I focus on Kevin Flyod's idea of historicizing the emergence of (alternative) erotic communities in some specific moments of American history in the late 19th and early 20th century where he tries to demonstrate the reification of 'erotic'. This reified 'erotic community' intensified its claim to sexual citizenship and sexual identity which did not show any connection to class politics and the totality of structural and/or systemic arrangements determining the material conditions of life. What enables erotic subjects to form collectives in this specific time period in the US is the material conjuncture of an engineered rationalization of production known as Fordism (Flyod 1999: 173). The gradual rise of techniques of scientific management in the late 19th and early 20th centuries led to such dramatic increase in productivity that inducing sufficient demands to avoid a crisis of overproduction soon became a persistent problem (ibid). Fordism propagated mass production and mass consumption. To Flyod, around the early 20th century in the US a confrontation between what he calls a residual Victorian manifestation of gender hierarchy and dramatically changing economic relations ultimately produced an unprecedented autonomization of the sexual. The Victorian ideas of gender primarily defined in terms of heterosexual and procreative sex was found inadequate in the age of overproduction where consumptive desire had to be induced; liberal gender and sexual norms become a precondition for consumption. Lukacs (quoted in Flyod 1999) mentions that as the articulation of the realm of production with the realm of consumption began to develop a simultaneous *disarticulation* of the two as the levels of cognition and ideology became "total" and reification became the dominant norm of society. The sexual and the erotic began to be articulated within the realm of consumption while being detached from the social. Flyod locates reification in the historical emergence of "sexuality" as a theoretically and ideologically autonomous object. Reification of desire surfaces further into distinctly modern categories of sexual subjectivity from the heterosexual/homosexual binary. Flyod argues that the formation of erotic communities through consumerism at this particular juncture of American history does constitute a reification of the social but it simultaneously triggered mobilizational politics of anti-heterosexism in the US. As the erotic and erotic identities get reified, the mobilization of sexually marginalized becomes more identitarian.

Flyod further engages with articulations of anti-heterosexist politics in the US and finds that they equally de-historicize and reduce the (erotic) subjects to abstract categories. He contrasts the pre-Stonewall minoritizing assimilationist emphasis on winning basic civil rights for a minority group[10] with the universalizing emphasis on polymorphous sexuality (Marcuse 1992) which questioned the hetero-homo divide. The post-Stonewall queer politics contests the hetero/homo divide by revealing the queer character of ostensibly heterosexual public spaces, most prominently in the shopping centres (ibid). Indeed queer politics tends to take its terrain, embodied spaces rather than abstract categories of citizenship (ibid). Lauren Berlant (quoted in Flyod 1999) critiques this terrain of Post-Stonewall queer politics as pseudo-revolutionary capitalist culture of identity exchange and tends to characterize it in terms of a hopelessly reified American nationality. While reiterating the ahistorical, mystified character of liberal, political subjective categories, Flyod blames these universalizing queer revolutionary projects of contesting hetero-homo divide as unproblematically engaging in other forms of dehistoricization and abstraction as well. The universalizing project which contests the homo/hetero divide fails to appreciate the fact that sexuality gets reified as it begins to articulate itself through a consumptive culture emanating in the late 19th and early 20th century US as a result of Fordist and Taylorist management of production leading to deskilling and passivity of the working class who were also slowly drawn into the culture of consumption and entertainment. So, the passivity of the working class and foundation of anti-heterosexist politics in the US are products of the same system.

Conclusion

Marxism and socialism as emancipatory projects have remained indifferent to sexual oppression despite Engels' concern for the women's question. Marxist politics discouraged incorporation of gender equality and 'erotic justice' in revolutionary agenda. Despite this disarticulation between Marxism and sexual oppressions, the communists and homosexuals were perceived as a "security risk" in the post- Second World War political culture of the US creating a moral panic which lasted twenty-five years affecting innumerable lives. The first gay associations which emerged in America in the 1950s, therefore distanced themselves from communist politics limiting themselves to influencing public opinions and 'civil rights'. The emergence of radical gay left politics in post-Stonewall times in the late 1960s and early 70s were influenced by the new left which was different from the old left in that 'class and labour' politics no more remained the prime focus; the 'counter-culture' and multiple forms and bases of oppression become the programmatic agenda of the new left (see Davis 2016). So, the question of class and historical materialism remained absent from the theoretical inquiries and political mobilizations. *The Gay Left* magazine of the Gay Left Collective in Britain focused their attention on family and sexual division of labour as the basis of gender oppression without a thorough incorporation of class and political economy. The 1980s experienced the assertions of 'cultural studies' in American academia with the dominance of Judith Butler's queer theory–the disruption of the heteronormative through counter performances of gender. Though Butler discusses materiality of body, her articulations are completely different from the Marxist understanding of (historical) materialism. For Butler, the materiality of body emerges through the reiteration of regulatory norms of gender through performativity which is the field of power. This simultaneously reveals that the naturalized state of gender is a fiction and there is always a possibility for improvisation (Odin 2016). Queer theory continues to be disruptive in orientation through performativity, as the editorial introduction of the recent *Routledge Queer Studies Reader* articulates (Hall 2013: xvi)- '...[Q]ueer Studies is the institutionalization of a new– or at least newly visible- paradigm for thinking about sexuality...in the early 1990s, constituting a broad and unmethodical critique of non-normative models of sex, gender and sexuality'. Despite this overarching concern, a group of scholars located within queer theory have been going against the grain to incorporate the issues of class, political economy and historical materialism in critiquing the mere performative in queer theory while proposing queer emancipation beyond the capitalist and neoliberal framework.

NOTES

1. Despite underscoring reproduction Engels upholds the primacy of production by subsuming the former under the latter; his unilinear evolutionism and naturalizing of the sexual division of labour and his model of economic liberation have equally received feminist disapproval (see Sayers et al., 2009).
2. See Neumann, Caryan. 'Labouchere Amendment (1885-1967)' http://www.glbtqarchive.com/ssh/labouchere_amendment _S.pdf, retrieved March 11, 2017.
3. During the 1940s and 50s the communist subversion at home and abroad seemed frighteningly real to many people in the US and the most enduring symbol of this scare was the Republican Senator of Wisconsin Joseph P. McCarthy. McCarthy's accusations were so intimidating that few people dared to speak out against him. See http://www.history.com/topics/cold-war/joseph-mccarthy, retrieved March 11, 2017. The homosexuals were thought to be drawn to the communist party because of their 'subversive' behaviour and partly on account of their being amenable to blackmail, and so, subsequently divulge official secrets to

the communists, the enemy camp.

4. Alfred Dreyfus was the son of a Jewish textile manufacturer; he joined the military and rose to the rank of captain. He was accused of selling military secrets to Germans and convicted of treason in December 1894. See 'Critical Essays Three Trials: Oscar Wilde Goes to Court' https://www.cliffsnotes.com/literature/p/the-picture-of-dorian-gray/critical-essays/three-trials-oscar-wilde-goes-to-court-1895, retrieved April 2, 2017
5. Going against the grain of queer theory implies here that this group of scholars does not reduce queer theory to performativity and articulation of queer self and identity through making the consumer products and consumptive spaces 'queery.
6. A few transgender autobiographies have recently emerged in India which demonstrate that cross-dressing and defying the gender binary is not so easy and playful but have very violent consequences for many who choose transgender identity. See Revathi's (2011) *Truth About Me* and Vidya's (2013) *I Am Vidya.*
7. Drag refers to practices of one gender dressing in the clothes of the opposite gender, often adopting the conventional mannerisms of that gender. Ball culture emerged in the 1920s in and around New York city. See http://haenfler.sites.grinnell.edu/subcultures-and-scenes/underground-ball-culture/retrieved March 29, 2017.
8. Willi Ninja is considered as the 'godfather' of the dance art called "voguing". He was the inspiration for Madonna's Vogue music video. See http://www.imdb.com/name/nm0632466/bio?, Retrieved March 30, 2017.
9. Queer Nation is an LGBT activist organization founded in New York City in March 1990 by AIDS activists from ACT UP New York (The AIDS Coalition to Unleash Power). The founders were outraged by the escalation of violence against LGBT people in the street of New York and the continued existence of anti-gay discrimination in the culture at large. See Queer Nation NY History http://queernationny.org/history. Retrieved March 30, 2017.
10. I refer here to the politics of Mattachine Society in pre-Stonewall times which was engaged with the politics of influencing public opinion about homosexuality in the hostile climate of the Lavender Scare.

REFERENCES

Adkins, Judith. 2016. 'Congressional Investigations and Lavender Scare'. *National Archive,* Summer, Vol. 48, No. 2. https://www.archives.gov/

publications/prologue/2016/summer/lavender.html.

Altman, Dennis. 1993. *Homosexual: Oppression and Liberation*. New York: New York University Press.

Butler, Judith. 1997. *Gender Trouble*. New York: Routledge.

Chrislove. 2012. 'Remembering LGBT History: How World War II changed Gay and Lesbian Life in America'. Daliy KOS, May 26. http://www.dailykos.com/story/2012/5/25/1094817/-Remembering-LGBT-History-How-World-War-II-Changed-Gay-and-Lesbian-Life-in-America.

Davis, Madeleine, 2016. 'New Left'. https://www.britannica.com/topic/New-Left.

D'Emilio, John. 1983. 'Capitalism and Gay Identity'. In Ann Sanitow Christine Stansell and Sharan Thompson (eds), *Powers of Desire: The Politics of Sexuality*. New York: Monthly Review Press, pp. 100-114.

Duggan, Lisa. 2004. *The Twilight of Equality: Neoliberalism, Cultural Politics and Attack on Democracy*. Boston: Beacon Press.

Ebert, Teresa L. 2016. 'Alexandra Kollontai and Red Love'. https://www.solidarity-us.org/node/1724 Retrieved on February 9, 2017.

Escoffier, Jeffery. 2015. 'Gay Left'. GLBTQ pp. 1-7. http://www.glbtqarchive.com/ssh/gay_lesbian_left_S.pdf.

Flyod, Kevin. 1998. 'Marxism, Queer Theory and Contradiction in Future of American Studies'. *Cultural Critic*, No. 40, pp. 167-201.

Hartman, Heidi. 1979. 'The Unhappy Marriage of Marxism and Feminism: Towards a More Progressive Union'. *Capital and Class*, July 1.

Hennessey, Rosemary. 1995. 'Queer Visibility in Commodity Culture'. *Cultural Critique*, pp. 31-76.

———2000. *Profit and Pleasure: Sexual Identity in Late Capitalism*. New York: Routledge.

Kissack, Terence. 1995. 'Freaking Fag Revolutionaries: New York's Gay Liberation Front'. *Radical History Review*. 62, 104-34.

Marcuse, Eric. 2002. *Making Gay History: The Half Century Fight for Lesbian and Gay Equal Rights*. Sydney: HarperCollins.

Marcuse, Herbert. 1992. *Eros and Civilization: A Philosophical Inquiry into Freud*. Boston: Beacon Press.

Namaste, Vivian. 2000. *The Erasure of Transsexuals and Transgendered People*. Chicago: University of Chicago Press.

Odin, Jaishree K. 2016. 'The Performative and Processual: A Study of Hypertext/Post-colonial Aesthetics'. http://www.postcolonialweb.org/poldiscourse/odin/odin2.html. Retreived October 19, 2016.

Porter, Cathy. 2016. *Alexandra Kollontai: A Biography*. Chicago: Haymarket Books.

Revathi. 2011. *Truth About Me: A Hijra Life Story*. Delhi: Penguin (Trans. From Tamil V. Geetha).

Sayers, Janet et al (eds). 1987. *Engels Revisited: Feminist Essays*. Abingdon: Routledge.

Valocchi, Stephen. 2001. 'Individual Identities, Collective Identities and Organizational Structure: The Relationship of Political Left and Gay Liberation in United States'. *Sociological Perspectives* Vol. 44, No. 4, pp. 445-467.

Vidya, Living Smile. 2013. *I Am Vidya: A Transgender's Journey* Hyderabad: Rupa and Company.

Wiley, Andrea and Josh Burke. 2008. 'The Lavender Scare'. http://www.edb.utexas.edu/faculty/salinas/students/student_sites/Fall 2008/6/Retrieved on September 21, 2016.

11

Countering 'Alienation': Re-reading Subversion in Discursive Practices

Rachna Chaudhary

The legal subject at the core of the judicial imagination is the autonomous, liberal individual born with certain inalienable rights. The core of this epistemology needs to be probed to bring out the 'partial and contingent content of their universalizing discourses.' (Conaghan 2000: 364). This paper has undertaken such *probing* based upon critical reading of various judgments delivered by the Bombay High Court and the Supreme Court of India in *Indian Hotel & Restaurant Association & Anr. v. State of Maharashtra & Anr.* (also known as Bar Dancers' case). Both Marxism and feminism as epistemic categories have been used to analyse judicial construction and treatment of the figure of the bar dancer/prostitute/sex worker.[1] The bar dancer is thus both the effect of discursive power and what Naffine calls the element of its articulation (Naffine 1997). The first section of the paper focuses on the content and the context of the judgments to lay down the issues of concern. The second section focuses on a review of the existing literature to assimilate the diverse perspectives and to explore the possibility of re-envisaging justice.

Judging Dance and the Bar Dancer

Briefly, the facts of the case are that the Maharashtra Government brought in an amendment in the Bombay Police Act 1951 in 2005, to prohibit the performance of dance in eating houses or permit rooms or beer bars.[2] The Amendment to the Bombay Police Act of

1951, introducing Sections 33A and 33B, was challenged as being unconstitutional in several writ petitions before the High Court of Bombay, by various stakeholders like the Bar Dancers' Union, the owners of establishments affected by the amendment and women's organizations among others. The High Court struck the amendment down and the Government of Maharashtra filed an appeal in the Supreme Court. The Supreme Court upheld the Bombay High Court's order in 2013. Since then there has been a continuous struggle between the state government and the Supreme Court adopting adversarial positions with the court upholding the right to livelihood in case of bar owners and dancers and the government has been trying to circumvent the court orders by drawing upon its executive powers and legislative support. The state legislature has even enacted a new legislation in 2016 titled Maharashtra Prohibition of Obscene Dance in Hotels, Restaurants and Bar Rooms and Protection of Dignity of Women (working therein) Act, 2016 (Mah. Act No. XII of 2016) to govern the dance bars in the state.[3] This is a rather sad illustration of the 'different and sometimes conflicting objectives' of various units of the state (Vance 2011: 934). The focus of the law seems on not allowing obscene dance or exploitation of 'any working woman for any immoral purpose in any place'.

There are multiple 'portraits' being portrayed by different groups involved in opposing and supporting the ban. The Bar Dancers' Union, the owners of establishments affected by the amendment and a few women's organizations among others are mainly the ones opposing the ban. The state is representing its view and justifying the ban through its counsels and then the judges who get to decide which claim is to be recognized by the law and which would be dismissed. Discursive subject formation is important in this context because the law and legal agents not only regulate the 'subject' of their discourse but also produce it by supplying terms of description and references.

While the impact of the law, the judgment, and the legality of the issues have been discussed from different perspectives ranging from 'Hindu puritanical anxiety' (Makhija 2010), 'good governance' (Pandit 2013), 'caste governance' (Sameena Dalwai 2013), to 'reproductive labour' (Prabha Kotishwaran 2014), among others, this paper focuses upon discursive subject formation.

When the matter first came up in the Bombay High Court, the Union of Dance Bar Owners, one of the petitioners, was duly registered under the Trade Union Act, 1926. The fact that sex-workers' collectives cannot be registered under the Trade Unions Act, but the bar dancers can, changes the mode of interaction with the legal system (Kotiswaran 2014: 3). In that sense, the court recognizes the dancer as a worker right from the outset. Even in the new law, the reference is to the dancer and working women. Even though the Sexual Harassment of Women at Workplace (Prevention, Prohibition and Redressal) Act came into force from December 2013 only, the campaign around the bill was quite visible and yet the arguments in the judgments are almost always couched in terms of morality since that was the dominant recourse available to working women other than the *Vishakha* Guidelines.[4]

The Union of Owners and Dancers' main line of argument was that the amendment was discriminatory towards artists (girls/women) dancing in bars and the viewers visiting these bars compared to the artists associated with the exempted establishments and the visitors to those establishments. Dances, even if vulgar and obscene, could go on in the exempted establishments. The petition emphasized—'The state, it is set out, is adopting double standards by allowing these activities where indecent clothes, movements and immoral activities in the name of high society are permitted, whereas establishments where there is no physical contact are sought to be closed down. The ban seeks to completely wipe out the performance of dances which as a form of entertainment/amusement, is accessible to the common man while the same dancers can perform the same dances for the rich audiences in three star hotels and above.' It is a 'fraternal dispute' in the sense that the emphasis is on the male sex-right, the access of the common man vis a vis the affluent man to the dancing bodies (Pateman: 1989). The government is thus guilty of upholding the (sexual) privileges of upper caste/class men by normalizing these privileges/'public secrets' through the differential rule (Anupama Rao 2011: 623). It was also claimed that 'the dance was merely wild gyrations to the tune of Hindi film songs in the presence of men and not traditional dance forms of Bharatanatyam, Kuchipudi, Kathak; ....Indian culture does not approve of this kind of business, which treats women as a commodity.' Rege has problematized such 'institutional reproduction of the 'distinctions' between the elite and the popular' culture and also highlighted the impossibility of politics in the face of such cultural reductionism (Rege 2002: 1049).

The petitioners argued that 'ladies undertaking dance performance for the entertainment of men is part of the cultural tradition of Maharashtra' and Lavani, Tamashas, etc., were cited as examples of the same. The marginalization of such caste and region-based cultural practices by the so-called elitist forms is now well documented (Banerjee 1989; Rege 1995, Rege 2002]. Such attempts at naturalizing women dancing for men as a part of Maharashtrian culture, simultaneously negate and affirm the violence inherent in such practices.

The court observed: 'It is normal in the hospitality and tourist related industries to engage young girls.' Unabashed fetishization of femininity as a commodity is evident in the normalization of young girls being employed by the hospitality and tourism industry. The dance bars were seen by the court as better sites of work for semi-literate/literate girls 'who may be beautiful, knows how to dance or tries to dance prohibited from earning a better livelihood or should such a girl, because of poverty and want of literacy, be condemned to a life of only doing menial jobs?' Menon alerts us to the dangers inherent in such reasoning as they 'reinforce sexualized images of women in the public sphere' (Menon 2012: 187).

The bar owners presented themselves as catering to tourists from all over the world and that their models of running bars and restaurants were being emulated in other parts of the world. This was an attempt at legitimizing the bars as revenue-generating business concerns since the exempted categories were seen as cultural hubs with foreigners visiting them and dance performances being of artistic rather than erotic or rather obscene category.

The counsel for state emphasized that dances in exempted establishments were performed by persons 'who have acquired skill in Western classical and Indian classical dance forms' and this was in keeping with the objective of the government to encourage tourism. 'Even otherwise five star hotels are a class by themselves and cannot be compared with dance bars. It is a distinct category. The persons visiting these hotels or establishments stand on a different footing and cannot be compared with people who attend the establishments which are popularly known as dance bars. ..... The class of establishments covered by Section 33(B) are those conducted by responsible persons/management who are conscious of their social commitments and obligations. These are the types of establishments, which have never conducted any activity of the kind that was being conducted at the dance bars.' These differential assessments were criticized by the court as well.

The petitioners counter claimed that 'obscene and indecent activities in the form of fashion shows and beauty pageants, dance and performances by dance troupes from abroad are considered to be 'decent' only because the venue is in star hotels and high class places which are visited by film stars, the very rich and elite families.'

The prime concern that emerged from those in favour of the ban was that many of the girls dancing in the bars were being trafficked from outside Maharashtra. This was thus projected as a security issue also along with other concerns. The lack of perspective is evident in such slippery framings of issues as these women were projected as victims of trafficking and also as threats to security. The genesis of such arguments can be traced to the anti-migrant politics followed by some political parties within the state.[5] The claims of a huge majority of helpless women being trafficked for sexual exploitation are now a recognized strategy of individuals and groups involved in anti-trafficking efforts. Numbers do communicate a lot and in the Indian context, they are still accorded 'occult respect' by the government (Kaviraj 2012: 27-28). But it is also well acknowledged that the data on trafficking is highly unreliable owing to the 'hidden nature' of the crime, reluctance of victims to report or share their experience which can be attributed to both fear of the state's repressive policies and the violence of traffickers (Lobasz 2009). The graphic descriptions of women's exploitation in dance bars strengthen the fetishized 'victim' subject of liberal discourse who can then be 'rescued' by well-intentioned lawyers, legislators, ministers and judges.

Lobasz alerts us to the danger of conflating different categories of people like those trafficked, the smuggled, and the refugees among others (Lobasz 2009: 324). By extension, seeing all trafficking as leading to sexual exploitation is problematic as theoretically it leads to reification of gender stereotypes about women's purity and helplessness and the practical aspect of such conflation leads to invisiblizing those trafficked for other purposes and hampers developing a perspective for sex workers' rights (Lobasz 2009: 344).

The State of Maharashtra through its Deputy Secretary, had filed an affidavit in reply which pointed out among other things that 'The dancing girls invariably used to be clad in dresses, apparently for name's sake traditional, but truly revealing female anatomy. These girls would dance in a peculiar manner with constant eye contact with certain customers and with such body movements so as to attract the attention of customers and entice them, so that they would be showered with currency notes by the customers.... These girls were found to be using various tactics to lure the customers and attract their attention. ...During the dance performance, these female dancers come close and in physical contact with the customers present.' These ideas about 'loose' women date back to the earliest ideas in mainstream criminology wherein, female offenders including prostitutes were treated as biological throwbacks and hence quite unlike 'normative' conformist ordinary women (Lombroso and Ferrero 1959). One social implication of being a biological throwback is that prostitutes are considered to be oversexed and shameless and hence the males are victims of the temptress.[6] This victim/agent ambivalence/conflation of the bad woman is nothing new in judicial discourse.[7] It was further argued that 'These dance performances were neither entertainment nor art. ....Performance of these dances was nothing but exploitation of women at a very young age many of whom were minors.' Such reconstructions help to secure the status of these women as being in need of control as well as protection since the figure of the bar dancer challenges the binary of offender and victim, collapsing both into a single entity. Kalsem rightly points out, 'In the legal text, the "evidence" (the voice) is exclusively male and "the body" is female (Kalsem 2012: 48).'

Dalwai draws attention to the fact that most of the bar girls come from the Bhatu caste cluster of north India, known traditionally for earning their livelihood through sexual and erotic labour including dancing, singing, entertaining and sex work (Dalwai 2013: 131). In the contemporary context, these women redeploying their "caste capital" for socio-economic mobility is not only conducive to handling the stresses of the situation as Dalwai enumerates (Dalwai 2013: 131), it results in carrying the burden of a stigmatized past to the present occupation as well.

The court sided with the petitioners and pointed out 'dancing as a form of art and expression has been known to our civilization from times immemorial. It is reflected in our cultural activities, carved out in stones and is a source of a large number of books. The dance and sculptures many a times are erotic or bordering on the erotic. Dance, therefore, by itself per se, cannot be said to be an activity which would be res extra commercium.' Dance does not seem offensive to 'official standards of propriety' in this case as only obscene or immoral dances can be prohibited or restricted (Willis 2009: 466). Through these detailed yet problematic and unnecessary evocations, Law also performs the function of rhetoric here thus rendering itself 'redundant' (Tambe 2009: 123).

The court seems to be upholding 'Indian culture' which has a tradition of dance as a form of art and expression and also because it falls within the ambit of res commercium rather than res extra commercium like sex work. It is the exchange value of dance in this instance which requires judicial protection. If a homogenized cultural identity for the neoliberal nation has to be carved out, it has to be a balanced combination of tradition and modernity. The appropriation of the dancer's body is not just discursive, it is a socio-cultural appropriation as well. Through her body, dance as a medium of communication is being re-recognized and the inscription is then of normalizing this 'other' body. And thus the court wanted to continue with 'our' tradition of dance and also to be more tolerant to 'skimpy dressing and belly gyrations' as Bollywood has helped us in pushing our limits of tolerance for the same. The myth of catering to collective interest helps in maintaining the ideological sanctity/ rather pretence of a liberal democratic society.

The Advocate General arguing on behalf of the state, claimed that bar dancing is a de-humanizing process and most of these women and girls are victims of trafficking. Thus there is no 'element of conscious selection of a profession' in this regard. Nussbaum rightly urges us to be extremely reflexive about 'our social views about money making and alleged commodification' to avoid harbouring class prejudices unjust to working people (Nussbaum 1999: 280). The inverse relationship between comparatively inflexible labour markets and employment generation in the Indian context is well theorized (Das et al. 2015). Svati Shah's work is also relevant in understanding the 'complexities of negotiating a livelihood' and also the fluidity of categories like 'choice' (Shah 2014).

Creating a Hierarchy of Victims[8]

Pandit locates the reasons of the government's stance in the larger picture like the pressure of sanctions from the US under its regime of stringent anti-trafficking laws, its waning power and influence in the era of economic liberalization which leaves the option of muscle flexing only in the cultural domain (Pandit 2013: 37). In this instance, the state government was responding to the moral panic around the dance bars and their harmful effects on youth, families, women and girls in and around Mumbai. The Home Department claimed to have even received complaints by alleged victims' families against illicit relations with bar dancers. While the sex worker can be given up as beyond redemption, the bar dancer symbolized the 'potential threat' and hence figured on the agenda of the state for cultural purification. Interestingly, within these establishments, there were other female workers working in different capacities. While the state claimed that the vulgar and obscene dances by bar dancers put these women also in danger of sexual exploitation, the ban did not include banning women from working in these establishments. The Minister responding to a calling attention motion in the State Assembly pointed out that 'the possibility of needy ladies amongst the lady-waiters also cannot be ruled out. If the lady-waiters are banned, then in that case, there is a possibility of questions pertaining to the women's rights arising.' A further distinction is made between bad girls and very bad girls here as the bar dancers are seen as the transgressors while the 'needy' ones try to work on jobs other than dance. The need to feed the family and children is emphasized as a cultural compensation for doing something that is otherwise morally or socially unacceptable, like bar dancing and commercial surrogacy. Here poverty and need to, paradoxically, be a responsible mother/daughter/wife/sibling (again as an individual responsibility), is a culturally acceptable explanation for taking up such 'reprehensible' profession (s). Constructing the women workers as 'needy' helps in 'normalization' of the client by the lawyers since 'need' happens to be subjective and not a valid ground for lenience, poverty is a social category over which the individual has no control (Worrall 1990: 21).[9]

The government also claimed that since many dance bars functioned from ground floors of residential buildings, women and young girls from those buildings and in the surrounding areas were subjected to daily harassment, stress and mental trauma whenever they returned home in the evening or late at night as 'a crowd of lascivious men' would make indecent comments and also inappropriate gestures. Borrowing from G. Pheterson, O'Neill asserts that the 'whore stigma' is transferable to all women but particularly to those who transgress the rules and norms that 'control' women morally and socially (O'Neill 2001: 186). That these women were approaching the court for assertion of their socio-economic rights outside the family/community dyad as citizen subjects not necessarily as mothers, daughters and wives made it easier to position them in opposition to the 'good women'.

Whither Sex?

The bar dancers are simultaneously being sexualized (by objectifying them) and desexualized (by re-presenting them as victims). The descriptions included by the government in its petitions are indicative of the sexism and tokenism that has dominated policy intervention while dealing with transgressive women.

The 'postcolonial sexual subaltern subject-in-pleasure' is nowhere in sight in these formulations (Kapur 1999). In fact, the multiple subjectivities of these women are 'muted' under the larger imagination of victimization framework. Their 'dancing' bodies are recuperated in a more materially productive and conformist way by benevolently refashioning their lives in a domesticated way by leaving them without (immoral) work or by asking them to wear decent clothes, putting up railings to avoid intimate contact with the audience, and by putting men in-charge of collecting the reward money from the men visiting these bars. If their dance is the commodified economic value produced by them, giving away the right to receive cash rewards on their behalf to the owners/managers of the dance bars is equivalent to alienating the dancers from the product of their labour. The stance of the court, seeped in liberal logic, chose affirmative remedies over transformative ones by recognizing the right to livelihood of the bar dancers but not moving beyond that mere recognition.

The production and circulation of accounts that see these bars as sites of opportunity and desire are restricted to academic or activist spaces.[10] The entire discourse is based on the idiom of paternalist protection of the liberal state and barely moves away from the logic of obscenity and the protection of dignity of women. Even though certain essentialist assumptions around these expendable bodies are questioned within the liberal frame of rights, the reconfigured identity is put back in the domain of the victim versus agent framework debates that are now well known. The problem inherent in the tendency to invoke an internally consistent category of "woman" and the failure to take account of the heterogeneity shores up tokenist claims of reforms. The state government offered to set up a cell under the Women and Child Welfare Department for their 'effective rehabilitation' and provide them with a 'dignified' alternative vocation and was also agreeable to setting up a Special Committee for the purpose. The idea of dignified 'work' for women needing rehabilitation has not moved from providing skills for stitching, sewing, embroidery, bakery products, add to it those needed to be a beautician or a data operator if one stretches the imagination. Even the court made it clear that while the bar dancers were recognized as engaged in a legitimate profession, the same rights would not be extended to a person engaged in an immoral activity like sex work (Bombay High Court, para 35). By accepting the dancers as 'freely consenting and economically active subjects', the judges absolve themselves and the state of the responsibility to ensure their well-being (Dickenson 1997: 124).

Interestingly, the much talked about safe existence of sex within legal discourse seems to have disappeared as sex itself is barely mentioned in these judgments (John and Nair 2000: 1). This is in stark contrast to the predominant presence of sex and its importance that has been regularly stressed in successive judgments related to matrimonial disputes.[11] Denial of bar dancers being sexual subjects is problematic as this entrapment within the victimization framework will hamper any attempts at transcending the subject/object binary (Sutherland 2005: 120).

Countering Alienation

The criminal justice system has always served as an effective tool in controlling or even getting rid of what Chomsky calls 'superfluous population' (Chomsky 2003). This is evident in the case of bar dancers as their construction along a negative work identity only and as 'fallen' women or victims to be rescued and not as citizens/workers firmly entrenches their alienation from the system which continues to marginalize them and also from the society that the system claims to mainstream them with.[12] The idea of justice then seems a fallacy as their own voices get 'muted' in a system that thrives on 'listening' only through authorized experts like lawyers.

As mentioned earlier, the case is still sub-judice with the court insisting on granting the bar dancers their right to livelihood and the state government continues to side-step the judicial orders by non-compliance, delaying the grant of licenses, harassing the bar owners, and even bringing in fresh legislation to undo the effects of the court orders.

The costs of *'emotional labour'* are manifold as the exchange value of the dance is contingent upon the ability of the dancer to evoke desire in the audience (Hochschild 2003: 7).[13] Yet that desire, if seen as the product, is alienating as it is a transgressive desire and not the normative one. The alienation or estrangement is also at multiple levels as personally there is an internalization of the stigma attached to dancing in the bar and often the dancers do not disclose it to their families, the working conditions are poor as is evident from the range of issues that came up throughout the judgment. The alienation within the legal system is by accepting, legitimizing and reinforcing the stigmatization of their work. Work hazards like sexual violence, long working hours, competition amongst the dancers, addiction, lack of any type of socio-economic security and harassment by the police have been mentioned in works focused on bar dancers. While dance necessarily need not be the source of alienation, the conditions under which the dance is being performed are definitely alienating and the judgment does little to change those conditions.

The attempts to politicize the figure of the bar dancer are also counterproductive since the needy 'worker' is barely able to transcend the victimization framework and gets further entangled into the circuit of protectionism.

Against this background, the paper tried to bring the focus back on work as identity and issues of livelihood. In that sense, it is also an attempt to align with the larger struggle of 'expanding the category of (gendered) labour' (Weeks 2007). The work of bar dancers expands our imagination of work and employment and also our understanding of the changing embodied experiences of sexualized identity-based work like bar dancing (Wolkowitz 2006).

The need to reconceptualize work in the differential context of value-production when the site of work is these dance bars is evident. There have been crucial attempts at the rethinking required and a brief recollection would help in better assimilation of diverse perspectives. A starting point could be to replace the totalizing and unidimensional figure of the (ideal) woman by 'multifaceted nature of identity' (Thornton 2011: 29).

If one looks at the arguments presented in the bar dancers' case, the terms of discourse are changing discernibly. In the Supreme Court, Catherine MacKinnnon's work has been evoked to argue in favour of the ban.[14] Not surprising as she has been at the helm of the anti-porn lobby in the US and has been influential in getting many policies and laws against the porn industry in place.

This selective appropriation of a voice from the feminist world lends credence to the lawyer's pro-women stance and also sounds a politically correct way of arguing in face of a remarkably visible sex worker's movement. Sutherland, while analysing the limitations of MacKinnon's conflation of woman with commodity, points out that 'Women's status as commodities rather than authors of commodities ultimately forecloses the possibility of consciousness raising and of praxis' (Sutherland 2005: 120).

Thus feminists and critical theorists have to be cautious and avoid inadvertently producing the 'impotent victim' as subject of their discourse (Morrissey 2003: 65). Morrissey observes that such feminist projections could be legally effective occasionally but are 'also naive and culturally dangerous in their continued activation of restrictive and disempowering stereotypes of women' (Morrissey 2003: 24).

The arguments also focused on the different standards of 'tolerance' applied to obscene dances and revealing clothes worn by female actors in Hindi films. That exploitation 'exists in all forms of employment including factory workers, building site workers, housemaids and even waitresses' was also mentioned. The differential treatment extended by the state in not banning men from visiting bars and consuming liquor but prohibiting the dancers from performing was also questioned. The problem inherent in the legislation by patronizingly seeking to protect women at the cost of their 'liberty, autonomy and self-determination' was also a subject of discussion. All this was definitely indicative of changing perspectives. But the overall framework within which these arguments were acceptable to the court remained the same.

The paper's core concern has been that though the judiciary did favourably dispose of the petition in both the High Court and Supreme

Court but the framing of the discourse remained couched in a liberal capitalist frame. Dance bars as sites of consumption are to be protected in a modern 'liberal' capitalist economy and dance is than re-presented as emblematic of tradition. Thus presented, 'the rhetoric of tradition and modernity' is simultaneously employed to symbolize both, the Indian nation and the Indian woman (Chaudhuri 2012: 278, 287-88). Thus the judges would uphold the right of women to take up 'moral' activity as a source of livelihood and the government would be chastised for still complaining about scantily dressed women.

The caution at work while regulating women's presence and access as the split between the public/private is continuously being reworked, is evident in the alternative/simultaneous exclusion and inclusion that is being strategized within the discursive space.

The pretence of seeking redistribution through labour laws is maintained by both the aggrieved groups like the bar dancers in this case and the judiciary/executive as the case maybe. Even though the outcomes hardly fall within the purview of labour laws.

Resisting these dominant constructions around femininity, chastity, work, identity, culture and sexuality is thus crucial for epistemic as well as political reasons.

Theorizing the Political

Foucault while stressing the importance of discourse for any effort towards societal change, has also warned against its counter-productivity and suggests that 'We must make allowance for the complex and unstable process whereby discourse can be both an instrument and an effect of power, but also a hindrance, a stumbling-block, a point of resistance and a starting point for an opposing strategy (Foucault 1998: 101).' It is thus imperative to approach the issue of discourse analysis as well as re-construction and deconstruction, cautiously and politically.

This section of the paper outlines the salients of more nuanced theorizations that can be used in the cases in question to re-envisage a different outcome not only in terms of the effect of the judgment but also in terms of theorizing the issues. Despite the greater fear of co-optation by the government, using a labour framework in the case of bar dancers is possible because prostitution here is implicit and not explicit. The fact that both the dancers and the re-presenters are denying prostitution and claiming a work identity only which might be oppressive and stigmatized but not as 'bad/immoral' as prostitution itself increases the possibility of being within the purview of licit rather than illicit. Kotiswaran's emphasis on seeking remedies within the existing and exhaustive framework of labour laws is significant in that sense (Kotiswaran 2014).

Since power lies in our understanding of the situation, relationship or contexts, power-knowledge can be used as the 'matrices of transformations' (Foucault, 1998: 99). The judges seem to see the bar dancers as the autonomous, unencumbered and willing as well as flexible workers prepared to be a part of the market in a global economy. The chastity, sexual passivity expected of women is being provided for as the directions in the judgment provoke us to believe. The feminist challenges to the victimization trope as the only recourse available to women coming in contact with the judicial system are rendered invalid. In that sense, the liberalization of the market can only be credited with a refashioning rather than a change in the structuring of gender relations.[15]

The recasting of the bar dancers as victims is necessary to keep the liberal contract of protection alive. The opening up of the workplace for scrutiny, even though rather belated but has been a part of the women's movement in India. The campaign from *Vishakha* to the anti-sexual harassment law in 2013 bears testimony to that struggle. The support extended to the bar dancers by organizations like Aawaz-e-niswaan among others have helped in identifying it as a women's issue without trying to judge the women involved. The women in the bar are not equal employees, they are women employees which makes them vulnerable and also a threat. While the threat is not evident in case of other women, who are re-presented as chaste women, struggling to support their families. These new sexualized identities can be a ground for political solidarity and also an expansion of women's rights including the right to be counted as human (Stewart 2011: 259).[16] Even though, a sizeable scholarship has seen potential in positing a relational subject located within networks of familial and community relationships and not just an atomic individualized subject (Stewart 2011: 261), in a post-colonial context, these deployments have to be overlapping/ simultaneous/independent depending on the context in question.

Sutherland suggests rethinking the 'possibility of female participation in processes of objectification' and she pushes us to turn to the concept of surplus through looking at 'excess of desire' as a radicalizing force especially to counter the victimization framework (Sutherland 2005: 130). This can have some use while the figure of the bar dancer is being re-presented. Both, Dalwai and Makhija's work helps us in rethinking the questions of agency in this context. Makhija argues that the figure of the bar dancer, openly and actively making an eye contact with patrons 'challenges the notion of the female dancer as a spectacle' and thus constituted as a source of anxiety for the state (Makhija 2010: 21). This gaze-reversal is seen by Makhija as constructing an active and hence threatening female subject who needs to be controlled.

Dickenson's quest is directed at finding the possibility of transforming the 'notion of alienation to fit women's typical *propertylessness in their labour* ', since the '*ownership* of property in one's labour' is crucial to a Marxist analysis (Dickenson 1997: 119). The resolution lies in refusing to adhere to the androcentricism of philosophy by concluding 'Lacking property in things, or even in soul or will, women have nothing to lose by dissociating themselves from property in their own bodies....Woman in this condition is outside the Hegelian sphere of moral agency.'(Dickenson 1997: 114)

The need for exercising caution is evident in Sangari's work who sees red in the tendencies to connect women's agency to direct participation in the capitalist labour process as 'it is based on a devaluation of women's labour and an overvaluation of their social passivity' (Sangari 1993: 867). But the class specificity of such analysis needs to be kept in mind.

Rajan's proposition of re-envisaging a 'new dance bar phenomenon with mixed in terms of genderwise–dancers and clientele, as well as a wider pattern of ownership' in order to rethink the links between 'freedom of expression, sexual freedom, and equality' is another useful strategy (Rajan 2007: 474).

Conclusion

As mentioned earlier, the paper has tried to push the understanding of gendered labour through the figure of the bar dancer and bring out the complexities of using classical theorizations of work/labour or even the rhetoric of classical patriarchal oppression for such new sexualized work identities especially when there is a continuum between apparently separate aspects of life. It also responds to scholars like Kotiswaran's call for feminist rethinking of the issues around 'reproductive labour' performed by women for the market from a labour perspective and in that sense address the lack of 'well articulated materialist feminist position' on sex work, exotic dancing and commercial surrogacy (Kotiswaran 2014). The politics behind the reconstitution of the dancers' bodies in response to the scrutiny of institutional powers, has been theorized using critical perspectives. Law emerges as a representational practice in its discursive management of the dancing body, in order to remove the threat posed by the possibility of transgression. The dancing body seemingly posits a threat only as long as there is a cultural production of that threat but it was the body that was obliterated while culture remained intact. The trope of victimization is useful in constitution of an ethical subject necessary to uphold the 'official policy' of regulation and criminalization though the socio-economic conditions that produce these dancing bodies as a commodity remain unaddressed.

NOTES

1. This 'putting together' of all three categories of women as they appear in the selected judicial pronouncements is not indicative of a conflation but is to acknowledge that different women are in conversation with the legal system.

   Given that there is a history of an 'unhappy marriage' between Marxism and feminism, one is cautiously attempting to use both the epistemic frames simultaneously or independently and not claiming the use of a Marxist Feminist perspective. A few references that have dealt with this relationship include : Barrett and McIntosh 1979; Hartmann 1981; Delphy 1984; Barrett and Hamilton 1986; Barrett 1988; Hartsock 2006; Howe 2010; Arruzza 2013.

2. The provisions inserted by the 2005 Amendments were:

   '33A(1) Notwithstanding anything contained in this Act or the rules made by the Commissioner of Police or the District Magistrate under sub-section (1) of Section 33 for the area under their respective charges, on and from the date of commencement of the Bombay Police (Amendment) Act, 2005:

(a) Holding of a performance of dance, of any kind or type, in any eating house, permit room or beer bar is prohibited.

(b) All performance licences, issued under the aforesaid rules by the Commissioner of Police or the District Magistrate or any other officer, as the case may be, being the Licensing Authority, to hold a dance performance, of any kind or type, in an eating house, performance, of any kind or type, in an eating house, permit room or beer bar shall stand cancelled.....

   .....33B. Subject to the other provisions of this Act, or any other law for the time being in force, nothing in Section 33A shall apply to the holding of a dance performance in a drama theatre, cinema theatre and auditorium; or sports club or gymkhana, where entry is restricted to its members only, or a three starred or above hotel or in any other stablishment or class of establishments, which, having regard to (a) the tourism policy of the central or state government for promoting the tourism activities in the state; or (b) cultural activities, the state government may, by special or general order, specify on this behalf.

   Explanation.—For the purposes of this section, "sports club" or "gymkhana" means an establishment registered as such under the provisions of the Bombay Public Trusts Act, 1950, or the Societies Registration Act, 1860 or the Companies Act, 1956, or any other law for the time being in force.'

3. Available at http://bombayhighcourt.nic.in/libweb/acts/Stateact/2016acts/2016.12.pdf.
4. Section 354 of the Indian Penal Code makes it a cognizable offence to assault or use criminal force with the intent of outraging the modesty of a woman. The other prominent Section in this category was 509 which listed word, gesture or act intended to insult the modesty of a woman as a cognizable offence. The *Vishakha* Guidelines were a set of procedural guidelines to be used in cases of sexual harassment pending promulgation of any law. The Supreme Court issued these in *Vishaka and Others v. State of Rajasthan and Others* (JT 1997 (7) SC 384).
5. The state has a history of politically motivated violence against migrant workers from other states, prominently from Bihar and Uttar Pradesh.

The Shiv Sena and Maharashtra Navnirman Sena workers have been occasionally charged with involvement in violence against north Indian migrant workers working in the state.

6. See review of such biases in earlier works on female criminality in Carol Smart (1976), E.B. Leonard (1982) and Larry J. Siegel, 1995).
7. As an illustration, in a 1975 judgment, *Chintan J. Vaswani and Anr. v. State of West Bengal and Anr.*, the judge described the men found in a bar as 'willing male victims', who were being seduced by the girls soliciting 'carnal custom flit'. And these male victims were alternately described as 'takers of virginity who sip every flower and change every hour.' See *Chitan J. Vaswani v. State of West Bengal*, (1975) 2 SCC 829.
8. I have borrowed the phrase hierarchy of victims from Lobasz 2009: 341.
9. I disagree with Worrall here since according to her, 'need' is the permitted redefinition of poverty as part of 'normalization' of the defendant.
10. Dalwai has undertaken the study of bar dancers for her doctoral work submitted to the University of Keele. Majlis, a Mumbai based feminist group has brought out a report on Bar Dancers. The Prayas (TISS - Mumbai) report and the SNDT reports have been extensively used to support adversarial positions and are continuously referred to in the judgments.
11. The Division Bench in the case of *Rita Nijhawan v. Balkrishan Nijhawan* in AIR 1973 Delhi 200 observed:
"Marriage without sex is an anathema. Sex is the foundation of marriage and without a vigorous and harmonious sexual activity it would be impossible for any marriage to continue for long. It cannot be denied that the sexual activity in marriage has an extremely favourable influence on a woman's mind and body. The result being that if she does not get proper sexual satisfaction it will lead to depression and frustration. It has been said that the sexual relations when happy and harmonious vivifies the woman's brain, develops her character and trebles her vitality. It must be recognized that nothing is more fatal to marriage than disappointment in sexual intercourse."
12. This is not to argue that the self was unalienated before coming into contact with the legal system.
13. Hochschild defines emotional Labour as that 'requires one to induce or suppress feeling in order to sustain the outward countenance that produces the proper state of mind in others...' p. 7.
14. Not surprising as she has been at the helm of the anti-porn lobby in

the US and has been influential in getting many policies and laws against the porn industry in place.

15. Ann Stewart sees the feminist contestations against the victimhood narrative in the works of scholars like Ratna Kapur as having the potential of restructuring of gender relations but the case in question pushes towards a less optimistic understanding (Stewart 2011: 238).
16. There have been substantial works exposing the dark side of the project of human rights but the critique is more relevant in terms of de-centring androcentricism and Euro/American centricism rather than an abandoning of the project. See Grewal 1999; Kapur 2006.

REFERENCES

Arruzza, Cinzia. 2013. *Dangerous Liaisons: The Marriages and Divorces of Marxism and Feminism.* London: Merlin Press.

Banerjee, Sumanta. 1989. *The Parlour and the Street: Elite and Popular Culture in Nineteenth Century Bengal.* Calcutta: Seagull.

Barrett, Michèle and Mary McIntosh. 1979. 'Chistine Delphy: Towards a Materialist Feminism?', *Feminist Review,* pp. 95–106.

Barrett, Michèle and Roberta Hamilton. 1986. *The Politics of Diversity: Feminism, Marxism and Nationalism.* London: Verso.

Barrett, Michèle. 1988. *Women's Oppression Today: The Marxist Feminist Encounter.* London: Verso.

Chaudhuri, Maitrayee. 2012. 'Indian "Modernity" and "Tradition": A Gender Perspective', *Polish Sociological Review,* 2 (178): 277-289.

Conaghan, Joanne. September 2000. 'Reassessing the Feminist Theoretical Project in Law', *Journal of Law and Society,* 27(3): 351-385.

Dalwai, Sameena. November 30, 2013. *Economic & Political Weekly,* Vol. 48(48): 131-132.

Das, Sonali, Sonali Jain-Chandra, Kalpana Kochhar, and Naresh Kumar. March 2015. 'Women Workers in India: Why So Few Among So Many?', *IMF Working Paper,* Asia and Pacific Department, WP/15/55, pp. 1-31.

De Beauvoir, Simone. 2011. *The Second Sex.* translated by Constance Borde and Sheila Malovany-Chevallier, London: Vintage.

Delphy, Christine. 1984. *Close to Home: A Materialist Analysis of Women's Oppression.* London: Hutchinson.

Dickenson, Donna. 1997. *Property, Women and Politics: Subjects or Objects.* Cambridge: Polity Press.

Dworkin, Ronald. 2002. *Law's Empire.* Delhi: Universal.

Foucault, Michel. 1998. *The Will to Knowledge: The History of Sexuality*-Vol. 1, translated by R. Hurley. London: Penguin.

Gangoli, Geetanjali. 2007. *Indian Feminisms: Law, Patriarchies and Violence in India.* Eldershot: Ashgate.

Grewal, Inderpal. 1999. "'Women's Rights as Human Rights': Feminist Practices, Global Feminism, and Human Rights Regimes in Transnationality", *Citizenship Studies*, 3:3, 337-354.

Hartmann, Heidi. 1981. 'The Unhappy Marriage of Marxism and Feminism: Towards a More Progressive Union', in Lydia Sargent (ed). *The Unhappy Marriage of Marxism and Feminism: A Debate on Class and Patriarchy*, pp. 1-41, London: Pluto Press.

Hartsock, Nancy. 2006. 'Globalization and Primitive Accumulation', in Noel Castree and Derek Gregory (eds). *David Harvey: A Critical Reader*, 167–190. Oxford: Blackwell.

Howe, Gillian. 2010. *Between Feminism and Materialism: A Question of Method.* New York: Palgrave Macmillan.

John, Mary E. and Janaki Nair. 2000. *A Question of Silence: The Sexual Economies of Modern India.* New Delhi: Kali for Women.

Kalsem, Kristin. 2012. *In Contempt: Nineteenth-Century Women, Law, and Literature.* Columbus: The Ohio State University Press.

Kapur, Ratna. 1999. 'A Love Song to Our Mongrel Selves: Hybridity, Sexuality and the Law', *Social & Legal Studies*, 8(3): 353-368.

Kapur, Ratna. 2006. 'Human Rights in the 21st Century: Take a Walk on the Dark Side', *Sydney Law Review*, 28: 665-687.

Kaviraj, Sudipta. 2012. *The Trajectories of the Indian State: Politics and Ideas.* Delhi: Permanent Black.

Kotiswaran, Prabha. 2014. 'Abject Labours, Informal Markets: Revisiting the Law's (Re)Production Boundary', *feminists@law*, 4(1): 1-9. Accessed on October 16, 2016 https://journals.kent. ac.uk/index.php/feministsatlaw/article/view/104/270.

Leonard, E.B. 1982. *Women, Crime and Society: A Critique of Theoretical Criminology.* New York: Longman.

Lobasz, Jennifer K. 2009. 'Beyond Border Security: Feminist Approaches to Human Trafficking', *Security Studies*, 18: 319–344.

Lombroso, Cesare and William Ferrero. 1959. *The Female Offender.* New York: Peter Owen.

Makhija, Sonal. September 25, 2010. 'Bar Dancers, Morality and the Indian Law', *Economic & Political Weekly*, 45(39): 19- 23.

Menon, Nivedita. 2012. *Seeing Like a Feminist.* New Delhi: Penguin.

Morrissey, Belinda. 2003. *When Women Kill: Questions of Agency and Subjectivity.*

London: Routledge.

Naffine, Ngaire. 1997. *Feminism and Criminology*. Cambridge: Polity Press.

Nussbaum, Martha C. 1999. *Sex and Social Justice*. New York: Oxford University Press.

O'Neill, Maggie. 2001. *Prostitution and Feminism: Towards a Politics of Feeling*. Cambridge: Polity.

Pandit, Maya. August 10, 2013. 'Gendered Subaltern Sexuality and the State', *Economic & Political Weekly*, 48 (32): 33-38.

Radford, Lorraine. 1987. 'Legalising Woman Abuse', in Jalna Hanmer and Mary Maynard (eds.), *Women, Violence and Social Control,* pp. 135-151, London: MacMillan Press.

Rajan, Nalini. February 10, 2007. 'Dance Bar Girls and the Feminist's Dilemma', *Economic and Political Weekly*, pp. 471 – 474.

Rege, Sharmila. 'The Hegemonic Appropriation of Sexuality: The Case of Lavani Performers of Maharashtra' in *Contributions to Indian Sociology*(1995) 29, 1 and 2, pp. 24-38.

Rege, Sharmila. Conceptualising Popular Culture: 'Lavani' and 'Powada' in Maharashtra, *Economic and Political Weekly* March 16, 2002, pp. 1038-1047.

Rao, Anupama. Summer 2011. 'Violence and Humanity: Or, Vulnerability as Political Subjectivity', *Social Research,* 78(2): 607-632.

Ross, Hamish. 2001. *Law as a Social Institution*, Oxford: Hart Publishing.

Sangari, Kumkum. May1, 1993. 'Consent, Agency and Rhetorics of Incitement', *Economic and Political Weekly,* pp. 867-882.

Siegel, Larry J. 1995. *Criminology,* 5th edn. Minneapolis/St. Paul: West Publishing Company.

Shah, Svati P. 2014. *Street Corner Secrets: Sex, Work, and Migration in the City of Mumbai*. New Delhi: Orient Blackswan.

Smart, Carol. 1976. *Women, Crime and Criminology: A Feminist Critique*. London: Routledge and Kegan Paul.

Spender, Dale. 1990. *Man Made Language*. London: Pandora.

Stewart, Ann. 2011. *Gender, Law and Justice in a Global Market*. Cambridge: Cambridge University Press.

Sunder Rajan, Rajeshwari. 2003. *The Scandal of the State: Women, Law and Citizenship in Postcolonial India*. Delhi: Permanent Black.

Sutherland, Kate. January 2005. 'Marx and MacKinnon: The Promise and Perils of Marxism for Feminist Legal Theory', *Science & Society*, 69 (1): 113–132.

Tambe, Ashwini. 2009. *Codes of Misconduct: Regulating Prostitution in Late Colonial Bombay*. Minneapolis: University of Minnesota Press.

Thornton, Margaret. 2011. 'An Inconsistent Affair: Feminism and the Legal Academy', in Martha Albertson Fineman (ed). *Transcending the Boundaries of Law: Generations of Feminism and Legal Theory*, pp. 25-39, Oxon: Routledge.

Vance, Carole S. Fall 2011. 'States of Contradiction: Twelve Ways to Do Nothing about Trafficking While Pretending To', *Social Research*, The Body and the State: How the State Controls and Protects the Body, Part II, 78(3): 933-948.

Weeks, Kathi. 2007. 'Life Within and Against Work: Affective Labor, Feminist Critique, and Post-Fordist Politics', Ephemera: *Theory & Politics in Organization,* 7(1): 233-249.

Willis, Ellen. 2009. 'Feminism, Moralism and Pornography', in Ann Snitow, Christine Stansell and Sharon Thompson (eds). 2009, *Powers of Desire: The Politics of Sexuality*, pp. 460-467, Delhi: Aakar Books.

Wolkowitz, Carol. 2006. *Bodies at Work*. London: Sage Publications.

Worrall, Anne. 1990. *Offending Women: Female Lawbreakers and the Criminal Justice System*. London: Routledge.

List of Cases

Rita Nijhawan v. Balkrishan Nijhawan in AIR 1973 Delhi 200

Chitan J. Vaswani v. State of West Bengal., (1975), 2 SCC 829.

Vishaka and Others v. State of Rajasthan and Others (JT 1997 (7) SC 384).

State of Maharashtra & Anr. v. Indian Hotel & Restaurants Assn. & Or. 2006 (3) BomCR 705.

State of Maharashtra & Anr. v. Indian Hotel & Restaurants Assn. & Or. (2013) 8 SCC 519.

12

Creative Construction: Imagining New Pathways of Worker Control

Manas Ranjan Bhowmik

"The tomorrow in today is alive," wrote Ernst Bloch. But it has to be excavated.
–Prashad 2015: 28

Section I. Introduction

This article is an attempt on excavation for a better tomorrow. Bloch's assertion is important to qualify a few definitional aspects initially. At the very outset it must be mentioned that while coining the term 'creative construction' the cue has been taken from Schumpeter's prodigious idea 'creative destruction'[2]. An idea that is excessively used yet seldom problematized. A cogent summary of the problems concerning the process of creative destruction can be found from the insights provided by Karl Marx. According to Marx's (1894: 363-364) exposition, under capitalism '...by employing new machinery, new and improved methods ... produced and continue to produce, a relative surplus population, a surplus population of workers who are not employed...'. Recent scholars like Thomas Piketty (2014), and Joseph Stiglitz (2012), while studying inequality have shown rigorously and repeatedly how capitalist development[3] is creating a huge surplus as well as unemployed population on the one side and this process is generating an enormous profit for a few capitalists on another side.

The idea of creative construction entails new, creative and innovative ways of constructing and reorganizing institutions of production not for profit but for strengthening workers' control.

Creative construction is a process that will not generate a mountain of profit at the cost of huge unemployment and exploitation of workers'; rather it ought to generate a non-exploitative, worker-controlled, community-centric and environmental-friendly production process. Here in concrete terms it is argued that workers' cooperatives can potentially subsume the idea of 'creative construction'.

The objectives of this article are the following. This article provides a microcosmic idea of a production organization form and cooperatives, which are different from the capitalist firm-organization. It is important to note that this alternative form of organization may provide some valuable insights about a non-capitalist, non-exploitative production process. In this article focus is on experimenting with alternative organizations of production (cooperatives) that aims to promote a democratically controlled and more humane production process. Also simultaneously this article is an attempt to reconceptualize worker control. It has studied the peculiar relationship between the two essential components of worker control—workers' union and workers' cooperative.

So far various scholars have studied cooperatives but mainly in the Western context. Developing country-specific works on cooperatives are limited. Hence this article is an attempt to study cooperatives and worker control with a special focus on developing country context. This article is an attempt to reconnect the theory of cooperatives with praxis. Also an attempt has been made in connecting economic logic with political implications.

The following questions are of importance. Is it possible to imagine a creative way to construct and experiment with alternative[4] producers' organizations which encapsulates better qualities than the existing capitalist firms? In this context how do we define a cooperative and how do we distinguish it from a traditional capitalist firm? Why should we consider the idea of workers' cooperatives as a valid alternative to capitalist firms? What are the advantages of cooperatives? What are the challenges of cooperatives and why are cooperatives so rare? What do experiences or empirical studies on cooperatives from all over the world teach us?

Further some intriguing political economy questions have also been raised. Can workers one day become their 'own capitalists'? Is it possible to re-conceptualize the concept of 21st century socialism based on cooperative principles? What do ground realities of the Indian economy and specificities of the Indian political economy context teach us about the cooperativist[5] path?

This article is organized as follows. In Section I introductory arguments are provided. The topic is introduced. Objectives of this article, the methodology followed and research gap have been pointed out. In Section II cooperatives are defined, different types of cooperatives are delineated and then cooperatives are compared with traditional capitalist firms. Section III argues for different perspectives that provide rationale for promoting and developing cooperatives. In Section IV a synoptic representation of theory on cooperatives especially focusing on the efficiency aspect, has been made. Also in this section a synoptic representation of empirical evidences of successful cooperatives has been offered. Section V explains the general rarity of cooperatives vis-à-vis capitalist firms. In addition to that, in this section specific factors responsible for rarity of cooperatives particularly in India have been summarized. Section VI is about new pathways of workers' control. Here while rethinking new pathways of worker control interfaces between labour unions (trade unions), state and cooperatives have been explored. Section VII is the concluding section of this article. Also in this section future areas of research have been pointed out.

Section II. Definition and Types

According to the International Cooperative Alliance or ICA (established in 1895)—'a cooperative is an autonomous association of persons united voluntarily to meet their common economic, social and cultural needs and aspirations through a jointly-owned and democratically controlled enterprise'.

As a norm, for decision-making in a cooperative–one person one vote rule has been followed (ICA principle). The fundamental difference between a cooperative and a traditional capitalist firm is the following. A cooperative is managed by the worker working in the firm at present, i.e. the decision-making right is based on the employment or labour supply, rather it is not based on the capital supply (not by shareholders). Cooperatives are also called 'Labour Managed Firm's or LMFs and capitalist firms are called 'Capital Managed Firm's or KMFs. In this article these terminologies have been used interchangeably. Here it is important to mention that in practice cooperatives are heterogeneous. Hence it is difficult to capture cooperatives under a single definition. Yet for the sake of simplicity and expositional purpose here I have considered the above popular definition of cooperatives provided by ICA.

As it is shown in Figure 1 mainly there are four types of cooperatives–producer cooperatives, consumer cooperatives, credit cooperatives and marketing cooperatives. Here in this article our main focus is on producer cooperatives.

Figure 1: Types of Cooperatives

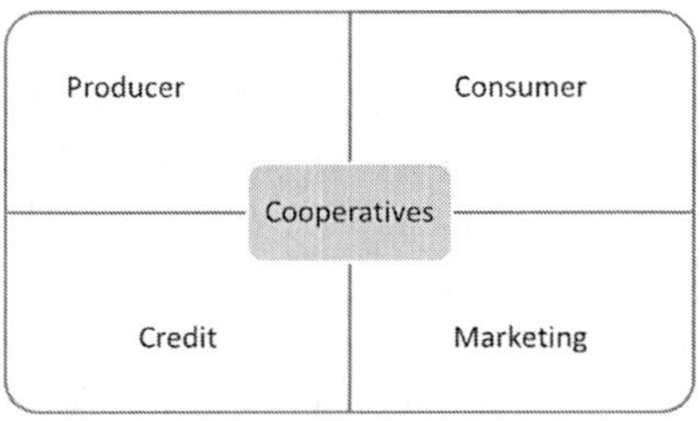

Table 1 compares LMFs and KMFs. All major decsions are taken in cooperatives through voting (one person one vote) and following a horizontal decision-making structure. On the other hand in KMFs or capitalist firms all the decisions are taken via a top-down authoritative structure. Also representation or appointing professionals or managers, is possible in cooperatives. But the difference is that here in cooperatives managers remain under supervision and answerable to workers. Due to the one person one vote principle in cooperatives power sharing, worker autonomy all these aspects are satisfied. Moreover profit sharing in cooperatives is also obligatory. In terms of worker alienation as well cooperative firms are better than capitalist frms. Wage inequality and monitoring costs would also be lower in cooperatives compared to capitalist firms. Usually cooperatives are formed using the localized workforce hence they would have an added interest in serving the local community well.

Table 1: Comparing LMF and KMF

Issues	*LMFs*	*KMFs*
Decision making	Voting- through assembly-horizontal	Top-down managerial decision-hierarchic
Power-sharing	Yes	No
Profit-sharing	Yes	No
Worker autonomy	Yes	No
Alienation	No or limited	Yes
Community participation	Obligatory	Dubious
Wage inequality	Low	High
Monitoring cost	Low	High

Section III. Rationale for Cooperatives

Marx on cooperative factories emphasizes:

> ...the cooperative factories... By deed, instead of by argument, ... shown that production on a large scale, and in accord with the behest of modern science, may be carried on without the existence of a class of masters employing a class of hands; ...like slave labour, like serf labour, hired labour is but a transitory and inferior form, destined to disappear before associated labour plying its toil with a willing hand, a ready mind, and a joyous heart (Marx 1864: 11).

Lenin even after the experience of the 1917 revolution in his article 'On Cooperation' emphasizes—'cooperation is socialism' (1923). Moving beyond Marx's and Lenin's emphasis on cooperatives here some other contemporary normative issues are discussed below that makes experimenting with cooperatives important.

First, importance of cooperation[6] is to be understood with respect to the issue of rising inequality. As per the Oxfam report (2016: 1) 'in 2015, just 62 individuals had the same wealth as 3.6 billion people—the bottom half of humanity'. Also it points out '... richest 1 per cent now have more wealth than the rest of the world combined'. In the latest International Cooperative Summit (October 2016) Nobel laureate Joseph Stiglitz claims that in USA, CEOs earn up to 300 times more than that of the average American worker. Within a typical firm the pay ratio between CEO and an average worker is skyrocketing in capitalist firms in countries like USA and various Western European countries. On the contrary most of the cooperatives follow the obligatory norm of keeping the pay differential between the highest and lowest paid worker, within the range of 6:1. Hence intra-firm wage inequality is lower in cooperatives. This feature of lower intra-firm inequality in cooperatives may have an impact on overall inequality in the society with an increase in the number of cooperatives. Moreover with the growing number of cooperatives the inequality of power on the whole in the society between the capitalists and working class might also decline.

David Schweikart (2002) has argued in favour of 'Economic Democracy', i.e. democratic management of firms and democratic management of investment. In order to reap the advantages of workers' better knowledge about shop floor information economic democracy or democratic management of firms is advocated here.

Bowles and Gintis (1990) have argued that workers' participation in governance inculcates an attitude of cooperation and concern for the others. This is because of the positive 'feedback' from output to input. Here the argument is that there is a feedback mechanism operating from production relations to the individual worker's attitude. And workers' participation in cooperatives could lead to a higher level of cooperation within the society as a whole by inculcating an attitude of cooperation among the workers.

Ruccio (2011) points out that exploitation happens in the capitalist production process in which surplus produced by the workers is appropriated by a group of people who has not produced it. In case of cooperatives, workers produce surplus value and make the decision of how to distribute the surplus value. Hence in cooperatives there is no scope for any other group to appropriate the surplus produced by workers. Hence in cooperatives exploitation does not take place.

Ellerman (1992) compares the capitalist employment contract with slavery. He and various other scholars have objected to the treatment of labour just like any other commodity. Yet there is agreement about the fact that in a capitalistic employment structure the relationship between boss and subordinates is just like the master-servant kind of relationship. A paper by Bowles and Gintis (1993) points out that such a relationship is not conducive to dignity or self-respect on the part of the subordinate. Hence in this regard the cooperative system of production owing to equal power sharing (one person one vote) is supposed to generate more equal status among workers.

Various scholars point out that KMF (capital managed firm or traditional firm) and LMF do not have equivalent implications for the surrounding community. As Dow (2003: 39) observes: '...worker-controlled firms usually favour stable employment and locally oriented investment, reinforcing the stability of the residential communities in which members live. The greater willingness of LMF members to supply local public goods, and to restrict local public bads such as pollution, also serves the interests of the surrounding community.'

Scholars like Rawls (1971), Bowles and Gintis (1996) observe that if freedom is considered as a value in itself irrespective of the economic consequences in one's life then a KMF is unable to deliver this value. Hence in this regard an LMF due to its fundamental democratic set up is potentially able to deliver this value to its worker-member.

All these issues regarding the normative perspective have encouraged this study. But a few positive issues are also pertinent. Capital has become largely unregulated at the global level since the 1970s. After this with the fall of the Soviet bloc in the world wide scale the employment situation has deteriorated. Formal sector employment, working conditions, job security on the whole–the safety net for the working class–all these have been torn apart by the neoliberal policies since then. Since the 1990s in the Indian economy many formal sector jobs have been declining. And there is a surge in the informal and unorganized sector jobs. In 1991 the formal sector employment in India was approximately 8 per cent, which was reduced to 7 per cent (approximately) around 2010 (Basu and Basole 2011). On the other hand within the formal sector also informalization is taking place. It implies that within formal sector sub-contracting of jobs to the informal sector has started (Basu and Basole 2011). Subcontracting to the informal sector has become the order of the day in the formal sector companies. Through subcontracting jobs to the informal household self-employment type enterprises, the big companies are benefiting in three ways. First, companies can reap the benefit of economies of scale while procuring the raw material. Second, by subcontracting these companies are able to cut down their labour cost or the cost related to establishing factories. Third, in this way big corporations can bypass labour regulations and workers' safety standards. Basically other than extracting surplus value through 'relative surplus value' extraction at present surplus extraction is happening through extracting the 'absolute surplus value' (Basu 2011). This absolute surplus value extraction is happening through subcontracting the work to self-employed household level by paying extremely lower piece rate wages to the worker. As a result under self employment paradigm labour has become increasingly vulnerable, de-unionized and end up working under inhuman working conditions for bare minimum subsistence wages and for longer hours. In this situation a need for an alternative model of production has become necessary. An alternative model of production which is more humane in terms of working conditions and better wages, where workers are entitled to a higher level of dignity, which could potentially transcend the workers' role far from a mere 'appendage of machines' (Marx 1867). In this regard experiments in line of the cooperative form of firm organization should be considered as a worthwhile endeavour.

As a historical perspective I need to mention that historically it has been observed that whenever capitalism faces a crisis the experimentation with alternative modes becomes imminent. The most prominent example is the Argentinian E.R. or 'occupy factory' movement after the collapse of neoliberalism in Argentina in the early 2000s (Dinerstein 2015). Also after the financial crisis of 2007 in USA unemployment surged and worker occupation of closed factories and formation of cooperatives started (Bryer 2012). In the mass movements like Occupy Wall Street and other similar movements in Europe or other developed nations, a search for an alternative economic system was intertwined with a search for an alternative production system. Hence at present the global economic crisis of capitalism is providing one more very important historical perspective to the study of the cooperative form of firm organization.

Section IV. Theory and Empirical Evidences

In discussing theoretical trajectories it is important to understand first the issue of ownership and control.

Ownership and Control

Table 2: Ownership and Control as Independent Dimensions of Firm Organization

	Asset Ownership	
	Private	Public
Control Rights	Control by capital capitalist firm	Socialist firm
	Control by labour labourist firm	Self-managed firm

Source (Dow 2003: 3)

Table 2 shows that it is possible to distinguish four separate economic systems by considering two independent dimensions of firm organization–one, the ownership of the physical assets and two, control over production. Standard capitalist firms and socialist firms, usually both types of firms assign ultimate managerial control to the capital suppliers. These capital suppliers may be private or state players. Labourist firms refer to such an arrangement in which physical assets are privately owned but firms are controlled by their employees or labour suppliers rather than capital suppliers. Self-managed firms can be identified with the Yugosloav system (1949-91) in which physical assets remain state-owned but workers control each enterprise.

Advantages of Cooperatives

A paper by Bowles and Gintis (1993: 92-93) identifies three reasons for LMFs to be more efficient than KMFs. They name them as—participation effect, mutual monitoring effect and wage incentive effect.

Figure 2: Advantages of Cooperatives

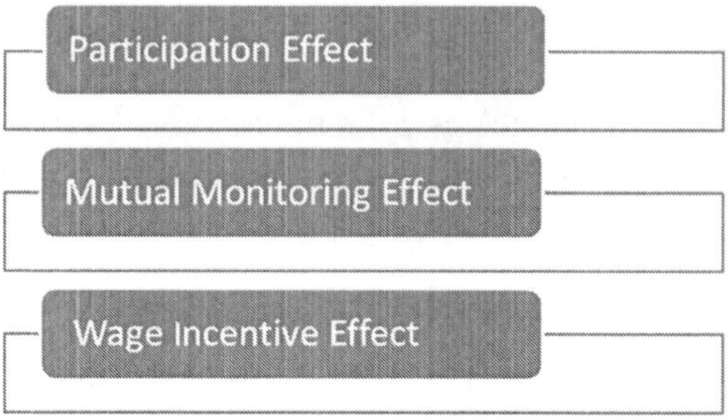

The first is the participation effect. There it is argued (Bowles and Gintis 1993: 93)–

> Our reasoning is simply that the alienation of the worker from the capitalist firm, specifically the exclusion of the worker from managerial decision-making and from ownership of the products of labour, and the contrasting integration of the worker in the democratic firm (even if quite imperfect) give the democratic firm important motivational advantages. We refer to this as the *participation effect* entailing greater efficiency in the democratic firm.

In other words here the authors try to point out the problem of alienation of workers in a KMF and impact of participation in decision-making and control, through motivational advantages for the workers in an LMF. This motivational advantage of workers potentially leads to higher productivity per worker in LMFs.

The second reason they point out, is the mutual monitoring effect. Here it is argued (Bowles and Gintis 1993: 93)—

> Workers frequently have virtually costless access to information concerning the work activities of fellow workers, and in the democratic firm each has an interest in the effort levels of other workers.The residual claimancy status of workers thus provides a motive for mutual monitoring.

Hence in LMFs due to the potentially non-existent worker-management antagonism there should be a spontaneous and free-flow of the shop-floor information. This kind of information sharing which is quite costly for KMFs would potentially make cooperatives more efficient.

The third reason is the wage incentive in cooperatives. Here it is argued (Bowles and Gintis 1993: 93)–

> ...wage offered in the capitalist eqilibrium is too low and monitoring expenditure too high. The reason is that the capitalist firm faces two prices in selecting its enforcement structure. One, the price of monitoring, correctly measure a social marginal cost, for the use of monitoring equipment or personnel entails real opportunity costs. But the other price, the wage, does not measure a real social cost. The payment of a higher wage is redistributive; it does not entail the greater use of scarce resources with alternative uses in production.

Hence KMFs keep their wage cost too low and monitoring cost too high. KMFs provide a lower wage incentive and depend on 'too much monitoring relative to an efficient alternative' (Bowles and Gintis 1993). Hence the potential gain regarding this issue is referred as wage incentive for LMFs by Bowles and Gintis.

Empirical Evidences

Empirically it is often correctly pointed out that the Mondragon Cooperative Complex in Spain is considered as one of the most successful cooperative endeavours in the world. Other than this, cooperatives in Italy's Emila Romagna region are extremely successful. Also since the early 2,000s cooperatives are flourishing in Argentina. In India sugar cooperatives of Maharashtra, dairy cooperatives of Gujarat and Andhra Pradesh have been running successfully for a long time. Kerala Dinesh is another large successful industrial cooperative complex in India, at present providing full-time employment to 6,000 people.

Section V. Boolean Analysis

A Boolean analysis has been conducted using QCA or the Qualitative Comparative Analysis technique. The fundamental concept is that cases can be denoted by formal logical statements in which the independent variables (conditions) for each case, in combination, are seen as logically implying the score of the dependent variable (outcome) for that case.

These combinations can be contrasted with each other and then logically simplified through a bottom–up process of paired comparison (Ragin 1987).

Table 3: Case Studies

Cases	*Survival (Successful)*	*Closed (Failure)*
1.Amul (Dairy)	✓	X
2. Mulkanoor (Dairy)	✓	X
3. Kerala Dinesh (Food products)	✓	X
4. New Central Jute Mill (Jute)	X	✓
5. Sonali Tea Estate (Tea)	X	✓
6. Dhaniakhali Cooperatives (Handloom)	✓	X
7. Somospur Cooperatives (Handloom)	✓	X
8. Hasnabada Weavers Society	✓	X

Conditions (Independent variable)

> MEMMOTI= Members' Motivation
› MEMSKIL= Members' Skill
› PRODINTER= Production Interdependencies
› MANAGSKI= Management's Skill
› EXTSUP= External Support

Here the dependent variable is a categorical one, measured by survival of a firm. Here survival implies success and is denoted by 1 and failure or close down of a firm is denoted by 0. And independent variables or conditions are- members' motivation, members' skill, production interdependencies, management skill, and external support. Findings of the QCA analysis using the TOSMANA software can be summarized as follows. With interdependencies in production and some amount of external support survival of cooperatives depend either on management skills or on members' motivation. With less interdependency in production just like handloom weavers' cooperatives survival may be easier.

Rarity of Cooperatives

'The cooperative factories run by workers themselves are, within the old form, the first examples of the emergence of a new form, even though they naturally reproduce in all cases, in their present organization, all the defects of the existing system, and must reproduce them. But the opposition between capital and labour is abolished there...These factories show how, at a certain stage of development of the material forces of production, and of the social forms of production corresponding to them, a new mode of production develops and is formed naturally out of the old' (Marx 1894: 571–2).

Table 4: Causes of Rarity of Cooperatives

Sl. No.	*Cause*	*Explanation/Description*
1	Horizon Problem	The horizon problem arises, for example if most of the workers in a cooperative are going to retire soon then most likely in a general assembly the majority will not vote for any such investment project which will start to yield after they retire.
2	Portfolio Problem	The portfolio problem refers to the problem of the cooperative members regarding diversification of their investments.
3	Control Problem	Issues regarding monitoring in general and evaluating managerial performance in particular.
4	Free Rider Problem	This problem arises regarding monitoring and physical asset utilization.
5	Influence Cost Problem	Due to existing diversities among members' interests in cooperatives decision-making and influencing the firm's final decision may be costly.
6	Capital Constraint	Credit rationing, inability of providing collateral may put cooperatives in a disadvantageous position while in need for credit.
7	Capitalist Takeover	Financial success may bring an end to cooperatives as it may fetch capitalist buyers with a premium price for the firm. Or it may attract capitalists to take over the firm via some other means such as power, pressure, etc.
8	Nature of Technology	Technology that cooperatives inherit is not neutral, but tends to be biased against democratic labour management of the firm, for example 'assembly line' kind of technology that produces hierarchic production structure.
9	Impact of Social Relations	Practical everyday activity of labour in capitalism reproduces and expands capitalist social relations of production, including the reproduction of authoritarian decision-making and reproduction of classes.

10	Cultural and Social Backgrounds	Hierarchical patterns are so prevalent in our society and so deeply ingrained in our minds that we are almost incapable of looking objectively at the available evidence and admit that democracy in business and in other types of organization is indeed an economically–and certainly humanely–superior structure.
11	Role of Education	From the very childhood days of schooling hierarchy is injected in the minds of the people under capitalism. And the hierarchic system in capitalist firms also basically reinforces the same effect.
12	Ideological Bias	Employees' newly revealed ability to carry more responsibility sometimes becomes too big a threat to the established way of doing things and to established power patterns.
13	Role of Government and Union	The role of government remains somewhat disappointing in promoting cooperatives. Also in multiple cases workers' unions have acted against workers' occupation of factories.
14	Shelter Organization and Cooperative Culture	Linkages with support organization for input procurement, credit availability, and marketing support–all these are important for the success of cooperatives.

The horizon problem may be best explained by using the following example. If most of the workers in a cooperative are going to retire soon then most likely in a general assembly the majority will not vote for any such investment project which will start to yield after they retire. The portfolio problem refers to the problem of the cooperative's members about diversification of their investments. Issues regarding monitoring in general and evaluating managerial performance in particular come under the control problem. The free rider problem arises regarding monitoring workers and optimally using physical assets. Prevailing diversities in members' interests in cooperatives may make decision-making costly and difficult. Credit rationing and inability of providing collateral may put cooperatives in a disadvantageous position while obtaining loans. Financial success may also bring an end to a cooperative as it may fetch capitalist buyers with a premium price for the firm. Or it may attract capitalists to take over the firm via some other means such as power, pressure, etc. Technology that cooperatives inherit is not neutral, but tends to be biased against democratic labour management of the firm, for example 'assembly line' kind of technology that produces a hierarchic production structure. Practical everyday activity of labour in capitalism reproduces and expands capitalist social relations of production, including the reproduction of authoritarian decision-making and reproduction of classes. Hierarchical patterns are so prevalent in our society and so deeply ingrained in our minds that we are almost incapable of looking objectively at the available evidence and admit that democracy in business and in other types of organization is indeed an economically–and certainly humanely–superior structure. From the very childhood days of schooling hierarchy is injected in the minds of the people in capitalism. And the hierarchic system in capitalist firms also basically reinforces the same effect. Employees' newly revealed ability to carry more responsibility sometimes becomes too big a threat to the established way of doing things and to established power patterns. The role of government remains somewhat dismaying in promoting LMFs worldwide. Also sometimes workers' unions have acted against worker's occupation of factories. Linkages with a support organization for input procurement, credit availability and marketing support are essential ingredients for the success of cooperatives.

Table 5: Factors Specific to India

SL. No.	*Factors*	*Description*
1.	Management	Crucial for a cooperative's success
2.	Government intervention	Important for credit provisioning and tax benefits
3.	Interlinked market -dyadic	Exercise of power when at least two markets are inter-linked
4.	Interlinked market –triadic	Exercise of power with interlinkage and third party
5.	Leadership	Charismatic leadership a key element for a successful cooperative
6.	Identity	For cohesion and motivation

Table 5 summarizes factors that play a crucial role for the success of cooperatives in India. Management either hired or exogenously provided or provided by the government has remained very important for the success of the cooperative. Government intervention remains important especially at the time of formation of cooperatives, through provisioning of concessional credit and other benefits such as tax benefits. Inter-linked markets in rural areas actually have acted as a barrier to entry for agricultural cooperatives. If a farmer takes a loan from a moneylender and has to sell the crop to that moneylender and in the process the price of crop and the interest on loan would be adjusted then this kind of transaction is an example of dyadic inter-linked transaction. Through the channel of credit provisioning here the moneylender may create a barrier for the farmer and narrow his window of selling and also can act as an entry barrier for agricultural cooperatives. It implies that owing to the debt trap designed by the moneylender even if the farmer wants then also he may not be able to join a cooperative. Moreover due to the prevalence of dyadic inter-linkage a third party or another seller of inputs may prevent the small farmer from selling input in order to satisfy and safeguard his interaction with the big moneylender. This is called triadic inter-linkage problem. Such types of dyadic and triadic interlinkages are prevalent in rural India afflicting Indian agriculture and acting as strong barriers to entry for agricultural cooperatives. Also this analysis of interlinkage can explain the lower formation rate of agricultural cooperatives in India. Other than these, sometimes charismatic leadership acts an important ingredient for the success of cooperatives. Similarly leadership issues have remained responsible for failure of cooperatives in India. Also caste, religion, and political party membership sometimes play a crucial role in harnessing coordinated group behaviour among workers and remain important for the performance of cooperatives.

Section VI. New Pathways of Worker Control: Trade Unions, State and Cooperatives

Theory and empirical evidences say that the relationship between cooperatives and trade unions is not so straightforward. A few contentious issues initially are considered here. One, if workers can address all their problems through cooperatives then why do they need trade unions? Two, is there any potential conflict of interest about forming and promoting cooperatives from a trade union's perspective? Three, the role of workers within a cooperative may confuse their relationship with the trade union. This is because a worker in a cooperative is not merely a wage-worker, rather here he becomes a worker-owner. Hence his usual class position is perturbed here and usual class enemy, i.e. the management is perturbed.

Theoretically Moene (1989 : 93) compares two different systems–one a system of capitalist firms with strong unions (Social Democracy) and two a system of worker cooperatives. He shows that the former system would suffer from two issues– one, comparatively unstable employment in the short run and two, the problem of underinvestment. Empirically as well instances of promoting cooperatives by trade unions remain limited in India and abroad. Yet some empirical evidences are necessary to point out here. In the 1990s due to the crisis of neoliberalism in South America hundreds of worker-owned enterprises emerged with full support of unions. A specific case is the example of Forja, the largest forge in South America formed with the backing of ABC Metalworkers' union of the Central Unica des Trabalhadores *(CUT)*. In Argentina workers taking over and running bankrupt and closed factories became a movement, 'Empressas Recuperdas' since 2000. Here also unions played a crucial role in some cases (Laliberté, 2003). In India Self-Employed Women's Association (SEWA) is a case in point.

Figure 3: Role of Trade Unions

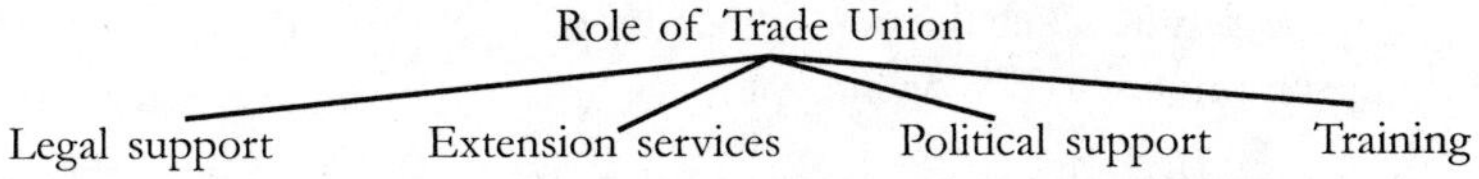

Based on my field work and the literature it is possible to point out at least four concrete ways of intervention of unions in promoting cooperatives. Here legal support refers to the legal need that arises especially during the formation of new cooperatives or restructuring and taking over old companies. In this period unions may play an active role in leading workers to become their own capitalists. Second, specifically workers in general and particularly in India lack vision and necessary skills of marketing and accounting (author's field work and Bryer 2012). Hence in this regard unions may guide cooperatives. Third, in order to form new cooperatives a larger political support is often necessary in order to obtain credit and tax support. Hence unions through their machinery and networks can create a political mobilization that can strengthen the case for cooperatives. Fourth, it is extremely important to provide training to the worker-owners in cooperatives so that they can adapt to their new roles and responsibilities.

Moreover it is also reported by many scholars that especially in the Indian context too much government intervention and politicization have also acted against the interest of cooperatives (Mukund, Shyamsundari 1998). Hence in this regard unions may provide practical guidelines about the extent of government intervention.

Political Implication, 21st Century Socialism- Utopia, Dystopia, Ray of Hope

Following Lebowitz's argument (2016: 1) it is possible to conceptualize 21st century socialism :

> Often the best way to begin to understand something is to consider what it is not. It is not ...capitalism. Nor is it a statist society where decisions are top-down and where all initiative is the property of state officeholders...Also socialism for the 21st century is not populism. A society in which people look to the state to provide them with resources and with the answers to all their problems...It is not totalitarianism. It is not a society in which the state demands uniformity in productive activity, consumption choices, or lifestyles.

Now the relevant question here is how to go there from here? Here in this article an attempt has been made to propose the cooperativist path to go there. In this article the argument is that the cooperativist path is absolutely central to this particular idea of 21st century socialism. And in this article one of the central arguments is that cooperatives need not only be considered as the final goal, rather development of cooperatives and associated political mobilization should be considered as a viable means to achieve this goal. As Lenin (1923) says 'cooperation is socialism', this article also argues for a radical reconceptualization of the 'goal' that is 21st century socialism as well as 'means' which is the cooperativist path. In this section 'alleged utopian' conceptualization, dystopian experiences and the possible way forward are analysed. Here a concrete example of decline of the traditional left movement in West Bengal, India is considered as a case in point.

After achieving remarkable success in the assembly election in West Bengal, the Left Front government has ruled the state continuously for 34 years (1977-2011). After that it has lost an election in 2011 for several reasons. My contention here is not to judge or analyse this long left regime of the state of West Bengal. Rather in this section my contention is to judge the decline of this left regime with respect to the central argument of this article. Only two related questions are addressed here. What economic rationales explain the decline of the left regime in West Bengal? Can worker cooperatives offer help in engineering a resurgence of the left movement in future?

About the first question two points need to be mentioned–one, in villages this regime was popular among farmers due to its land reform policies–'operation barga', patta. And two, in urban and semi-urban areas this left regime was popular among industrial workers due to its successful penetration in trade union activities. Eventually since the mid-1990s agriculture has become unviable and trade unions also have lost their glory due to enormous expansion of the unorganized sector. Widely reported present ground reality in West Bengal is on the one hand agriculture which has become unviable for many farmers and a pool of unorganized un-unionized workers searching for decent employment opportunities. Hence providing land right or the old slogan of 'land to the tiller' is not enough. On the other hand it is even more difficult to unionize unorganized workers. Hence the question arises–what is to be done to engineer a resurgence of left in West Bengal. This particular issue leads us to the answer to our second question.

Can we not think of a left resurgence following a hitherto uncharted route in West Bengal? With respect to agrarian questions, Bidwai (2015: 340) proposes : '...collective farming based on sharing labour and other inputs and resources in agricultural production...

Cooperatives could play a central role in such an effort.' Also about organizing the unorganized sector workers, Bidwai points out (2015: 343):

> ...a better strategy, which might consist in creating associations or cooperatives of workers in the unorganized sector, which are treated favourably in respect of government contracts and credit through an explicit affirmative action programme.

This type of activism would potentially generate a social embeddedness for the left parties and dividend from this type of embeddedness would go far beyond narrow calculation of vote share and seats. With respect to the recent rout of the left parties in West Bengal and in India this social embeddedness with the community through the cooperativist path, according to this author, is a quintessential point to ponder over. According to various scholars moving beyond the electoral calculation left parties in Kerala has been able to establish this kind of social embeddedness through their struggle for literacy and education. As a result of it even after electoral loss the LDF (Left Democratic Front) in Kerala was not routed like the case of the Left Front in West Bengal. Here the point is that through the workers' cooperative movement it is possible to establish the social embeddedness with the masses.

Section VII. Conclusion

> The future, like the present and the past, belongs to mixed economies in which public and private are braided together in one way or another. But how? That is the problem for everybody today, but especially for people on the left (Hobsbawm 2009).

Following Hobsbawm this article is an attempt to develop Marxian reconceptualization about future organizations 'in which public and private are braided together in one way or another'. And it is argued here that 'workers' cooperatives may be considered as one of these forms. In this article a synoptic presentation of the theoretical literature on cooperatives is provided. Delving in detail in any of these theoretical paths remains beyond the scope of this article. Rather the focus remains in connecting theory and praxis. Practically useful interconnections are developed in this article. New pathways of worker control have been considered. Crucial linkages between trade unions and cooperatives are studied. Moreover probable interfaces between the two and concrete ways of building alternative paths of struggle have been pointed out. The QCA technique is used to perform an exploratory Boolean analysis and the result of the analysis has actually strengthened the central argument of this article. Also factors responsible for rarity of cooperatives have been studied. Moreover factors specific to the Indian economy posing further challenges to cooperatives have been highlighted here.

In India unavailability of systematic longitudinal data sets on cooperatives is acting as an impediment to undertake any systematic empirical analysis on cooperatives. In order to do empirical analysis on cooperatives one has to depend on case studies or primary survey methods. This study can be extended by including more case studies. Also using the categorical variables a logistic regression may be conducted. Other than this sector-specific institutional comparison can be done using methodologies of New Institutional Economics.

Many future works may come about in the above mentioned areas. And this article may act as a threshold of those endeavours in providing an overview and delineating fundamental problems. With this robust theoretical and empirical understanding, it is attempted to nurture and chalk out new pathways of organizing workers for revolutionary praxis in the long run.

NOTES

1. This article is a result of research undertaken by the author under a Minor Research Project grant provided by the University Grants Commission. Hence the author is extremely grateful to the UGC for financial support. Also for the invaluable all-round support the author is thankful to the institution Ramakrishna Mission Vidyamandira.
2. 'The fundamental impulse that sets and keeps the capitalist engine in motion comes from the new consumers' goods, the new methods of production or transportation, the new markets, the new forms of industrial organization that capitalist enterprise creates' (Schumpeter 1942: 82).
3. 'The opening up of new markets, foreign or domestic, and the organizational development from the craft shop and factory to such concerns as US Steel illustrate the same process of industrial

mutation—...—that incessantly revolutionizes the economic structure *from within,* incessantly destroying the old one, incessantly creating a new one. This process of Creative Destruction is the essential fact about capitalism. It is what capitalism consists in and what every capitalist concern has got to live in' (Schumpeter 1942: 83).

4. Here alternative implies alternative to capitalist firm organization.
5. Two paths of worker control are considered here – 1) trade unionist path and 2) cooperativist path. First is attaining and exercising worker control through workers' unions. And second is attaining and exercising worker control by developing workers' cooperatives.
6. In this article cooperation and cooperatives have been used interchangeably. The usage of the term cooperation must be understood with respect to cooperatives and not in general.

REFERENCES

Alchian, Armen A. and Harold Demsetz. 1972. 'Production, Information Costs, and Economic Organization', *American Economic Review* 62(5): 777-795.

Bardhan, Pranab K. and John E. Roemer. 1993. eds., *Market Socialism:The Current Debate.* New York: Oxford University Press.

Bardhan, Pranab. 1993. 'Economics of Development and the Development of Economics', *The Journal of Economic Perspectives*, 7(2): 129-142.

Basu, Deepankar and Amit Basole. 2011. 'Relations of Production and Modes of Surplus Extraction in India: Part I- Agriculture', *Economic and Political Weekly*, XLVI(14): 41-58.

Basu, Deepankar and Amit Basole. 2011. 'Relations of Production and Modes of Surplus Extraction in India: Part II- 'Informal' Industry', *Economic and Political Weekly*, XLVI(15): 63-79.

Basu, Kaushik. 2000. *Analytical Development Economics*. New York: Oxford University Press.

Bidwai, Praful. 2015. *The Phoenix Moment: Challenges Confronting the Indian Left.* New Delhi: HarperCollins Publishers.

Bowles, Samuel. 1985. 'The Production Process in a Competitive Economy: Walrasian, Neo-Hobbsian, and Marxian Models', *American Economic Review* 75(1): 16-36.

Bowles, Samuel and Herbert Gintis. 1976. *Schooling in Capitalist America: Educational Reform and the Contradictions of Economic Life.* New York: Basic Books.

Bowles, Samuel and Herbert Gintis. 1990. 'Contested Exchange: New Microfoundations of the Political Economy of Capitalism', *Politics and Society* 18(2): 165-222.

Bowles, Samuel and Herbert Gintis. 1993. 'A Political and Economic Case for the Democratic Enterprise', *Economics and Philosophy* 9(1): 75-100.

Bowles, Samuel and Herbert Gintis. 1996. 'Is the Demand for Workplace Democracy Redundant in a Liberal Economy?', in Ugo Pagano and Robert Rowthorn, eds., *Democracy and Efficiency in the Economic Enterprises*, pp. 64-81. New York: Routledge.

Bradley, Keith and Alan Gelb. 1983. *Cooperation at Work: The Mondragon Experience.* London: Heinemann Educational Books.

Braverman, Harry. 1974. *Labor and Monopoly Capital: The Degeneration of Work in the Twentieth Century.* New York: Monthly Review Press.

Bryer, Alice R. 2012. 'The Politics of Social Economy: A Case Study of Argentinian E*mpressas Recuperadas'*, *Dialectical Anthropology* 36(1-2): 21-49.

Coase, Ronald H. 1937. 'The Nature of Firm', *Economica* 4 (16): 386-405.

Coase, Ronald H. 1960. 'The Problem of Social Cost', *Journal of Law and Economics* 3: 1-44.

Craig, Ben and John Pencavel. 1993. 'The Objectives of Worker Cooperatives', *Journal of Comparative Economics* 17(2): 288-308.

Doucouliagos, Chris. 1990. 'Why Capitalist Firms Outnumber Labour-Managed Firms', *Review of Radical Political Economy*, 22(4): 44-67.

Doucouliagos, Chris. 1995. 'Worker Participation and Productivity in Labour-Managed Firms and Participatory Capitalist Firms: A Meta-Analysis', *Industrial and Labour Relations Review,* 49(1): 58-77.

Dow, Gregory K. 2003. *Governing the Firm: Workers' Control in Theory and Practice.* Cambridge: Cambridge University Press.

Dinerstein, Ana Cecilia. 2015. *The Politics of Autonomy in Latin America: The Art of Organizing Hope.* UK: Palgrave Macmillan.

Ellerman, David P. 1992. *Property and Contract in Economics: The Case for Economic Democracy.* Oxford: Blackwell.

Hobsbawm, Eric. 'Socialism Has Failed. Now Capitalism is Bankrupt. So What Comes Next?' 2009. *The Guardian.* April 10.

Jossa, Bruno. 2005. 'Marx, Marxism and Cooperative Movement', *Cambridge Journal of Economics*, 29: 3-18.

Laliberte, Pierre. 2013. Editorial, *International Journal of Labour Research*, 5(2): (172-177).

Lenin, V.I. 1923. 'On Cooperation'. https://www.marxists.org/archive/lenin/works/1923/jan/06.htm (accessed on September 25, 2016).

Marglin, Stephen A. 1974. 'What Do Bosses Do? The Origins and Functions of Hierarchy in Capitalist Production', *Review of Radical Political Economics* 6(2): 60-112.

Marx, Karl. 1864. Inaugural Address of the Working Men's Association The First International. https://www.marxists.org/archive/marx/works/

1864/10/27.htm (Accessed on September 25, 2016).

Marx, Karl. 1867 [1977]. *Capital: A Critique of Political Economy*, Vol. 1, New York, Vintage Books.

Marx, Karl. 1894, *Capital,* Vol. 3, London. Penguin Classic Edition.

Moene, Karl. Ove. 1989.'Strong Unions or Worker Control?', in Jon Elster and Karl Ove Moene (eds.), *Alternatives to Capitalism*, pp. 83-97. Paris: Cambridge University Press.

Mukund Kanakalatha and B. Shyamsundari. 1998. 'Doomed to Fail? 'Handloom Weavers' Coopearatives in Andhra Pradesh', *Economic and Political Weekly*, 33 (52): 3323-3332.

Prashad, Vijay. 2015. *No Free Left: The Futures of Indian Communism*. New Delhi: LeftWord Books.

Putterman, Louis and Randall Kroszner. 1986. eds., *The Economic Nature of the Firm: A Reader,* 1st Edition, Cambridge: Cambridge University Press.

Ragin, Charles C. 1987. *The Comparative Method: Moving Beyond Qualitative and Comparative Strategies*, Berkeley: University of California Press.

Rawls, John. 1971. *Theory of Justice*, Cambridge: The Belknap Press of Harvard University Press.

Ruccio, David F. 2011. 'Cooperative, Surplus and Social', *Rethinking Marxism*, 23(3): 334-340.

Schumpeter, Joseph. 1942. *Capitalism,Socialism and Democracy*, London and New York: Routledge.

Schweickart, David. 2002. *After Capitalism*. Oxford: Rowman & Littlefield Publishers, Inc.

Stiglitz, J. 2012. *The Price of Inequality: How Today's Divided Society Endangers Our Future*. USA: W.W. Norton & Company.

Web sites

https://ica.coop/en/what-co-operative

Reports

Oxfam report 2016

https://www.oxfam.org/sites/www.oxfam.org/files/file_attachments/ bp210-economy-one-percent-tax-havens-180116-en_0.pdf (Accessed on September 20, 2016).

Software

Cronqvist, Lasse. 2016. Tosmana [Version 1.521]. University of Trier. Internet: https://www.tosmana.net/

13

Reworking Notions of the 'Trade Union' and Organized Labour: Issues of Identity, Ecology and Technology in Imaginations of the *Chhattisgarh Mukti Morcha* in Central India*[1]

Radhika Krishnan

The decades of the 1970s and the 80s were a period of interrogation in India, characterized in many ways by intense contestation of the reigning notions of 'development', 'technology' and progress. It was an era when the so-defined 'social movements'—spearheaded in Ghanshyam Shah's articulation by peasants, Adivasis, Dalits, Backward Castes, women and the industrial working class—attempted to rework the existing social, economic and political discourse.[1] If the period saw intense and diverse challenges to notions of 'development' and technology, it is not surprising that the working class too was a part of this process of questioning and dissent. This period saw a variety of working class mobilizations; for instance, apart from factory and workplace-based trade union struggles for wages and better working conditions, there were also attempts to mobilize workers in the unorganized sector (such as home-based garment workers and street vendors) and protracted

* This paper, whose draft was presented at the International Conference on 'Marxism and Contrremporary South Asia: References and Issues' organized by the South Asian University and the Rosa Luxemburg Stiftung, appeared in the *Economic & Political Weekly* (5 August 2017, Vol. LII, No. 32), 62-70.

militant struggles by fisher people in Kerala, Odisha, Goa and elsewhere. In the context of the larger churning that was happening, one is however also prompted to ask: how was organized labour responding to new issues that were emerging—issues of ecological conservation and environmental damage, issues of technology, and issues of identity, for instance? For struggles happening in resource-rich areas where local economies are heavily dependent on the use of natural resources, how were concerns of the working class articulated? When a massive industrial project comes up in a predominantly rural area with a largely agrarian economy, when peasants enter the factory shop or the mine pit in search of a livelihood, do contradictions arise in their minds? It is precisely in this context that the experiences, experiments and campaigns of the Chhattisgarh Mukti Morcha [the Chhattisgarh Liberation Front, henceforth referred to as the CMM] need to be examined.[2]

Moving Beyond "Economism": Envisaging Workers' Struggles in Chhattisgarh

Existing analyses of the CMM's campaigns amongst workers have pointed out two striking features: the CMM's efforts to organize contractual labour and address their problems, and the attempt to move beyond what is often termed as 'economism' in the trade union movement. Niyogi's efforts to mobilize contractual labour was arguably a new experiment in the 1970s and 80s. It was a period when casualization and contractualization of the workforce had not yet reached contemporary levels, and in the existing culture of trade union practice in Chhattisgarh, contractual labour was more often than not outside the vision of the 'traditional' trade union. In choosing to organize contract workers, Niyogi was in a sense moving out of the comfortable confines of the organized labour sector, and foregrounding issues of identity and dignity in the process. As we shall see in the following sections of this paper, the CMM's attempts to merge the social and the political with the 'economic' was not confined to organizing contractual labour—rather, it played out in several other interesting ways.

Niyogi argued that trade unions "need the illumination of social emancipation *along* with economic struggles, not just the darkness of economism".[3] Clearly, the CMM's campaigns reflected at least some of this understanding, prompting various observers of this movement to take note. A report published by the People's Union for Democratic Rights (PUDR) mentions that the workers' struggles led by the CMM "transcended the much narrower traditional boundaries of trade union movement" and went beyond the routine demands for wages and better working conditions.[4] Reviewing *Sangharsh aur Nirman* (a compilation of Niyogi's writings, speeches, interviews and campaigns which includes commentaries by people who worked closely with Niyogi), Subramaniam writes, "In an era in which trade unionism is drawn more and more into the mire of economism, Niyogi and his Chhattisgarh Mines Shramik Sangh (CMSS) stand out for their political commitment to the revolutionary transformation of every conceivable aspect of life."[5] He adds that Niyogi combined the trade union movement struggles for wages and better working conditions "with the political goals of the democratic movement."

Dr. Binayak Sen, who was involved in various ways with the CMM's programmes, makes a similar observation. According to Sen, Niyogi created a "counter-culture" in Chhattisgarh through his attempts to construct a new 'model' of development and through campaigns where economic struggles went hand in hand with political-social-cultural efforts touching almost all aspects of people's lives.[6] For Sitaram Shastri too, an important aspect of the CMM's work was its ability to see a person not merely as a mineworker or an employee in a factory fighting for his/her economic rights.[7] In describing the CMM's struggles in Chhattisgarh, Anil Nauriya is even more explicit: "A trade union which isolates itself from the problems of society at large soon finds that the rest of society too does not stand by it...The Chhattisgarh movements have made an important contribution in this respect...[here] there is no contradiction between trade union activities and larger areas of concern.[8]

The debate on economism, in fact, has a long history. At the beginning of the 20th century, Lenin had warned trade unions not to focus exclusively on "the relations between the workers *in a given trade* and their employers."[9] Lenin also asserted here that trade unions should not feed "on the thin gruel of 'economic' politics alone"; they should rather "learn the details of *all* aspects of political life" and "take part *actively* in every single political event", he added.[10] What is interesting in the CMM's campaigns is not merely the fact that attempts were made to break away from economism. Surely there have been several attempts in the long history of workers' struggles to move beyond issues of wages and working conditions. What is interesting is the unique shape that such attempts took in a place like Chhattisgarh in Central India where a mega industrial project such as the Bhilai Steel Plant (BSP) had shaken the social and economic lives of people, for better or for worse. What was the exact nature of the "counter-culture" that Sen refers to? When the CMM tried to link the trade union movement with the larger "democratic movement", when it addressed "every conceivable aspect of life", did it see 'workers', 'peasants' and 'Adivasis' as neat and distinct categories that had little to do with each other?

Weaving Red with Green

In the 1970s and 80s, the CMM's campaigns in Chhattisgarh against the BSP management and the private companies in and around the Bhilai-Durg area, and against the Madhya Pradesh government, highlighted several demands. Abolition of the contract labour, fair wages, enhanced bonuses, provident funds, gratuity, leaves, better working conditions and more facilities for workers and their families – all these figured in the CMM's campaigns. But this was by no means their only focus. The 'red and green' flag of the CMM perhaps indicates how Niyogi and the CMM chose to frame their response to the industrial and technological regimes that the BSP stood for. For the CMM, basic needs of the worker could no longer be ensured merely through militant struggles for industrial employment, wages and bonuses. Implicit in the CMM's campaigns was an understanding that one also needed to confront managements for ruining local economies, for destroying rural livelihoods and endangering local resources.[11]

The narrative of how the CMM began its engagement with the

environmental question is fascinating, even as it is instructive for those concerned with the theory and practice of the battle against 'economism'. Headloads of timber collected by villagers in the Dondi Lohara forests surrounding the Dalli Rajhara iron ore mines had been confiscated by the local forest department and removing of timber by peasants was deemed "illegal" by the state's fiat. A disgruntled peasant came to the union office asking for help. As the CMM sought to intervene, it found itself searching for a response to questions of ecological balance, resource use and misuse, and human interventions within local ecosystems. Gradually, the debates and discussions that followed led to the articulation of an official "environment policy". We find in this narrative an intriguing story of how a 'trade union' came to realize that its members were not only mineworkers. Even as workers dug iron ore from the bowels of the earth, they were simultaneously members of a community which had to deal with water rendered bloody-red as a result of their toils; their neighbours and families were being hounded by the police, declared "trespassers" of the nearby forest; agricultural inputs in their village were getting more expensive by the day. The demands they began to articulate underwent a gradual metamorphosis, in an expression of this changed understanding of the role of a "trade union".

For the CMM, the "eminent domain" policy of state control over forests went against the traditional Adivasi culture and custom of community ownership and community responsibility over resource use and resource protection. The CMM thus argued that forest dwellers themselves were best suited to look after and protect forests from "thieves" and poachers, rather than forest rangers employed by the state. It came up with a proposal to convert the ubiquitous police stations in the forests with *paryavaran thanas* (environmental stations), replacing the figure of the police and the much-hated forest ranger with the forest-dweller. It was a move which the CMM felt would simultaneously help in ensuring proper protection of the environment and providing employment opportunities.[12]

Flowing logically from this criticism of forest policy was the

CMM's opposition to the idea of captive plantations and monocultures.[13] The CMM started the "*Apne Jungle ko Pehchano, Apne Parivaar ko Pehchano*" [know your forest, know your family] campaign, to rethink connections with the local forest, in the process local forest ecologies were recognized for their ability to sustain and nurture. The CMM's somewhat romantic equation of the 'forest' with the 'family' apart, the actual nature of the campaign however was not quite within the same idealist frame, grounded as it was in an attempt to discover and reclaim material connections with the forest. Use and misuse of water and forests as an industrial resource also entered the CMM's agenda. Rejecting economistic "common sense" that would possibly argue that a trade union should defend workers' jobs by demanding an assured water supply for industries, the CMM opposed excessive water extraction as well as industrial water pollution.

Opposition to the big-dam project—an opposition equally based on displacement of lives and the ecological destruction caused—was a central part of the CMM's ecological framework. '*Baandh nahi banega*' [the dam will not be built] was one of the CMM's slogans, as it launched campaigns against large dams, and built a critique to bolster its arguments for construction of small-scale stop dams, lift-irrigation systems and borewells. Besides, the 'Green Revolution' package came in for criticism, with the CMM predicting that it would lead to "failed dreams", farmers' woes and ecological destruction.[14] Thus, what began as a response to an indigenous peasant's problems with the local forest ranger, gradually developed into a larger perspective.

Exploring Technological Choice: Addressing Production, Employment and Technology

At the CMM office, close to the now abandoned mines, one is confronted with multiple narratives of how and when the "red and green" came together in the local imagination to frame a fresh ecological engagement with the industrial project. At another level, however, the story of Dalli Rajhara is simultaneously a narrative of skills, learning, systematic deskilling and relearning. The introduction of capital-intensive technology and industry in a predominantly agrarian, subsistence economy is rarely an uncontested process. New technological regimes and knowledge systems often collide with existing ones, and this process can result in the creation of new structures, knowledge and methods of interaction. The manner in which this played out in the Dalli Rajhara mines has been explored in some detail elsewhere.[15]

One has to point out that the CMM was operating in a context where large-scale mechanization and subsequent mass retrenchment was an ever-looming spectre as far as organized labour was concerned. When the CMM started operating in the Dalli Rajhara mines, manual mining was employed to extract the iron ore. The manual mining operations were to be subsequently replaced, after some decades, by completely mechanized operations. In between however the CMM—working with some engineers who volunteered to make the Dalli Rajhara mines office their home and assist the workers in working out fresh technological choices – came up with the idea of '*ardh-mashinikaran*', semi-mechanization. What was this option of "semi-mechanization"? It was essentially an innovation in the industrial process; a reordering, if you like, of the process in order to ensure more participation of human labour. It involved a restructuring of the production lines, replacement of machinery, as well as a reallocation of duties performed by labour. In this semi-mechanized process, it is the jaw crusher rather than human labour which is now rendered obsolete.

In this debate on mechanization with the Bhilai Steel Plant management, mineworkers had to deal with the alien vocabulary of 'efficiency', 'productivity' and 'quality'. The workers moreover saw an essential and interesting difference between technique/technology and the machine, stating that 'taknik', technique or technology was not solely resident in the machine, and in fact human labour was the primary repository as well as keeper of 'taknik', technique and technology. In dealing with the shifting technological paradigms, the mineworkers and the CMM articulated a curious, and perhaps nebulous desire, to 'internalize' technology. Labour cooperatives, workshops and garages were opened; workers assured the management they would handle part of the mining cycle themselves through their labour cooperatives and without the intervention of labour contractors. The cooperatives faced various challenges, and had to constantly improvise, innovate and create technological solutions to keep production going.[16] In the process, a counter-culture of cooperation was sought to be created, where competition would be replaced with collectivity and constructive activity. It was, moreover, a dialogue that refused to see "technology" as a static entity that had to be "received" passively by labour.

Rather than an uncritical acceptance of technological choices presented to the working class as *fait accompli*, the CMM thus attempted to change the frame of the debate by posing an alternative model of technology and industrialization. For the CMM, genuine needs could be met by protecting the livelihoods of farmers and workers in various small-scale industries—the potter, the weaver, the ironsmith and the manual mineworker were to be the mainstay of economy in the CMM's framework.[17] Industrial development was thus sought to be seen as a seamless part of a larger project which included rural and agricultural development, a project whose complex contours was articulated in several ways. Moreover, the CMM rejected the notion that technology could be "value-neutral"; it identified two kinds of technologies: *deshpremi* [patriotic] and *deshdrohi* [anti-national] while choosing the employment-generating capacity of technology to be one of the important benchmarks to identify its suitability and "patriotic" content. Unlike the All India Trade Union Congress (affiliated to the Communist Party of India), which tended to see inherent "socialist" benefits accruing to labour due to technology imported from the then USSR, the CMM sought to evaluate technology through the prism of workers' experiences.

"Dhartiputra" versus "Shramputra": Creating an Alternative Discourse on Identity[18]

In the 1950s and 60s, technicians, engineers, bureaucrats, workers, traders and businessmen from different parts of the country swarmed to Bhilai and the neighbouring industrial centres which mushroomed in the BSP's wake. Migrants came to settle in these villages, drawn by the prospect of employment or displaced from their own villages. The dynamics of labour in the region around Bhilai, and in other parts of Chhattisgarh too, could thus hardly remain impervious to the complexities that the migrant labour inevitably posed.

The "outsider" in the dominant Chhattisgarhi discourse is a source of shame, hurt and anger; the archetypal trader, industrialist, "skilled" worker or educated "officer" from "outside" who makes a living in Chhattisgarh at the cost of the "local" *Chhattisgarhiya*. This economic subjugation and dominance apart, matters are not mended by a long history of a sense of lost esteem, fuelled by the picture painted by the "outsider" of an 'uncivilized' *Chhattisgarhiya* who is lazy and unenterprising and eats *baasi* [spoilt rice] to boot.[19]

The landscape, economy and livelihoods in several villages in and around the Dalli Rajhara region where the CMM began its work, nested between the Killekoda, Dalli, Jharan Dalli, Rajhara and Mahamaya hills, had been irrevocably altered by the establishment of the iron ore mines. These villages—Aramukasa, Burkalkasa and Adjal for instance—had been home to land and forest-based communities. As their very names (which are in Gondi) suggest, these villages were predominantly inhabited by the *Gond* Adivasis. Even in the surrounding plains, a sizable portion of the population was made up by Adivasis and the "lower caste" Dalits, Kurmis and Kalars. With the establishment of the Bhilai Steel Plant and the iron ore mines in Dalli Rajhara, the local Adivasi and 'backward caste' population found themselves working as contract labour in the mines, as opposed to the non-*Chhattisgarhiya* migrants who were permanently employed. The CMM, concentrating as it was on organizing contract labour which was largely drawn from the "local" *Chhattisgarhiya* population, was well aware of the *Chhattisgariya* sense of hurt and humiliation, and also of the real material foundations on which this sentiment was built.

The CMM movement in Dalli Rajhara began as an expression of dissent against the differential wages paid to contract and permanent labour in the mines. The existing demographic reality of the area however ensured that this dissent was necessarily embedded in tensions over identity. The perceptions of injustice were fostered not just by the differential wages, but by a strong sense that the "local", the Adivasi and *Chhattisgarhi/Gondi* speaking worker was not welcome even in the local union office, then controlled by the AITUC.[20] As the CMM sought to organize the (predominantly "local", Adivasi) contract labourers, it framed their demands as a question of dignity: for the CMM, the quest for homes and equal wages was essentially a quest for self-respect. At the root of the unrest in Dalli Rajhara was a clear sense of alienation and discrimination that was far more than merely "economic", and it was precisely this sentiment that the CMM grappled with. In the process, dignity and wages came together as combined concerns; the "economic" and the "social" intermingled and transmutated.

The CMM moreover attempted to address the perceived sense of inferiority of the Chhattisgarhi by invoking and encouraging respect for the Chhattisgarhi identity, its people, its languages, metaphors and traditions. The CMM movement ensured that Chhattisgarhi men and women, such as Anasuya Bai and Janaklal Thakur, emerged as leaders within the organization. The resistance of the *Chhattisgarhi* workers employed in contractual jobs (due to the purported lack of "skill" that the educated outsiders possessed) occasionally led to the defence of the "local", the *Adivasi/ Chhattisgarhi* way of life. The CMM, in its attempt to articulate the concerns of contractual workers, was driven to appreciate certain facets of the local "culture", skills and livelihoods that were threatened and marginalized by the juggernaut of large industry. Witness for instance, its concern to revive knowledge of the local forests and of indigenous paddy varieties. The question of language too was embedded in the CMM's responses. The CMM leadership, including the non-Chhattisgarhi "outsider" and well-known trade union leader Shankar Guha Niyogi, thus communicated in Chhattisgarhi as a matter of routine. Chhattisgarhi was in fact the most commonly used language in speeches, songs and plays, a practice that was notably not part of the political culture in Chhattisgarh in the 1970s and 80s. It was not just Chhattisgarhi, but the other local dialects of the region that were sought to be accorded importance, as is evident from the CMM's demand that Chhattisgarhi, Gondi and Halbi be made the medium of primary education in Chhattisgarh.[21] Clearly, the CMM was also wary of Chhattisgarhi dominating over the other predominantly Adivasi dialects of the region.

However, when ethnic and regional identities assumed a common-sense interpretation in the dominant discourse, the CMM found the mere respect of Chhattisgarhi identity inadequate. It was a period when the Shiv Sena, for instance, was running an aggressive anti-outsider campaign, invoking the *Marathi Manoos* sentiment, and claiming that Maharashtra was "only" for Maharashtrians. Responding to a similar *Chhattisgarh Chhattisgarhiyon ka* [Chhattisgarh for Chhattisgarhis] campaign in Chhattisgarh, the CMM termed it as a fascist idea which should evoke disgust and hatred.[22] The CMM thus thought it necessary to differentiate "Chhattisgarhi" identity from such "son of the soil" formulations. Progressive forces should never make this distinction between "inside" and "outside" forces, said the CMM in a pamphlet issued by it. The CMM, in fact, countered the notion of "*dhartiputra*" [son of the soil] with its vision of "*shramputra*" [son of labour]. For the CMM, it was only through combining labour and soil that real "progress" takes place; when the labourer internalizes the culture of the soil, then he/she becomes the real "son of the soil".[23] It attempted to carve a fresh definition for what it was to be 'Chhattisgarhi'. This is how the CMM went on to define a 'Chhattisgarhi':[24]

- A Chhattisgarhi is one who is making an honest living through his/her labour in the geographical area of Chhattisgarh.
- A person who is committed to Chhattisgarh's *mukti* [freedom].
- A person who does not engage in feudal oppression.
- A person who desires the end of the capitalist system.
- A person who wants the people's development in Chhattisgarh.
- A person who believes in and practises international solidarity of the working class.
- Someone who has traditionally been a resident of Chhattisgarh, but has subsequently left the region to earn a living, and who does not exploit anyone.

- A person from any other nationality, who is earning an honest living in Chhattisgarh's industrial area through his hard work, who wants to permanently live in Chhattisgarh and who works with commitment towards Chhattisgarh's economic, social and cultural development.

This multifaceted definition was a clear break from dominant ideas of ethnic or regional identity, rooted as it was in a vision of solidarity of workers, peasants and farmers. To further make its definition clear, the CMM identified Chhattisgarh's "enemies" in those who represented and stood for local feudal structures (the *malguzaars* and the *sahukaars*), the semi-feudal contractors and the comprador bureaucratic class.[25] More importantly, for the CMM, these people were enemies of Chhattisgarh, even if they had been born in Chhattisgarh and spoke the local languages. One thus sees an interesting attempt to redefine identity, to isolate it from an uncritical invocation of ethnicity and regionalism. And in the process, solidarities were forged across linguistic and regional borders, while contradictions with representatives of a feudal, colonial and imperialist order were sought to be intensified.

"Social Movement Unionism" and the CMM

It was in the 1970s and 80s that 'social movement unionism' (SMU) emerged as a phenomenon in the Global 'South'. During this period, a critique of the 'Northern' form of unionism gained momentum, characterized as they were by an economistic worldview. As a challenge to "business unionism", social movement unionism in contrast, engages equally with the factory/mine 'workspace' and the larger community where workers reside, in a significant change from the traditional trade union practice of separating the two. Social movement unionism is however not merely a 'shift' of working area or of mass bases; it represents a more fundamental philosophical shift in 'labour' as a category. Social movement unionism sought to redefine the meaning of labour, expanding the concept to include the process of "collective action of working people" to transform workspaces as well as communities, and reduce inequality.[26] In this process, struggles over wages and working conditions go together with struggles for better living conditions in working class areas. Not just the factory owner and the industrial management, but the local state machinery and the government are then challenged by the SMU.

In the absence of any serious engagement with the implications spawned by the CMM moment within labour narratives in India, one might be tempted to draw analogies between the *Chhattisgarh Mukti Morcha* and the broader experiments that were part of social movement unionism. Workers who see no contradiction between 'their' struggles in the factory floor and the mines and 'others'' struggles for healthcare and schools; a union for whom protest was not merely a strike; for whom creating alternative structures was as much a political 'protest' as a shutdown; a union which saw anti-dam activists and Adivasis protesting for their land rights as friends and partners—there are indeed instances which can encourage characterizations of the CMM as a 'social movement union'. Any uncritical analogies, however, would perhaps be misplaced, if one were to understand what the CMM was striving to achieve in Chhattisgarh.

Social movement unionists frame labour as a transformative "social" and "political" entity rather than as a "commodity to be bargained over". The CMM, while possibly agreeing with this framing, was in fact seeking to redefine labour's social and political engagement. Therefore, even as workers moved out of the mine pits and factory floor to forge fresh connections with peasants and the local community of subsistence farmers, they sought to interrogate the prevalent discourse on 'development' and technology. This coming together of workers and peasants in Chhattisgarh was, in a sense, the pivot around which ideas on resource use and misuse and technological choice were constantly deliberated upon. The 'red and green' in the CMM's imagination was not merely an expression of solidarity between workers and peasants (which it undoubtedly was)–it was moreover an attempt to create a vision for 'development', livelihoods and technology that would simultaneously speak to the imaginations of the adivasi, the peasant and the industrial worker.

The nature of the factory floor was sought to be reshaped, technological choices presented to labour were made to pass the test of 'suitability', and moreover 'labour' was envisaged not just in the factory and the mines, but also, equally, in the field and the forest. Working with imaginations that were part-worker, part-peasant and part-Adivasi, the CMM's outlook on 'development', technology and livelihoods refused to work in the binaries provided by the dominant discourse. For the CMM, industrial 'growth' could not be easily equated with jobs, nor was mechanization synonymous with 'efficiency', 'growth' and development. The CMM's emphasis on healthcare, water and education were therefore part of a larger framework and perspective on 'development'—to read in the CMM moment a simple and uncritical reflection of 'social movement unionism' in fact frustrates the process of understanding the paradigm and imagination which Niyogi chose to speak from.

Expanding Spaces and Scope of Resistance

"Ours was a 24-hour union, which was open all the time, to address all problems, domestic disputes, fights between husband and wives, caste disputes, police repression, corruption, anything that touched the lives of people in the area", explains CMM leader Sudha Bharadwaj (cited in www.indianlabourarchives.org). As we attempt to understand the impetus and nature of CMM's varied campaigns, Bharadwaj's assertions assume a crucial significance. Much has been written about the CMM's concern for ecology, for the "quality of working life", for public health and education. The engagement with questions of ecology, began, as we saw, with an Adivasi peasant entering the union office with his concerns. Enabling and underlying this narrative, lies a crucial philosophical and material foundation. The sub-text that allowed an indigenous peasant's concerns to enter the space of the trade union office was the CMM's reluctance to remain confined to the idea of an "eight-hour" union. This reworking of existing trade union practice, and the subsequent culture it helped to establish, had crucial repercussions for the CMM. The very process of continuous dialogue with the worker/Adivasi/peasant opened up fresh avenues for interrogation and engagement, and led the CMM to address issues as wide-ranging as forest rights, monocultures, dams and industrial pollution.

The many elements of the CMM's framework for trade union practice – introduction of ecology, education and public health in the trade union discourse, the complex engagement with questions of ethnicity and identity, the attempted reshaping of technology and technological choice—have occasionally been seen as 'aberrations' in working class politics and practice. To engage with these issues, one would have to be an 'unorthodox' trade unionist, this narrative suggests. We thus need to ask: does this engagement need to be seen as tantamount to a disavowal of working class practice? Is it indeed an "aberration", or is the reluctance and absence of this engagement the "aberration"? This question needs to be deliberated upon, if one seeks to understand the dynamics of the CMM. This question, moreover, is crucially connected with our understanding of what exactly constitutes the "working class". In other words, we need to ask if a worker is merely a person employed in a specific job. Equally, we need to think through our ideas of what constitutes "production".

For Marx, production is "not only a particular production"; and the production process is thus based on a complex web of connections, on organically related processes and structures of power.[27] Building on this premise, Ellen Wood convincingly argues that the "productive sphere" itself is "defined by its social determinants".[28] Economic categories thus "express certain determinate social conditions" and capital is impossibly enmeshed in its social determinations.[29] Given this framework, "mode of production" becomes a social phenomenon", where divisions between the 'economic', the 'social' and the 'political' seems particularly blurred.[30] Capitalist organization of production has indeed meant that the 'political' and 'social' conditions required for facilitating the process of production have been in some senses isolated (in the shape of the powers vested in the state, for instance) from the 'economic' process of what we usually see as "production". However, as Wood has noted, this isolation obfuscates, hides and undermines the deep and organic connections which together play crucial roles in constituting the entire process of production.

The 'economic', in the way it is usually constructed in our discourse, is 'material', as opposed to 'social'. This, however, is an inappropriate lens through which to view the complex set of relations in society, as E.P. Thompson argues for instance.[31] The material is indeed "irreducibly social," constituted by social relations and practices.[32] A complex web of human and non-human relations are embedded in the process and relations of production, and hence these interconnections need to inform our understanding of both 'production' and 'class'. As Wood puts it, there are two ways of thinking theoretically about class: "either as a structural *location* or as a social *relation*".[33] In analysing class and the process of class formation, it would be useful to see class as a phenomenon, a relationship and a process, to be observed as "patterns in social relations, institutions and values."[34] All the complex relationships of exploitation, conflict and struggle are crucial to the process of class formation.

Tithi Bhattacharya, in urging us not to "skip class", uses a framework of production and "social reproduction" to understand the dynamics of the working class.[35] This framework attempts to think about the working class as consisting of 'workers' who have an existence beyond the workplace; it attempts to understand the relationship between this (seemingly autonomous) existence and the process of actual 'production' in the workplace/factory floor/mine. Her reading of the complex processes and interactions involved in processes of production as well as social reproduction of labour thus complicates any simple understanding that 'production' is merely an economic category, beyond the pale of the 'social' and the 'community'. In this framework, the 'social', social structures, relations and the community thus become organically connected to the formation and the very idea of the working class.

How does the above discussion help us in our study of the CMM? If we expand the scope of what we see as the 'working class', if we qualify our understanding of the process of production by seeing its intrinsic connections with its counterpart in the social reproduction of labour, we are left with some crucially important insights. We have, in fact, a fresh understanding of what constitutes class and class struggle. Let us now evaluate the CMM's experiences in this light. Take, for instance, the CMM's insistence on being a 24-

hour union, rather than an 8-hour one. By expanding the scope of trade union practice and opening the doors to ensure that the entire gamut of the workers' experience could be addressed, the 'trade union' was essentially bringing in the sites of both production as well as its twin, the social reproduction of labour, into its vision. The 24-hour trade union practice can indeed be seen as a reflection of an understanding that 'class' is present, and formed and reinforced, in various ways including outside the actual site of 'production'. 'Class' is then equally seen in how labour is systematically denied access to public health. If ensuring public health services is seen as essential to the process of renewing labour power, then public health can very logically make an entry into trade union discourses. This entry then appears as logical, perhaps, as the addressing of wages and bonuses in trade union practice.

Let us also now re-examine the CMM's explanation for how the demand for housing and equal wages for contract workers entered the trade union discourse. As we have noted before, the CMM framed these demands as essentially questions of dignity and equality. The Chhattisgarhi contract workers were no less, in this imagination, than their counterparts who were permanently employed, and thus they too deserved homes and better wages. If class is seen as a social process and a relationship (rather than as a structure), impacting every possible arena, then this understanding provides us with a frame to view the denial of equal rights and dignity to Chhattisgarhi workers. As we have noted, the alienation of the Chhattisgarhi identity was a lived reality, evident in the discourses around the discrimination of the Chhattisgarh region and its people. The discrimination of the predominantly Chhattisgarhi contractual labour was hence rooted in existing social relations, power structures and lived realities. These social processes and relations of discrimination were hardly separate from the exploitative processes of production and class formation in Dalli Rajhara, embedded as they were in the existing practice as well as logic of 'economic' production. Indeed, we now find a perfectly logical explanation not just for the demand for housing and equal wages to enter the trade union discourse, but also for the framing of this demand as a 'social' question of dignity.

The 24-hour practice, as we saw, led to an engagement with environment, following the CMM addressing an Adivasi's experience of alienation from the now inaccessible local forest. The experiences of the Adivasi, now termed a 'trespasser' in the state's discourse, were once again rooted in social relations of domination and exploitation. At one level, a 'trade union' addressing the Adivasi's woes (which seem only loosely connected to the problems of the labourer on the factory floor and the mineworker) can be seen as an expression of social movement unionism—workers connecting with local communities and leading struggles related to demands of 'other' constituencies. On the other hand, perhaps, the connections between the worker and the beleaguered and disempowered Adivasi seem even more fascinating. After all, similar processes of discrimination of labour, and moreover of the "local" Chhattisgarhi, could surely be seen in the mines as well as in the local forest? In other words, were not similar social relations of discrimination being harnessed by the Bhilai Steel Plant and the state? Was not 'class' visible in the fact that factory owners were allowed access to forests, were allowed to use the forests as raw materials, while the Adivasis were penalized for doing so? The same play of class and identity was in fact visible in the Dalli Rajhara mines too. Once again, the entry of the Adivasi concerns, and subsequently of an entire gamut of ecological concerns in trade union practice seems not so curious.

It is an even more straightforward process to explain a trade union's engagement with questions of technology. Technology, as we have seen in some detail in previous chapters, is deeply connected with the issue of workers' employment, livelihoods and workplace experience. Technology is embedded in the discourse and politics of production, efficiency and retrenchment. In this sense, what needs explanation is not a trade union's engagement with technology, but the absence of this engagement. The question of 'identity' too needs some attention. The question for us is: are the so-termed "prebourgeois relationships", caste, religion and language, and the "culture" they are embedded in, paradoxical to the idea of a workers' organization, and to the idea of 'class' and class struggle, as Dipesh Chakravarty, for instance, suggests?[36]

The point that the "culture" and "consciousness" of the worker might play a role in the structuring of the relations of production is well taken. Even as Ranajit Das Gupta, for instance, expresses his criticism of Chakravarty's work, he asserts that these "complexities" have often been ignored in labour studies.[37] Indeed, there have been several influential studies dealing with the question of cultural identities and 'economic' categories. Ellen Wood makes the crucial point that capitalism while it ensures "formal equality" (which was often not possible in pre-capitalist societies), can "co-opt and reinforce inequalities and oppressions that it did not create".[38] In the process, capitalism can use and build upon, rather than suppress, existing social divisions and inequalities based on race, caste and gender. Thus, while capitalism can be "structurally indifferent" to the social identities of the people it exploits (as in there is no inherent tendency in capitalism towards casteism/racism or gender oppression), it can and most often does exploit the possibilities presented by existing oppressions based on social identities.

Nancy Fraser undertakes a detailed exploration of the supposed (and seemingly irresolvable) dichotomy between cultural identities and economic classes, between claims for "recognition" of social oppressions on the one hand and "redistribution" on the other. Fraser argues that neither redistribution nor recognition can be "subsumed" under the other; both categories are rather "co-fundamental and mutually irreducible dimensions of justice".[39] A strict division between 'economic' and 'social' dimensions of oppression, are tenuous at best and virtually impossible at times. In practice, these dimensions largely feed into each other to such an extent that invisibilizing any one dimension might be counter-productive even to the project of addressing and eradicating the other. Fraser therefore argues that in practice, "overcoming injustice in virtually every case requires both redistribution and recognition".[40]

The CMM experience can possibly help us to take forward the process of rethinking the complexities of labour's multiple and multifaceted experiences. If we look at the category of 'class' as being multi-dimensional (rather than a strict 'economic' category) as suggested by Fraser, Wood and others, we find a useful way of understanding the CMM. In Chhattisgarh, the social relations of oppression, based on the Chhattisgarhi regional identity, or the Dalit/Adivasi ethnic identity, were closely woven into the economic structure of the Bhilai Steel Plant and the mining project at Dalli Rajhara. In the industrial belt around the Durg-Raipur area too, these social relations were harnessed by the industrial project. The CMM's addressing of the identity question thus no longer appears an "aberration" for a trade union seeking to organize workers to demand their rights from the industrial management and the state. The multiple identities of the 'worker'—that of a Chhattisgarhi, a wage labourer, an Adivasi, a former peasant with memories of the oppressive *malguzari*—were recognized and consciously invoked. In the process, the interlinkages as well as the disjoints between these identities were located, even as a labour-based regional identity was sought to be framed as the basis of the struggle against oppression in Chhattisgarh.

Conclusion

'Alternative' trade unionism is hardly an unheard of phenomenon, even if one concedes its relatively subdued and marginal presence in trade union practice. The *Global Labour Journal* ran a special issue in 2015, carrying several articles on what it termed as "creative and (un)typical campaigns."[41] Moreover, in the 1970s and 80s, in India, within the milieu of resistance and contestation of dominant "development" and technological paradigms, several voices were, in fact, trying in myriad ways to "adapt" Marxism, so to say, to the specific situations they were confronted with. As they interrogated the intricacies of the diverse social and political landscape in India, they entered into a deep and even contentious engagement with ideas of class struggle in India. Many questions were subsequently asked as a part of this process of interrogation: how for instance could the well-entrenched caste hierarchies in India's society be understood, how did ruptures along caste, class and gender lines play out? It was indeed a period of reinvention and adaptation of ideas, and within the labour movement, too, there were surely signs of this churning and reinvention. The CMM can possibly be seen within this larger frame. Thus, dialectical materialism and Marxist-Leninist practice was not to be seen, in the CMM's imagination, as an orthodox, inflexible agenda set in stone.[42] Rather, a 'creative' engagement with this 'science' was in order, depending on social and political circumstances.[43]

In choosing a "red and green" framework to address what was seen as "backwardness" in Chhattisgarh, "class consciousness" hardly proved to be a deterrent for an engagement with ecology or with the vexed question of "appropriate" technology. Moreover, the foregrounding of identity and dignity resulted in rendering the category of "worker" more complex, for now the *Chhattisgarhi* or Adivasi worker and his concerns for recognition and dignity were identified separately from those of his non-*Chhattisgarhi* counterpart. This *adivasi*/non-*adivasi*, or the Chhattisgarhi/non-Chhattisgarhi insider/outsider dynamic added several layers of ideological complexity to the "workers" struggles in Dalli Rajhara. Labour was framed by the CMM as a significant indicator of Chhattisgarhi identity – *shram* [labour] rendered in Chhattisgarh, and not mere birth, was to be the defining characteristic of the '*Chhattisgarhiya*'—even as the Chhattisgarhi's palpable sense of hurt, humiliation and discrimination was sought to be addressed.

This attempted interrogation and reworking of the category of the worker was surely rendered all the more complex by the CMM's efforts to envisage labour not just in the factory and the mines, but also in the field and forest. In this imagination, therefore, the categories of the "worker" and the "peasant" were seen as being seamless and intermingling. It is these practical, academic, ideological and deeply productive implications for labour—the culture of a constant engagement with the "worker", and the subsequent reluctance to ignore any arena of engagement be it "environment" (however defined) or technology, the reframing of the very category of the worker, the foregrounding of identity and dignity, production and livelihood – that existing labour narratives have possibly tended to underplay.

NOTES

1. Ghanshyam Shah, *Social Movements in India: A Review of the Literature* (New Delhi: Sage Publications, 1990).
2. The CMM is no longer a unified movement—after the murder of Shankar Guha Niyogi, the original organization split into three factions. The three factions of the CMM are led by Sudha Bharadwaj, Bhimrao Bagde and Janaklal Thakur respectively. Janaklal Thakur's group continues to work from the original office in Dalli Rajhara. Bhimrao Bagde's faction is predominantly based in Rajnandgaon, while the Sudha Bharadwaj faction operates in Raipur as well as Bilaspur. All three groups claim to follow the ideology and principles of the original CMM, and we will include the campaigns and initiatives of all three in our analysis.
3. Personal translation, quoted in A.K. Roy, 'Vampanth ki Teen Dhaaraon se Alag, Ek Chauthi Dhaara', in Anil Sadgopal and Shyam Bahadur (eds.), *Sangharsh aur Nirman: Shaheed Shankar Guha Niyogi aur Unka Naye Bharat ka Sapna* (New Delhi: Rajkamal Prakashan, 1993), 649.
4. *Shankar Guha Niyogi and the Chhattisgarh People's Movement* (New Delhi: People's Union for Democratic Rights, 1991), 8.
5. C.N. Subramaniam, 'Experiments with Revolutionary Trade Unionism', *Revolutionary Democracy,* Vol. 2, No. 2, September 1996, http://www.revolutionarydemocracy.org/ (Website viewed on April 2, 2012).
6. Binayak Sen, 'Kranti ke Baad ka Aabhaas Karata Andolan' in Anil Sadgopal and Shyam Bahadur (eds.), *Sangharsh aur Nirman: Shaheed Shankar Guha Niyogi aur Unka Naye Bharat ka Sapna* (New Delhi: Rajkamal Prakashan, 1993), 548.
7. Sitaram Shastri, 'Sangharsh ka Kushal Saarathi' in Anil Sadgopal and Shyam Bahadur (eds.), *Sangharsh aur Nirman: Shaheed Shankar Guha Niyogi aur Unka Naye Bharat ka Sapna* (New Delhi: Rajkamal Prakashan, 1993), 512.
8. Anil Nauriya, 'What Chhattisgarh Movement Means', in *The Chhattisgarh Mukti Morcha: On a Rainbow in the Sky* (New Delhi: Centre for Education and Communication, 1998), 167-168. This article was originally published in the *Economic and Political Weekly*, November 30, 1991.
9. Vladimir Ilyich Lenin, 'What is to be Done? Trade-Unionist Politics and Social-Democratic Politics', http://www.marxists. org (Website viewed on April 25, 2012).
10. Ibid.
11. For a description and analysis of the CMM's multifaceted environmental engagement, see Radhika Krishnan, Red in the Green:

Forests, Farms, Factories and the Many Legacies of Shankar Guha Niyogi (1943–91), *Journal of South Asian Studies,* http://dx.doi.org/10.1080/00856401.2016.1216243.

12. Shankar Guha Niyogi, 'Hamaara Paryavaran', in Anil Sadgopal and Shyam Bahadur (eds.), *Sangharsh aur Nirman: Shaheed Shankar Guha Niyogi aur Unka Naye Bharat ka Sapna* (New Delhi: Rajkamal Prakashan, 1993), 232.
13. Captive plantations are vast tracts of forestland handed over to industries, mostly paper mills, for a long period of time for their exclusive use.
14. Green Revolution refers to an agricultural scheme characterized by the increased use of various technologies such as chemical pesticides, herbicides, and fertilizers as well as new breeds of 'high yielding'.
15. For an account of the challenges faced by the CMM in the Dali Rajhara mines, see Krishnan, Radhika, 'Rethinking Technological Choices and Knowledge Production in the Mines and on the Factory Floor', *African Journal of Science, Technology, Innovation and Development*, Special Issue on Informal Innovations, 2014, 6(3): 213-221.
16. For an account of the challenges faced by the CMM in the Dali Rajhara mines, see Radhika Krishnan, 2014, pp. 213-221.
17. 'Chote aur Sundar Chhattisgarh ki Or', in Anil Sadgopal and Shyam Bahadur (eds.), *Sangharsh aur Nirman: Shaheed Shankar Guha Niyogi aur Unka Naye Bharat ka Sapna* (New Delhi: Rajkamal Prakashan, 1993), 64.
18. *Dhartiputra* literally refers to "son of the soil", while *Shramputra* means the son of labour. The CMM was to coin the concept of "shramputra" to counter the anti-outsider discourse in Chhattisgarh.
19. In Chhattisgarh, there is a tradition of storing cooked rice in water overnight, which is then eaten throughout the next day. This is known as *baasi,* literally 'spoilt' rice.
20. Personal interview with Ilina Sen on April 5, 2012 in Raipur, Chhattisgarh.
21. 'The 'Other' Peasant Rally', *Economic and Political Weekly,* Vol. 24, Number 48, December 2 (1989), 2645.
22. 'Jeevan ki mrityu par vijay', *Nava Bhaarat Bar Nava Chhattisgarh* (Dalli Rajhara: Chhattisgarh Mukti Morcha, 1998), 48.
23. Ibid.
24. *Nava Bhaarat Bar Nava Chhattisgarh* (Dalli Rajhara: Chhattisgarh Mukti Morcha, 1998), 11.
25. Ibid., 11.

26. Edward Webster and Carla Lipsig Mumme, 'Recasting Labour Studies in the New Millenium', *Society in Transition* 2002, 33(2), 259.
27. Karl Marx, *Grundrisse* (London: Penguin Classics, 1993), 86.
28. Ellen Meiksins Wood, *Democracy Against Capitalism: Renewing Historical Materialism* (Cambridge: Cambridge University Press, 1995), 22.
29. Ibid., 23-24.
30. Ibid., 25.
31. E.P. Thompson, 'The Peculiarities of the English', in *The Poverty of Theory* (London: 1978), 81-82.
32. Ellen Meiksins Wood, *Democracy Against Capitalism: Renewing Historical Materialism* (Cambridge: Cambridge University Press, 1995), 61.
33. Ibid., 76.
34. Ibid., 81-82.
35. Tithi Bhattacharya, 'How Not To Skip Class: Social Reproduction of Labour and the Global Working Class', https://viewpointmag.com/2015/10/31/how-not-to-skip-class-social-reproduction-of-labor-and-the-global-working-class/(Website accessed on October 20, 2016).
36. Dipesh Chakravarty, *Rethinking Working Class History: Bengal 1890-1940* (New Delhi: Oxford University Press, 1989).
37. Ranajit Das Gupta, 'Indian Working Class and Some Recent Historiographical Issues', *Economic and Political Weekly,* Vol. 31, No. 8 (February 24, 1996), 27.
38. Ibid., 259.
39. Nancy Fraser and Axel Honneth, *Redistribution or Recognition? A Political Philosophical Exchange* (London and New York: Verso, 2003), 3.
40. Ibid., 25.
41. Michelle Williams, 'Transformative Unionism and Innovative Campaigns Challenging Inequality', *Global Labour Journal,* Vol. No. 6, Issue No. 3 (2015), 253.
42. Anil Sadgopal and Shyam Bahadur 'Namr', 'Ek asamapta yaatra ke shabdchitra', *Lokayat*, February 28, 2005, 27.
43. Shankar Guha Niyogi', '*Hamaare baad ki peedhi hamaara sthaan swayam hi le legi*', in *Samkaleen Teesri Duniya*, December 1991, New Delhi, 8.

14

Temple as a Site of Contestation: The Left's Engagement with Hindu Identity Politics in Kerala

Nirmala V.U.

The state of Kerala was known in academic circles for the victory of the Communists in democratic elections since 1957 and the impressive performance of the state in human development. But the literature in social sciences regarding Kerala state and society leaves the right wing currents in the social political life of the region in darkness. This paper tries to examine the growth and consolidation of right-wing Hindu religious politics in Kerala against the backdrop of their rising political visibility and expanding social base of mobilization. The growth of Hindu right wing parties in Kerala will be explained with a reference to certain unexplored dimensions of the politics forming around Hindu temples in the state and the left's political efforts to engage with it in various ways.

Since the 1980s the Hindu organizations have been vigorously pursuing Hindu identity politics in Kerala for which the mobilization of people of the religion against state control over temples has been imperative. The paper tries to understand how the various modes of state interventions lead to consolidation of religious identity by bringing into the light of discussion the following questions. How does the transformation of temples' previous role as a site of production and ritualistic authority to control a caste-ridden society into devotional centres become meaningful to both the political left and the right in Kerala? How do the left political parties engage with the idea of 'wounded Hindu self' propagated by the Hindu right-wing organizations? How do the left encounter the *Sangh Parivar* through engaging in temple administrative reforms from above and below? The prime objective of this paper is to examine the efforts of the left in engaging with the identity politics of the Hindu religion.

Transforming Temples and the Hindu Religion

Temples in Kerala today, are signifying or are easily identified with the worshipping practices of the Hindu community. But the life and meaning of temples was not the same across the history of Kerala society. Temples had undergone major transformations during the early medieval, early modern and in the contemporary history of Kerala. Historians hold different views regarding the exact period when temples emerged as central institutions of social life and the reasons for their emergence in history. One view suggests that Kerala had the system of worshipping in temples much before the emergence of the Brahmin-dominated caste system. The differing opinion is that Kerala witnessed the emergence of temples along with spread of Brahmin settlements only during the early medieval period (Gurukkal 1977; Gurukkal and Varier 1999; Nair 1992; Veluthat 1993). Institutionally and functionally these temples of medieval Kerala varied in their strength. Other than those temples that had an immense role in the economic, political and social life of the people, there were different worshipping places and gods for different caste groups. In a society divided into caste communities there was less centralization and unification in terms of a single religion. Different caste groups having different deities and shrines/sacred groves etc., were brought together (probably as Hindus) in the caste-based economy rather than in matters of common faith and worshipping practices. However the meaning of Hindu to denote a common religion to the people of those periods may be very weak.

The huge medieval temples with elaborate rituals based on *agamic* texts and architecture were the nerve centre of Kerala's agrarian system. The structure and functions of temples of medieval Kerala have stronger implications for the land and agrarian relations which continued in the modern period as well. Temples being the 'landed magnets' in the agrarian economy managed various economic functions in the realm of development, redistribution, surplus extraction, etc., along with acting as a major source of employment (Gurukkal 1977; Nair 1992; Veluthat 1993). The medieval temple was 'a manifestation of state or local government [....] institution expressed itself as a decentralized power structure having political, economic, cultural and ritual dimensions serving to integrate the village economy' (Nair 1992). Temples legitimized socio-political formations like feudalism, monarchy and the caste system. The religious idioms provided by the temples legitimized such power structures and thereby sustained order in the society which commanded allegiance from the people (Veluthat 1993). The interdependence of the rulers and temples for legitimacy of the political system was one of the major characteristics of the period (Ganesh 1990). Temples accelerated the crystallization of caste order as it promoted caste-based division of labour and at the same time, it also served the function of social integration by coordinating and controlling the caste-based division of labour. Temples were the base for social integration and differentiation simultaneously (Gurukkal 1977).

It was this role of legitimation of the caste hierarchy that placed the temple as the epicentre of demands for social changes in Kerala during the colonial period. The caste norms followed by the temples of Kerala became a point of reference for various anti-caste movements demanding reforms in the Hindu religion based on the values of equality. This period changed the life of the temple and moved the meaning of the temple from a restricted sense to a common place of worship. The leaders of anti-caste movements, who located themselves within the ambit of religion, like that of Sree Narayanaguru, identified the temple as a site of contestation for reform. He started an 'alternative temple' movement challenging the Brahmin caste monopoly over temple rituals, and gods. He demanded his followers to give up their practice of worshipping in shrines and sacred groves and also to abandon their traditional gods which were outside the Brahmin ideology. His movement projected an idea of the Hindu as a worshipper in temples. The temple's popular meaning as of today emerged from the transitions brought about by the social reforms in the 'Hindu way of life'.

Unlike the 'alternative temple movement', the temple entry agitations which sprang up from the 1920s were demanding entry rights to the 'lower caste' in the major Brahminic temples of Kerala. These movements were also considered as efforts on the part of Hindu leaders to sustain the religion in the wake of mass conversions to Christianity and Islam as a protest against casteism in the Hindu religion. Such movements tried to redefine the idea of Hindus in an inclusive manner which would be free from the malady of caste. In short the anti-caste Hindu reform movements of Kerala popularized the idea of the temple as the worshipping place of all Hindus irrespective of their caste identity. Though the anti-caste Hindu reform movements redefined the 'idea of Hindu' and shook the Brahmin caste's dominance in temples, it hardly questioned the economic dominance of Brahminic temples in the society. The material base of the temple remained unchallenged till the growth of peasant movements and the land reforms led by the state.

The various land reforms at the initiative of the rulers of the two princely states and later by the democratic and secular governments had affected the economic dominance of the temples in the Kerala society. In Kerala's feudal set up the Brahminic temples enjoyed superior land rights mostly in wet land area and private forests. They owned and operated the major share of land in the society known as *devaswom* lands. Possession of an immense amount of wealth in landed and mobile property had made the temples the point of reference in the struggle for land rights by the landless majority. The various tenancy proclamations by the princely states in the pre-independence period and the later land reform enactments by the Kerala government had destabilized the economic base of the temples, of which land revenue and rent were prominent.

As the economy was predominantly agrarian in nature, the land reforms focused mostly on wet lands became very disadvantageous to *devaswom* lands. The demands for the protection of *devaswom* land from peasants' movements which were growing in number and strength caused serious concern mainly among the wealthy and traditional sections of the 'upper castes', Hindu reformist organizations and devaswom boards. There was a significant section of Hindus, especially 'lower caste' Hindus remaining as landless and were looking for land reforms as a solution. Various legislations regarding revenue, tenancy, agrarian relations and *devaswom* lands passed by different governments, which got completed by the 1970s, had axed the material power of the temples all over the state. Though the temples were provided with compensation through annuities it displaced them from the status of owner to that of a recipient. This does not mean that the temples were pauperized but decline in their status was evident. Studies show that the chief resource base of the temple in the post land reform period shifted to income from rituals and temples were reduced to the status of carrying out functions as a 'cultural sub system of the village society' (Nair 1992). Gradually temples became an institution depending on devotees and the state.

The shifting of the temple from designer and manager of caste inequality to that of a commonly accessible place of community worship through a Sanskritization current of the Kerala renaissance had implications for both the left and the right in Kerala politics. The promotion of temple-centred worshipping culture by Hindu reformist organizations and the collapse of the economic base of the temple through land reforms had prevented the temple from gaining centrality as a direct promoter and partisan authority in the socio-economic relations of power. The 'temples of innocence' are gradually prevailing over the 'temples of a moribund culture and a hoarder of surplus of exploitation' for the new devotees. This transition has several meanings to the transformation of Hindu identity and its politics at a later stage. The material loss for the temple and its visibly insignificant place as the centre of power in the contemporary class and caste relations ironically helped it to re-emerge as a symbol having the character of a common cultural property in the popular imagination of Hindus even across the caste. The temple has been transformed from a centre of economic dominance and social monopoly to that of a cultural institution and a symbol of community identity assertion in the contemporary time. The impact of increasing remittance from Gulf migration and emergence of a new middle class in the 1980s had also contributed to this process. The rise of a new Hindu-hood was visible from many developments since the 1980s which aimed at giving a new meaning to the Hindu religion and culture. The isolated attempts regarding the renovation of deteriorated temples which largely stimulated short-term public attention began in the past became more regular in the 1980s. As any other locus of social identity formation the temple appearing in the new form defined and redefined the external other, aliens, nativity and foreignness, and enemies and 'common' challenges by bringing it closer to a device of a rightward politics of Hindu communalism. The strategy of state has to be looked at to delineate the trend, mainly with reference to the politics of the left with temples and its 'new community', which is the focus of writing this paper.

State and Temple Administration in Kerala

Temples came under the constitutional responsibility of the government of Kerala by a pretty long historical process. Temple administration in the three regions of Kerala, viz. Travancore, Cochin and Malabar exhibited greater differences due to the diversity in the character of the state structure and its administrative set up, and the differences in their cultural context. The only commonality among the temples was the ritual monopoly of the Brahmin caste that was too with exemption of temples under the control of different other castes. It is argued that the Brahmin monopoly over temple rituals was crystallized during the time of King Kulashekhara of the *Chera* dynasty (Narayanan 2013). The Brahmins enjoyed supremacy in the sacred areas of the temple and finality in deciding matters related to temple rituals. By virtue of their superior land rights, temples had enormous landed property managed autonomously by the proprietor of the temple that could be an individual/family or a trust.

The amassing wealth of the temples placed them in conflict with the state. The resulting rebellions led to the confiscation of the temple and its property to the state's revenue departments. The state of Cochin confiscated a number of wealthy rebelling temples and placed under the administrative disposal of the ruler in the 18th century. In Travancore it was under the leadership of Colonel Munro, the British Government's Resident to the princely state, temples were confiscated and placed under the jurisdiction of the revenue department of the state (Devaswom Separation Report 1920). The takeover of temples and their administration by the state caused some sort of standardization of temple administration. Though the rulers of the princely states attached the temples to the administrative machinery of the state with a secular objective of state power consolidation, the Hindu background of the rulers saved them from facing strong questions about legitimacy and authority. This also enabled the state to restrict the caste-wise hegemony of Brahmins to the realm of ritualistic authority alone. The rulers of Travancore and Cochin attached only those temples which were wealthy and in revolt against the state. Therefore there were various types of temple administrative systems in the said regions like incorporated *devaswoms*, unincorporated *devaswoms*, personal deposit *devaswoms*[1], etc., along with many temples under private individuals/families/communities (Devaswom Separation Report 1920). The *devaswom* departments of the princely states followed the exclusionary practice of appointing only 'upper caste' Hindus in the department. The inclusion of *devaswom* in the revenue department made it also exclusive in terms of caste and religion. Only 'upper caste' Hindus were appointed in the revenue services of the Travancore government as *devaswom* was under its purview. Against this, the civil rights movements were formed which demanded recruitment of 'lower caste' and non-Hindus to government services. The Travancore government constituted a committee to study the issue and the committee recommended the separation of *devaswoms* from the land revenue department (Devaswom Separation Report 1920). One of the major problems involved in separating *devaswom* from revenue was the lack of proper accounting of *devaswom* properties that made it difficult to differentiate between *devaswom* and state properties. This compelled the rulers to fund *devaswom* departments and placed them under the direct administrative disposal of the king. A separate *devaswom* department was established in accordance with the recommendations made by the committee through the Devaswom Proclamation of

1922 by the King of Travancore. Through these *devaswom* departments the state of Travancore followed an interventionist approach in temple matters, which also enabled state-led reforms like abolition of the *devadasi* system, animal and bird sacrifices, etc.

In the Malabar region, it was the British colonial government that legislated over matters of temple administration. In Malabar, the Madras Hindu Religious and Charitable Endowment Act (MHRCE, hereafter) of 1927 provided the legal basis for the administration of temples and related institutions. Unlike the princely states, the temples of the region lacked the potential to rise in revolt against the state as the temple proprietors were not in charge of revenue collection which had a separate department to manage it. It was the allegations of corruption and mismanagement that led to the state intervention in the affairs of temples in the region. The precedence continued in force even after independence and the temples (including the private ones) were under endowment administration in accordance with the said Act.

The Post-Independence Phase

Even in the post-independence period *devaswoms* remained as a vestige of continuing privileges of the Hindu rulers. The interim constitution of the Travancore state (1948) placed *devaswom* strictly under the control of the ruler and constituted a *devaswom* fund (Krishnamoorthy 1974). The Hindu ruler of Travancore made it mandatory for the independent state government to frame temple administration laws in a manner so as to retain his right over temples in the region. When the princely states of Travancore and Cochin merged to form the United State of Travancore- Cochin under the mediation of the Government of India, a covenant was signed. In the Covenant, Article 8 made it obligatory for the covenanting states to contribute a share of their general revenue to the *devaswom* fund. It also inscribed that the administration of *devaswoms* in the Travancore and Cochin region had to be vested with the Travancore Devaswom Board (TDB) and the Cochin Devaswom Board (CDB) respectively. The Covenant also detailed the composition and criterion for the creation of the boards (Travancore Cochin Gazette

Extraordinary 1949). Following the Covenant, the Travancore-Cochin Legislative Assembly introduced the Travancore-Cochin Hindu Religious Institutions (TCHRI) ordinance in 1949 and enacted the TCHRI Act of 1950 which detailed the constitution, powers, functions and responsibilities of the Travancore Devaswom Board and Cochin Devaswom Board to be formed for the administration of incorporated *devaswoms* in the region (M. Muralidharan Nair vs. State of Kerala 1990). The provision regarding the amount to be provided to the *devaswom* by the Travancore-Cochin government was also included in the Constitution of India under Article 238 which got replaced with Article 290 A after the state reorganization process in 1956.

The TCHRI Act of 1950 established the TDB and the CDB. It envisaged *devaswom* boards as autonomous bodies, though the government does have a crucial role in its creation. The Act acknowledged the hereditary rights of the erstwhile rulers of the two princely states in the boards (TCHRI Act 1950). The boards would have three members, who are Hindus. Among the three one each had to be nominated by the royal families of Travancore and Cochin (for TDB and CDB respectively) and one by Hindu members of the council of ministers of the state government and one to be elected by Hindu MLAs of the legislative assembly (TCHRI Act 1950). The Act did not define who should be a Hindu, though there were demands for defining Hindu as a theist, temple worshipping Hindu. Though the demand was rejected by the assembly, as they acknowledged diversity as a trait of Hinduism (Travancore Cochin Legislative Assembly Proceedings April 12, 1950) it remained as a major challenge to the communists in the state for many years. Thus there were many challenges in the offing for the democratic government of Kerala which inherited the responsibility of managing temple administration from its preceding political rulers who had made it a constitutional responsibility of the government.

Communists, State Power and Hindu Religion

The transformation of temple administration from the hands of Hindu rulers to a secular government raised practical and philosophical concerns which were elevated with the election of the communist party to power to form the first government of Kerala. Moreover the Communist Party of India (CPI) was facing the charge of 'destroyers of religion' from the early 1940s strongly from the Catholic Church as the Church had close collaboration with the Western world and its anti-communist propaganda. Among all the religions it was the Roman Catholic Church that demanded its people to keep the communist party at a distance because of the alleged atheism of the communists (Joseph 1951).

One of the most important criticisms against the CPI was that of atheism, others being crimes against the nation, violence and loose morality. The clergy identified communism as the 'path of Satan' and went to the extent of equating world communist leaders to Anti-Christ (Vadakkan 1952). The CPI on the other hand, was seen as trying to avoid such an image through publishing a number of works on communism and religion, communist parties and the governments' approach to religion etc., by citing examples from the Soviet Union and China, especially by K. Damodaran, E.M.S. Namboodiripad, N.E. Balaram and others. The collaboration of communists with the rationalist group of Kerala and their efforts to carry forward the renaissance strategy of critiquing religious rituals and superstitions also enhanced the suspicion. The leaders of rationalist and atheist organizations in Kerala such as M.C. Joseph and Pavanan used to publish articles criticizing religious rituals and superstitions in the party's journal *Navayugam*.

The communists were already familiarized with the different currents within the Hindu tradition owing to their experience with socio-religious reform movements (Namboodiripad 1994). This background of the leaders provided the party with an in-depth knowledge of Hindu religious texts, myths and traditions, which enabled them to effectively handle criticisms that equated communism to materialism/atheism. On the one hand, they were staunch critics of the illogical rituals, discriminatory practices and customs of the religion and on the other, they were successful in appropriating the Hindu traditions, festivals, temple arts, etc., for the propagation of their ideology and programmes (Vinodan 1990).

Temples remained as an important arena of their activity. The party book stalls at temple festival venues, the secularization and presentation of temple rituals like *teyyam* (trance dance) and arts like *Padakam, Ottantullal,* etc are some examples. When the party came to power, temples became a quandary problem for them as land reforms remained a major goal of the government.

The first communist ministry in Kerala attempted to make some moderate breaks in the conventional pattern of the state's relation with religion in the case of Hindu temples. Deviating from a convention of assigning the charge of revenue and *devaswom* to separate ministers followed in the erstwhile princely states and the United State of Travancore Cochin, the communist government of united Kerala decided to appoint the same person as Minister for both. The decision also underscored an administrative rationale. These two departments had considerable overlap in their responsibilities and jurisdiction regarding land administration in areas of the erstwhile princely states. Disputes were common between the two departments regarding the ownership of land. Moreover the revenue department which was in charge of land reforms had to deal with the land of devaswoms, and the same minister for the two was considered as helpful to avoid delay in administrative transactions. Moreover, better coordination between the two departments was necessary to help the government to conduct a land survey to assess the landholdings and to redistribute the land to the landless.

Since the communist ministers including the Minister for Devaswom did not take the oath of office in the name of God there was an apprehension looming large in the public that they would defy religion and God. Therefore, any decision of the government regarding temples could easily spark some flames. An amendment proposed to the TCHRI Act was the first instance. The amendment was part of the administrative necessity and intended only some nominal changes. In the view of the government the amendment bill to the TCHRI Act 1950 was necessary to cope with the provisions of the State Reorganization Act of 1956 (Kerala Legislative Assembly (KLA) Proceedings 1958). But when the bill was moved in the House, the members of the opposition demanded that the communists should attest their faith in God as a precondition to legislate in matters of gods, devotees and temples. When it was rejected the arguments from the opposition went on saying that the communists intend to destroy the temples and they would replace the gods with Lenin and Stalin, 'the murders' (KLA Proceedings 1958). They also alleged that by taking over *devaswom* boards the communists would convert the temples into study classes for devotees in atheism.

The communists defended their claim to manage *devaswom* mainly based on an administrative logic and constitutional reasoning. They engaged in a series of philosophical debates with their opponents through public meetings and media organs of the party. The fulcrum of their argument was that Hinduism was a system of plurality of faith and atheism was also in its corpus. The textual and oral traditions of Hinduism were brought in for debates. Lokayata and Sankhya from pan-Indian Hindu traditions and examples of folklore traditions of Kerala were also cited as evidence. They challenged the opponents to prove any of these traditions as non-Hindu. There was a concerted effort from the part of the CPI to portray their ideology in an Indian colour by claiming proximity to Hindu traditions (KLA Proceedings 1958). Though the opposition was not fully convinced by the arguments, there was no unified resistance from Hindus in any of these issues.

The distinction between sacred and secular was held high in their approach to temples. The government and the party also repeatedly assured people that their involvement would be limited to the material realm of temples including the routine administration and property rather than in matters of faith or worship. Devaswom, which literally means in Malayalam 'the property of God', was brought in for clarifying what was the objective of their administration (KLA Proceedings 1958; Pavanan 1958). In fact, the communists anchored their politics regarding religion in general, and temple administration in particular on an intellectually convincing separation of religion and secular. By taking into confidence their success in philosophical debates with opponents regarding the status of atheism in the inner-world of Hinduism, they elected an atheist, K.G. Narayanan, to the TDB as the nominee of Hindu MLAs of the Kerala Legislative Assembly (Nair 1983). Temples and the devotees in the 1950s was a weaker and disorganized rival to oppose such secular decisions.

The government largely left the realm of rituals untouched though it altered some of the administrative customs and conventions regarding the pattern of state intervention. Compared with this, the implications of the government's reforms concerning the landed property of temples by and large went against them. The legal steps taken by the government to prevent eviction of tenants and the proposed legislation for land reforms and the transformations envisaged in the realm of agrarian relations had more serious consequences to temples rather than the communists' secular ideological warfare against religion. In fact, the material power of the temple was related to its status as landlords with a class interest which is necessarily their secular reason for a serious rift with the communists. However, the communist government could not complete the legislation for land reforms. The Kerala Agrarian Relations Bill was referred to the President by the Governor which delayed its passing. The government was dismissed by the centre in 1959. It was in response to an agitation against the government for which the 'religion in danger' was a highlight. However, temples had neither become a major point of reference in the agitation nor were the base for mobilization of people against the government unlike the Catholic Church.

The party's engagement with the material realm of temples was also extended to the concerns of labour rights of employees. State intervention in temples was justified by the party to ensure better wages and welfare to the temple-dependent communities and the administrative staff (KLA Proceedings 1958). It shows that other than organizing many powerful agitations for land reforms and proceeding half-way to bring a legislation to affect the material base of the temples, the first communist government hardly attempted to change the realm of faith and rituals by using state power. But the attempts to axe the material power of temples over land and call for labour mobilization in temples prepared the ground for resistance by the opponents in the future. The unified Hindu resistance against any of these was impossible at that time since the individuals and social groups belonging to the landed and landless class of Hindus had been divided mainly over the distribution of temple land. The 'lower caste' population had no reason to believe that the temple land was their property to protect it from the state's encroachment. Any legislation to distribute land would be welcomed by them. The party's intervention in the administrative functions of temples or the extent of atheism in communism did not seem to be a major concern for them. Labour mobilization in temples and its administrative services by the party was aiming at providing relief to the employees which would not be a cause for any serious protest against the communists. The upper caste's wealthy sections, the only invariably fixed enemies of communists' class politics related to temples in land and labour relations, were not in a position to mobilize a majority of Hindus against the party. Temples could not attain the centrality to attract an anti-communist opposition to become a site of protest. The party could also by and large ride freely over the oppositional currents without suffering any serious loss in its support base, mainly from Hindus.

The coalition between the Indian National Congress (INC), Praja Socialist Party (PSP) and Indian Union Muslim League (IUML) that won the election in 1960 amended the Kerala Stay of Eviction Act of the communist government. It resulted in a large number of anti-eviction agitations by the tenants. Even though in some places the agitation implied a social polarization of classes the CPI was determined to take them all equally with reference to secular class conflict (Damodaran 1961). The movement by tenants for land from Kottiyoor *devaswom* was an event in this regard in 1961. The temple had held large tracts of land which it later gave in lease to the Nair Service Society (NSS), an 'upper caste' organization. The presence of Christians as tenants and migrant settlers was highlighted by the *devaswom* and the NSS as an attempt of non-Hindus to encroach the temple land. The involvement of a Catholic priest Joseph Vadakkan on the side of the tenants gave some force to their argument. The landlord accused the CPI for joining hands with the minority religion in waging an agitation to capture the 'land of Hindus'. The propaganda was however dormant at the period of the agitation to draw a major support. When the CPI was seen in the forefront of different land struggles against landlords of all religions and the government the plan of the opponents to project the agitation on communal lines did not work very well.[2] Meanwhile the Congress-led government also assured the assembly that it would include all *devaswom* land under the purview of the new land reform act to the dismay of temples.

In 1962, a few Hindu religious outfits, Devaswom Confederation, upper caste organizations (e.g. the Nair Service Society) and the *devaswom* boards demanded the exemption of *devaswom* land from the purview of the land reforms. They also pleaded to the central government, but failed to achieve the goal (Krishnamoorthy 1974 and Radhakrishnan 1989). The events show that associations with a common interest concerning the temples were becoming active in the state, though their influence on the decisions of the government was very moderate, if not very weak.

Compared with Travancore and Cochin the decline of temples in the Malabar region (north Kerala) was more widely a trend. In the 1960s some organizations for the protection of temples were formed. The first of this kind was Malabar Pradesh Kshetra Samrakshana Samithi (Temple Protection Council of the Malabar Region, MPKSS hereafter). It was founded in 1966 by K. Kelappan[3] (a Gandhian and leader of temple entry agitations) at a meeting convened in Kozhikode. The objectives of the organization included the reconstruction and renovation of Hindu temples, ensuring proper management and administration of temple property and the reorganization and rejuvenation of Hindu society (Tharamel Krishnan vs State of Kerala 1977). The organization mobilized people and resources for renovation of temples with an objective to save their property and grace from degradation. It was a Hindu revivalist organization. The interest of K. Kelappan in reviving the Hindu community was already visible in his leadership role in various anti-caste and *Sarvodaya* movements.[4]

Malabar Pradesh Kshetra Samrakshana Samithi organised its first agitation for reconstruction of the temple at Tali in Malappuram[5]. The temple was located in an area where the Muslims were a majority. A belief was persistent among the Hindus that the temple was destroyed when Tipu Sultan invaded Malabar (Jayasanker 1999). The communist-led coalition government opposed the demands of the agitation fearing communal clashes in the locality. Moreover the CPI (M) journal (*Deshabhimani*) published articles that openly condemned the agitation (see Joseph 1969). It added strength to the propaganda that the communists would not permit the Hindus to regain their temples' space. Besides this, since the Indian Union Muslim League (IUML) was a partner in the left-led coalition government, Hindu organizations argued that the left was succumbing to pressure of its political allies from the minority religion to prevent Hindus from any mobilization against past 'injustice meted out to them and their gods'.[6]

Compared with the government of 1957-59, the left government of 1967-69 had made some advances into the realm of Hindu rituals. It enacted the Prohibition of Animal and Bird Sacrifices Act in 1968 applicable to all the temples across the state. The Travancore Devaswom Board also introduced some reforms mainly by breaking the caste-based customs in the selection of priests in its temples. The TDB in collaboration with the Ramakrishna Ashram started an institute, Tanthra Vedantha School, to offer training courses to Hindu priests. Caste was not a bar for admission. TDB also decided to appoint non-Brahmin priests in its temples who had the certificate from the institute (N. Adithayan vs TDB 1996).[7] Another landmark decision by the government was the Thiruppuvaram Abolition Act in 1969 which stopped the convention of sharing a part of the state's revenue among various Thiruppu holders which included Hindu temples (Thiruppuvaram Payment Abolition Act 1969). In the Left's second term of power, the religion and the communists came into confrontation in the realm of both economy and rituals.

The coalition government led by the CPI and Congress initiated a vast number of reforms regarding *devaswom* administration in the 1970s. The legislations for tenancy reform were also completing a crucial phase in its tenure. It brought about a transfer of ownership of land from temples to tenants (Rajagopal 1995). Various village level case studies prove that the *devaswoms* incurred substantial loss due to the implementation of land reforms act[8]. The land reforms which had a far-reaching impact on the ownership of wet land and dry land in the regions affected the Hindu temples greatly.[9] Reports of government commissions even went to the extent of describing temples as 'victims of the Kerala Land Reform Acts' as it had wiped off the rights of temples as landlords (Krishnamoorthy 1974; Nair 1983). The loss of temple land and benefits of non-Hindus from its distribution among tenants were pointed out as grievances by the Hindu organizations. By hiding the differential consequences of land reforms for different castes among the Hindus, they argued that the greatest beneficiaries of the land reforms movement in Kerala were Christians and Muslims, and the greatest losers were the Hindu temples and Hindu people (Nair 2011). The idea of 'Hindus as the victims of a secular/communist injustice' was implanted in their political discourse, and it began to grow strongly in the coming period. Though the communists were not solely responsible for land reforms, their ideological background made them the focal point of right wing criticisms[10].

The CPI-Congress coalition government's relationship with the Hindu religion was mainly through legal and administrative means from above. The Guruvayur Devaswom Managing Committee Act (1971) introduced by the government to constitute a governing body for the Sreekrishnaswamy temple of Guruvayur met with opposition from the hereditary trustees of the temple and Hindu organizations. In 1972, the government amended the law but it was challenged by MPKSS in the High Court for violation of fundamental rights of Hindus, government's arbitrary intervention in internal affairs of temples and most importantly the possibility of atheists becoming the members of the managing committee. According to MPKSS, 'the full and absolute control over GDMC by the government reduced Devaswom to a limb of government. It empowered the government to nominate members to *devaswom* boards quite arbitrarily who might be born as Hindu but whose political creed or personal belief may be such as completely opposed to temple worship or even faith'(Tharammal Krishnan vs. GDMC 1977). The petitioner won the case. The Court in 1978 directed the government to incorporate specific provisions to ensure that the *devaswom* members are 'persons having an interest in temples'. The government in 1974 had also abolished the prerogatives of the royal families to nominate members of *devaswom* boards [TCHRI Amendment Act 1974].

The government of the same coalition in 1978 further amended the GDMC Act and decided to follow the court verdict by incorporating provisions to prevent non-believers from becoming members of GDMC. The Act also provided for reservation to Scheduled Castes in the managing committee and assured *devaswom* employees' participation in the administration as part of reform (GDMC Act 1978). These changes became imperative not only for the right, but also for the left in temple administration. For the right, the judiciary proved as a resort to solution; and for the leftists it signified the need for caution regarding their intervention in *devaswom* administration.

Giving a surprising twist to the events, in 1977 the MPKSS was taken over by the Rashtriya Swayamsevak Sangh (RSS) and renamed it as an all Kerala organization, namely Kerala Kshetra Samrakshana Samiti (Kerala Temple Protection Council, KKSS). Thus the politics of the sacred got invariably mixed with, and transformed into politics of the communal. The motto of the organization was 'temple-centred village and temple-centred life' (KKSS 2016). They mobilized people and resources for renovation of temples by working as a moderate wing of the RSS on the ideological front. In the eyes of a common Hindu devotee it was only a cultural and devotional organization aiming at reconstruction and renovation of their temples. The state interventions in temples as mentioned above had already united the hereditary rulers, trustees, etc., and they became more lenient towards the Sangh Parivar in this period. As the new laws were also aiming at social inclusion for different caste groups, the KKSS was cautious to avoid opposition to the affirmative action. They demanded reforms in temples in consultation with spiritual and community leaders. The state's top-to-down and bureaucratic approach aiming at reforms hardly sought for this option. The RSS gained benefits from the growing polarization between religion and the state. The coalition made by the left parties in 1967 and 1971 were also lacking in secular credentials, unlike the government of 1957. The political representatives of the minority religions were part of their governments. So the 1970s provided a favourable political environment for Hindu organizations in Kerala.

The KKSS petitioned in the court to define the term 'Hindu' to determine the eligibility of MLAs and Ministers who could elect and nominate the members to *devaswom* boards. The main objective was to prevent the communist MLAs and Ministers who would not be prepared for a self-identification as 'believing Hindus' (K.V. Narayanan Namboodiri vs. State of Kerala 1985). The judicial verdict came in favour of the KKSS also lent strength to a counter-ideological attack against the left's interpretation of the Hindu religion. The Communists' earlier strategy of defining Hindu in a manner so as to include the (Hindu) atheists in its realm by drawing examples from Hindu philosophy and history, was checked by the court. The Court defined Hindu in this context as persons having faith in God and temple worship (K.V. Narayanan Namboodiri vs. State of Kerala 1985). The Judiciary became the main battle ground for the Hindu organizations regarding temple administration and the Sangh Parivar always showed this legal back-up to gain more legitimacy. Their lack of electoral strength kept the legislature and executive out of their reach. Therefore their main activities focused on mobilization of devotees and intervention in *devaswoms* through a legal fight with the government invoking the right to religion.

The left-led government of 1980-81 seemed to be very cautious to avoid a direct confrontation with religion. While the RSS moved with cases in the court and mobilizing people and resources for renovation of temples, the left government was planning a strategy of more active mobilization of employees in temples. However, the efforts of the government were gaining attention neither in the media nor in public, and among the devotees as well.[11]

The energy, resources, reason and support of the Sangh Parivar was very limited to blow-up the temple-centred agitations to state-wide in the 1960s. But the scenario changed in the 1980s. An agitation against the land claims by the Christian church near Nilakkal Mahadeva temple was the testing ground for their influence. The Church argued that Nilakkal was once a place where Christianity flourished and the cross unearthed from the area was the one consecrated by Saint Thomas, the apostle in the first century. The UDF government granted permission to the Christian denomination to build a church in a land near the temple. It spurred a rebellion and the leadership of the two communities took antagonistic postures (Pillai 2013). The Sangh Parivar and Hindu caste organizations propagated that the government's mismanagement and appeasement towards minorities had caused the loss of temple land gradually in the past, and the allotment of land to the church was the latest development. They argued that Nilakkal falls within the ambit of Sabarimala, the pilgrim centre of Hindus. The issue brought the state on the verge of a communal clash. Though the problem got resolved, it was an indication of the Sangh's extent of influence on the Hindu devotees, and on the government ruled by the Congress.

In 1982, various Hindu organizations submitted a joint memorandum to the Governor of Kerala by raising their concerns about *devaswoms*.[12] In response to this, the government appointed a commission to study the matter (Nair 1983). The Hindu organizations contested the 1984 Lok Sabha election by forming the Hindu *Munnani* (Hindu Front). The alliance situated itself in the electoral politics against the Communists and the Congress by describing both of them as equally anti-Hindu[13]. The call for 'Hindu unity' compelled the Congress to issue an ordinance intending to free *devaswom* boards from the 'atheist communist party members' (TCHRI Amendment Ordinance 1984).

The said ordinance defined the term Hindu as 'a person who believes in God and professes Hindu religion'. It became mandatory for the members of the Kerala Legislative Assembly to file a 'declaration stating that he/she believes in God and professes Hindu religion to the presiding officer before voting in the election and nominations to *devaswom* boards' (TCHRI Amendment Ordinance 1984). The communist-led opposition challenged it in the court. In a petition to the court it argued that the new definition of Hindu was confusing and a self-declaration would not be an objective ground of validation of status of one's faith (K. Krishnankutty (MLA) and others vs. State of Kerala 1985). The left used the logic of reason and science, but the Court dismissed the petition in favour of the government and declared that the atheists had nothing to do with temple administration. Though the left failed in the Court, the ordinance by the UDF also lapsed because the government could not introduce a law before the expiry of its term in office.

State and secular parties acted as the external constraints on the expansion of Hindu identity politics in Kerala. But the nature of internal polarizations of Hindus was also a problem for the Sangh Parivar. By realizing this, the KKSS started engaging in reforms against caste-inequality by describing caste as an achievable status. They organized a congregation of Hindu *sanyasins*, scholars and Vedic *Pandits* who came forward with the 'Paliyam Declaration' in 1987 (Radhakrishnan 1999; Sadasivan 2000). The declaration states that *Brahmanyam* is related to Karma and anybody can attain *Brahmanyam* through Karma even if born in a non-Brahmin caste. They also made it clear that all 'such Brahmins' can become priests and perform rites and rituals in any temple (Tarabout 2016).

This event shows that the Hindu organizations under the guidance of the RSS started appropriation of the ethos of religious reform movements of the Kerala renaissance.[14] The left parties' mode of using the heritage of social reform movements was mainly with a secular/humanist objective of a forward-looking social revolution. They were also cautious to project them as a common heritage of all sections of Kerala. The emerging Hindu organizations mainly focused on the revivalist messages of the social reformers and interpreted their call for the construction of a new community as solely based on Hinduism. The social reformers' reluctance to adopt conversion as a means to fight caste inequality was treated as a reason for their confidence in the virtue of Hinduism. Both were available in the form of competitive schemes showing good imperatives in moulding the public opinion and tilting the political orientation of increasing the number of Hindus since the 1980s.

The Hindu Munnani formed an alliance with Bharatiya Janata Party in the 1987 state assembly election. The demand for liberation of temples from state control and the intervention by secular political parties were the prime points of their election manifesto (Parvathy 2003). The election debates and campaigns were polarized between communal and secular. The Left Democratic Front (LDF) projected itself as the champion of secularism and won the election. In fact, the Congress suffered from the consolidation of Hindu votes behind the Hindu Munnani.

Being very confident about the victory of their secular position in the election, the LDF and its leading party CPI (M) toughened their stand on religion. The government appointed T. Jacob Thampi, a Dalit Christian, as a member of the Guruvayur Devaswom Managing Committee (Rajagopal 1995), which invited scathing criticism by the Sangh Parivar. Such a secular assertion from the government indirectly enhanced the opportunity of KKSS in furthering the demands for temple liberation from the communists and the state. In retaliation, the KKSS formed a Guruvayur Temple Action Council (GTAC). The Council was successful in raising the point that Thampi was still living as a Christian and the government's claim about his reconversion to Hinduism is not on the basis of any proof other than the individual's confession. GTAC organized a parallel *devaswom* board and the government was later compelled to recall the member (Rajagopal 1995).

The right of atheists of the Hindu MLAs in voting for board members was again taken up to the Court by the Hindu activists. The left repeated its old arguments that it had no intention to intervene in the sacred arena of temples, and therefore the accusation of its intervention in religion had no base. The government also argued that the petitioner attempted to divide the Hindus on the basis of the nature of their faith which would lead to exclusionary practices. Internal diversity in matters of faith was long existing and characterizing Hinduism (M. Muralidharan Nair VS. State of Kerala 1990). But the Court quashed the elections to the *devaswom* boards and reaffirmed its earlier decision that Hindus as mentioned in the TCHRI Act refers to those Hindus having faith in God and temple worship.

To counter the verdict, the government adopted the legislative route and amended the TCHRI Act five times in 1990-91. One such amendment inserted a new clause in the act to define a Hindu thus: 'Hindu means a person who is Hindu by birth or conversion into Hindu religion whether or not such a person believes in God or temple worship', provided that a 'Hindu member nominated or elected to the board shall be a person who believes in God and temple worship and who shall make an oath before the secretary' (TCHRI Amendment Act 1990).

It was an attempt to retain the voting rights of all the Hindu MLAs irrespective of their nature of faith. The left changed its previous position, and faith in God and temple worship was made a mandatory qualification to become the members of the *devaswom* board. The effort of the left to incorporate atheists into the world of Hindus was unilateral by the government and its argument was alien to the popular way of reasoning. It only helped the Hindu right wingers to construct a 'wounded Hindu self' among the Hindus' public sphere with some political implications. The government also became proactive in protection of property of temples. It passed an amendment to include the property of *devaswoms* under the Kerala Land Conservancy Act to prevent further encroachment of temple land (TCHRI Amendment Act 1990).

The 1990s was a transition period for the left's engagement with religion. For a long time, the left parties discouraged its cadres from engaging with temple committees or the organizations having religious and spiritual connotations. Moreover the communists had been pursuing a static understanding of the Hindu identity and following mostly an approach suitable to engage with the Hinduism of the period of social reform movements. They mainly resorted to legal and administrative solutions to deal with religion from the government. The left belittled the emerging movement dynamics of Hinduism and there was no strategy to counter-appropriate the rising currents. The left parties were confident also about their Hindu base and the sufficient strength of their reformist pledge to bind them with the left. The predicament of left parties' engagement with religion came from facing two sources of criticisms. First, the rationalist groups who branded any engagement with religion as an ideological compromise. Second, the right wing religious identity groups that treated any intervention from the left in the realm of religion as unwanted and arbitrary because the communists are atheists. Ironically both these groups were united to portray Marxism as atheism. By realizing this conundrum as a hurdle to expansion of the party's political engagement with religion E.M.S. Namboodiripad in his works from the late 1980s had made some concerted efforts to distinguish between 'bourgeois atheism' and Marxism (Namboodiripad 1993). The strategy of the left was reoriented to build up a dialogic relation with the progressive factions of the religious groups.

The Congress coalition government (1991-96) once again amended the TCHRI Act to prevent the communist MLAs from participating in the election and nomination of members to the *devaswom*. The clause demanding the MLAs to declare their faith in God and temple worship was reinserted in the law. It was a point of opposition from the LDF which accused the action of the United Democratic Front (UDF) as an instance of following the aims and objectives of the RSS (KLA proceedings 1994). The LDF government that came to power in 1996 repealed the changes. However they refrained from expanding the clause to explicitly define atheists as Hindus (TCHRI Amendment Act 1999). It was in striking contrast with the act of the left government of 1987-91. In this period the government also scored a victory in the legal tussles with Hindu organizations. The High Court rejected the petition filed by the KKSS challenging the GDMC Amendment Act of the government (M.P. Gopalakrishnan Nair vs. State of Kerala 1999). Giving blues to the petitioner, the Court categorically stated that *devaswom* administration is a secular function of the government.

Many more changes in *devaswom* administration were brought in when the left ruled the state in 2006-11. The government introduced *devaswom* reforms in this period with strategies to regain the temple spaces from the Hindu right by promoting decentralized and participatory model in temple administration. The reforms in the MHRCE Act and TCHRI Act enlarged the scope of reservation in *devaswom* boards for Scheduled Castes, Scheduled Tribes and women (MHRCE Amendment Act 2008, TCHRI Amendment Act 2007). Communists were seen as proactively leading discussions in the assembly and taking actions in the interest of temples. State intervention in temple affairs was described as necessary to bring about social inclusion, labour welfare and social reform. The Court had also directed the government to constitute a separate *devaswom* board for the temples in the Malabar region.

Malabar Devaswom Board (MDB) was a major achievement of the government. One of the distinctive features of the *devaswom* amendments was the provision for temple advisory committees recognized by *devaswom* boards for all the temples in the Malabar region (MHRCE Amendment Act 2008). The Act provided for the participation of religious minded people in the administration of the board and faith in God and temple worship was inserted as a criterion for the members (MHRCE Amendment Act 2008). The Act gave the power to the government to appoint a commission of enquiry regarding matters of irregularities in temples and to recruit employees through the public service commission. Similar provisions were also included in the amendments to the TCHRI Act 2007. Though the government envisaged temple administration in a participatory and decentralized manner, the supervisory power given to the state government was viewed by the Hindu organizations as causing a decline in the autonomy of the *devaswom* boards. In response to a petition the High Court suspended certain provisions of the TCHRI Amendment Act (G. Raman Nair vs. State of Kerala 2007). Though the left moved slightly away from their very assertive stand on matters of faith, its dialogic relation with Hindu organizations, especially of the right was weak. In the question of temple entry for women of all the age groups to the Sabarimala temple, the left by falling back on its reformist pledge towards the religion filed an affidavit in the court stating that the government has no objection to the demand. On the other hand, the Congress and the Sangh objected to such a move by citing 'the emotions of the devotees' as the reason. Though the stand of the political left is very progressive and reformist in nature, their organizations having limited access points to connect with devotees in the internal realm of their faith fail to gain legitimacy.

The Temple in Between the Left and the Right

Temples remains as the pivot of mobilization of Hindus by the right wing in Kerala. Protection and renovation of temples and the state intervention in Hindu religion through *devaswom* administration forms their rallying cry. The politics surrounding the Hindu temples was important for the Sangh in Kerala, especially while it was facing political ostracism in the party system and the civil society circles. The RSS wished to appear in politics and civil society in a softer form, for which the activities associated with temples through the KKSS, provided them with productive options. While the temples under the control of state and the *devaswom* boards were largely out of reach to Hindu organizations affiliated to the Sangh Parivar, the innumerable number of non-*devaswom* temples provided them with ample space. The language of cultural revivalism used by the Sangh Parivar with the temple as a focal point of Hindu life was initially appealing mainly to the 'upper castes' in the period of the genesis of temple protection movements in the 1960s and 70s. But by the late 1990s it could widen its base among the 'lower castes' also through engaging with temples belonging to their communities, and by promotion of Hindu temple culture among many of the marginalized communities including the Scheduled Tribes (Ramachandran and John 2005). For its growth the Sangh was in need of various frontal organizations having a cause different from their visibly communal agenda. Leftists were not found competitive in this arena of their activism. The strategies of the right wing extended from redefinition of caste identity, festivals, rituals, etc., to that of facilitating pilgrimages.

The right wing was cautious to organize several programmes aiming at regeneration of Hindus as a religious community by realizing the challenge from the government's decision to provide for reservation to 'lower castes' in temple administrative bodies. The KKSS conducted a series of religious congregations to fulfil the ethos of the Paliyam Declaration 1987. The organization welcomed and celebrated the verdict of the apex court in a case that upheld the decision of the TDB regarding the eligibility of non-Brahmins to be appointed as priests in temples so long as they are properly trained and qualified to perform the rituals (*The Hindu* October 7, 2002). The KKSS also initiated steps to train priests and in various religious congregations converted several non-Brahmin children, including Dalits and tribes, to 'Brahminhood' (Mukundan 2001). The Sangh Parivar in its public communiqué moved away from the idea of caste as an ascribed status and defined it in relation to duty. Even though the number of qualifying candidates for priesthood from the 'lower castes' is on the rise, their actual appointment in temples was facing other hurdles. Though the Sangh Parivar was striving hard to paint itself in a caste-less colour in matters of selection of priests, in a number of temples where the priesthood was hereditary and belonging to certain Brahmin families, the Sangh's spokespersons highlighted the significance of age-old custom over caste and merit. In fact, the caste question related to priesthood is more easily overcome by the Sangh Parivar in the temples which came into being as part of their temple renovation programme. While the state seems to be isolated in its war against the vestiges of caste in temples by following a top-bottom practice, the KKSS is more able to coordinate with different caste associations[15] and Hindu spiritual forums to carry out the task in their way. For taking up the new mission of revivalism, the Sangh Parivar has a wider network and diverse auxiliary organizations at its disposal compared with the political left to engage with the believers.

The Sangh also employ a strategy of redefinition or introduction of rituals, and festivals as an effective way of countering the secularization of traditional ones by the communists and the progressives. Many of the festivals in temples in Kerala had a varying composition of religious and non-religious components. They were very rarely an exclusive sphere of a particular religion. Many festivals related to different religions had also been secularized by the state, market and the public. Many of them lost the exclusivity of a religion. The higher inclusiveness of festivals was a hindrance to the growth of the Sangh Parivar, which wanted to segregate the population by religion. Since the 1980s the Sangh Parivar was active in mobilizing devotees around certain new festivals detached from the local traditions of Hinduism in Kerala, for example, Janmaashtami procession (Sri Krishna Jayanti), Vinayaka Chathurthi, Raksha Bandhan, etc.

Over a short period of two decades the new Hinduism (Hindutva) promoted by the Sangh Parivar started gaining wide influence in setting the agenda of festival programmes in many local temples as well. Hindu spiritual gurus were appearing as a necessary component of these occasions. Festivals as a site of liberation and a chance to get together for the people living in the locality were gradually receding. Local art forms exhibited in the temples were refashioned to suit the centralizing and unifying themes of Hindutva. Such changes have made the festivals more religious than ever before. It shows a transformation of festivals as a space and an occasion to demonstrate the power of a single unified religion in a more explicit way and in competition with those of other religions.

Children and women were the emotional route that the Sangh Parivar chose to reach the Hindu popular mind in Kerala. It heavily popularized various festivals exclusively held for women devotees of the localities in many temples such as Attukal, Kadampuzha, Chakkulathukaavu as important sites for pilgrimage. Sabarimala was the only popular seasonal pilgrimage site to attract devotees from others states. But since the 1980s it grew in ability and popularity and the Sangh Parivar was very keen to capitalize it. The Parivar lacking in any direct control over the temple, which is governed by the Travancore Devaswom Board, sought for some new ways. It concentrated on devotees by forming associations like the Sabarimala Ayyappa Seva Samajam. Its activities include providing assistance to devotees, formation of pilgrim groups and taking study classes for pilgrims about the rituals and customs. All these efforts enabled them to describe themselves as the caretakers of the Hindu community. Despite having a limited number of the 'prominent' gods in their custody since most of them reside in the temples run by the *devaswom* boards, the Sangh Parivar is actively promoting new gods of many privately owned temples to compensate for this deficit. Even though the left can exercise a bureaucratic and legal control over all the major temples in the state only when it is ruling, competition is high for extending their influence to the local temples in which the Sangh Parivar has already spread its roots. In a middle class dominating society pilgrim tourist packages are increasing their supply. Many of them are combos of devotional and entertainment trips. Devotees were turning out to be the customary clients of the Sangh Parivar.

There has been a spurt in local level temple protection councils organized by the KKSS with varied objectives. It had approached the Court in many cases to protect the landed and mobile property of the *devaswom* boards. The organization appropriated the secular language in bringing forward its agenda while addressing the material interests of the devotees. The fading memory of the benefits of land reforms and the emergence of a sizeable middle class population from various caste groups enabled the Sangh to bring forward a religious unity between the gainers and the losers by concealing the real history of the land reform process and its differential impacts on the communities. Temples can be easily presented as the best examples for the state's 'secular injustice' before these groups.

In a predominantly left-liberal social space in Kerala, 'exploitation' and 'discrimination' have a greater thrust in the mundane political communication. The Hindu right wing is also projecting the issues of exploitation, discrimination, domination, etc., to find a place in the usual political discourse. The KKSS draws attention to the issues of 'exploitation' of devotees by pointing out the 'increased monetary charges' for rituals in the temples under the state's *devaswoms*. Later on they are able to propagate it as 'a looting of Hindu devotees sponsored by the secular/atheist governments which are running the temples'. Besides the accusation of recruitment of atheists to *devaswom* boards, the lack of autonomy, discrimination of Hindu community, corruption maladministration, arbitrary government interventions, bureaucratic mentality, constitutionality, communitarian rights, etc., also find a place in their propaganda for nurturing the idea of 'historical injustice to Hindus by the secular government'. Such terms used in conversation of a secular language is converted for communal purposes.

Conclusion

The left in Kerala have a basket of strategies in its engagement with the Hindu religion which can largely be classified as interventions from above in the form of legislative and administrative measures and interventions from below i.e., dialogue with socio-cultural organizations, secularization of rituals, festivals and unionization of temple employees. As it is in a position to win power in every consecutive election since the 1980s to the state assembly it can bring about legislative and administrative reforms so as to suit its politics. The introduction of temple advisory committees, reservation based on caste and gender in *devaswoms* are the important results. As discussed before the secularization strategy was in use from the very beginning. In addition to adding a secular dimension to Hindu rituals, festivals etc., the leftists found a radical in Lord Ayyappa and Lord Sri Krishna. The myths and traditions that have an element of exploitation and sufferings, as in the case of *teyyam* were incorporated by the communists to find a place in the religious realm. The equation of Onam as a remembrance of primitive communism is another example in this regard. Such methods enabled them in the 1950s and 60s to counter allegations from class interests that opposed communist interventions in religion, especially in a context where temples were the repositories of economic power.

A cursory glance at the mode of governance by the 1957 government shows that the left of the period was leaving matters of material relations involving temples to the administrative and legal decisions, while reserving their engagement with religion for cultural interventions from below. Their government was strong in matters where the party had a back up of movement of its initiative. But once the interventions in the cultural realm through movements got weakened the administrative and legal interventions in religion became bare. This was not dynamic enough to counter the evolving mobilization of Hindus by the right. By realizing this, the leftists retracted to encounter the emerging right wing mobilization of Hindus by cherry picking stories and themes from Hindu mythology, texts and folklore that have an element of radicalism. But unlike the past, such methods are largely laying ineffective, non-intellectual and is becoming counterproductive by nurturing criticism against them. It seems that the left's recent attempts are driven out of compulsions and as super-imposed interventions in the culture of religion. Labour in temple is another arena giving scope for the left's intervention. All the major *devaswoms* in Kerala have labour associations affiliated with trade unions including CITU. The CITU backed strike of the Sri Chakra Rajarajeshwari Velichapdu Welfare Association, an association of oracles in Malabar region demanding a wage rise is an example to the continuity and strength of the left in this regard (*Times of India* 2012).

The previous role of temples to assume the centrality in social relations of production and to make authoritative claims over it gave the scope for the communists to place them in the oppositional front of its agitations for land reforms. The temples, after land reform and the resulting collapse of feudal production patterns shifted their place to the realm of non-antagonistic contradiction. By using the support from the court verdicts the Sangh Parivar in Kerala ideologically reinforced the idea and meaning of Hindu as 'temple going theist'. It claims as normal by placing all other currents of the lives of Hindus as deviations. This discourse produced a powerful interlocking between a Hindu and temple. Hindu identity is getting fixated in the way the Sangh Parivar would like to have it.

Thus the temple emerged as a symbol of community identity by avoiding major tangible basis for accusation of caste/class monopoly. When the temples lost its material power of the previous days in production relations and in caste relations, the Sangh is trying to project it more as a common cultural property of Hindus. The temple is also luring the left as a stage of politics where it cannot play only the tune of class politics. It is a cultural challenge and the contestations around the temple are appearing largely as cultural. True, it is situated in an economy, but rarely gives a big chance to wage a singular economic fight.

NOTES

1. As per the Devaswom Separation Report of 1920, there were two classes of *devaswoms* under the management of the government of Travançore, viz. incorporated and unincorporated *devaswoms*.

Incorporated *devaswoms* were those institutions directly managed by the state. Unincorporated *devaswoms* also known as Personal Deposit Devaswom are the ones controlled indirectly by the state.

2. However the particular agitation was unearthed by the Sangh Parivar in later years, when the public memory about the secular role and goals of the communists in the land agitations was fading.
3. K. Kelappan, a former leader of the Indian National Congress (INC) was known for his efforts in fighting untouchability and other social discriminations that existed among Hindus. The movement for protection of temples under him helped in bringing together all castes because of his earlier involvement in the temple entry movements for the benefit of non-Brahmin lower castes. Kelappan also protested against the communist government's decision to create Malappuram district. He described it as a 'communal award' since the new district is a Muslim majority region of Kerala. But the government implemented the decision by citing under development as the reason.
4. The new interpretation of an old agitation and redefinition of an old organization's demand for a dignified space for Hindus equal with others into a call for political assertion of Hindus are the common chord of narrative exercises in the popular communiqué issued by the Sangh Parivar. It is part of constructing a political subject of Hindus, which was not on the agenda of leaders like K. Kelappan or MPKSS. Even though Kelappan would not have the same political/cultural objective of the RSS, reference to him in the agitations for renovation of temples has a great imperative for its agenda to gain legitimacy and to urge for continuity.
5. The historical background of the region needs to be mentioned. The region was under the rule of Tipu Sultan and the British. It included areas where the Mappila rebellion occurred. The Marxist explained the Mappila rebellion as a conflict of class interest between Muslim tenants and Hindu landlords. The political Islamists consider it as an identity assertion by the Muslim community. The Sangh and the colonial historians identified the Mappila rebellion as a communal clash. Many Hindu leaders of the INC also shared similar views.
6. After the split in the CPI in 1964 the hopes about forming a single party government by the left was bleak. In the 1967 election the two leading communist parties –CPI (M) and CPI formed a United Front (UF) with five other political parties including those claiming support of Muslims and Christians.
7. Prakkulam Bhasi, the leader of the Kerala Socialist Party (KSP) which

was a coalition partner in the UF government was appointed as the president of TDB.

8. See Franke 1992; Herring 1980; Radhakrishnan 1989; Scaria 2010.
9. The agitations for land reforms organized by the communist parties were mainly concentrated in areas containing paddy fields (Franke 1992). They had different approaches to capitalist and feudal landlordism. The land reforms were mainly intended to abolish vestiges of feudal landlordism. It avoided plantations from its ambit (Herring 1980). The party also hoped to bring about land reforms to facilitate capitalist relations in cultivation, and plantations were already capitalist.
10. The efforts of the governments of united Kerala came only at a later stage in the process of diminution of temples' material power. The left activated the conclusion but it was not alone responsible for it in the history. All the major political parties of the period had their role in framing and implementing land reforms. But interestingly, the left remains as the projected enemy of the Sangh in this regard.
11. Popular attention and debate on the party's stand on religion was surrounded by reactions to a sarcastic remark made by the Chief Minister in a speech related to the increasing number of burglaries in temples. His remark, 'why do gods need security?' was described as an indication of a communist's condemnation of gods and a justification for the lack of seriousness on the part of the government to ensure the security of temples.
12. The memorandum demanded the liberation of Hindu temples from political interference, creation of an administrative mechanism for them by involving spiritual leaders and religious scholars capable of leading the devotees in the right direction in matters of faith, increasing the annuity from government to temples, prevention of misuse of temples' land and resources for secular purposes, protection of the basic needs and legitimate demands of temple employees, banning agitations and demonstrations by temple employees that cause discomfort to the devotees, exemption of temple land from forest and environmental laws and proper administrative mechanism for temples in Malabar regions.
13. While the RSS seems to be equalizing both the Congress and the communists in their responsibility for increasing state encroachment in the 'internal affairs of Hindus', there was always a concession in their criticism of the former. The reason for the failure of Congress in their propaganda was corruption and pressure from minorities. It shows that the emerging Hindu organizations hardly have any reason to treat the

Congress as a considerable force to come against them. But, the approach towards communists was very different. Ideologically the communists were pinpointed by them as the arch enemies of Hindus.

14. Unlike the left politics that used such values of the Kerala renaissance viz. inclusiveness of Hinduism while addressing social disabilities, the right wing used the same values for glossing over their criticisms against the Hindu religion in the name of caste. This strategy of appropriation is evident today when the right wing claims their legacy from Sree Narayanaguru, Chattampi Swamikal, Ayyankali, Pandit Karuppan, etc. In the Sangh's view they are 'Hindu Monks' as opposed to the leftist interpretation of them as social reformers in the general fashion of secular humanism.
15. The urgency for Hindu unity against the ascendancy of minorities in state politics and economy was presented by the Sangh before the mutually competing caste organizations as an appealing reason in recent times. In the 2016 state assembly election a coalition of about 30 Hindu caste organizations, Bharatiya Dharma Jana Sena (BDJS) was formed with the leadership of the SNDP. Their alliance with the BJP provided a better show for the Hindu right in the election.

REFERENCES

1. 'Oracles Trade Trance for Union'. *Times of India*, February 1, 2012.
2. 'Sangh Parivar Outfit Hail Verdict on Temple Priests' *The Hindu*, October 7, 2002.
3. Damodaran, K. 1961. 'Manthri Velappanum Daivavum' (Malayalam) *Navayugam* August 11 (5): 5-6.
4. Franke, Richard. 1992. 'Land Reforms versus Inequality in Nadur Village, Kerala', *Journal of Anthropological Research,* 48(2): 81-116.
5. G. Raman Nair vs. State of Kerala 2007 AIR 2008 Ker 96.
6. Ganesh, K.N. 1990. 'The Process of State Formation in Travancore', *Studies in History,* 6(15):15-33.
7. Gurukkal, Rajan. 1977. 'The Socio-Economic Role of Temples in Kerala AD 800-AD 1200'. Unpublished M Phil Thesis, Jawaharlal Nehru University.
8. Gurukkal, Rajan and Raghava Varier. 1999. *Cultural History of Kerala*, Department of Cultural Publications, Trivandrum: Government of Kerala.
9. GDMC Guruvayoor Devaswom Managing Committee Amendment Act 1972 Kerala Gazette Extraordinary No. 776 dated 20/03/1972.
10. GDMC Guruvayoor Devaswom Managing Committee Amendment

Act 1978, Kerala Gazette Extraordinary No. 193 dated 19/03/1978.
11. GDMC Guruvayoor Devaswom Managing Committee Amendment Act 1998 Kerala Gazette Extraordinary No. 639 dated 24/04/1998.
12. GDMC Guruvayoor Devaswom Managing Committee Amendment Act 2001 Kerala Gazette Extraordinary No. 2092 dated 31/12/2001.
13. Herring, Ronald J. 1980. 'Abolition of Landlordism in Kerala: Redistribution of Privilege', *Economic and Political Weekly*, 15(26): 59-69.
14. Jayasanker, S. 1999. Temples of Malappuram District- Census of India- Special Studies—Kerala, Trivandrum: Directorate of Census Operations.
15. Joseph, O.J. 1951. 'Vella Lohayude Ullil Kallapetti' (Malayalam) *Navayugam*, December 8 (27): 14-17.
16. Joseph, M.C. 1969. 'Gandhi Bakthiyum Tali Prakshobhavum' (Malayalam) *Deshabhimani*, Vishu Special Edition. 114-115.
17. K. Krishnankutty vs. State of Kerala. AIR 1985 Ker 148.
18. K.V. Narayanan Namboodiri vs. State of Kerala AIR 1985 Ker 160.
19. Kerala Legislative Assembly Proceedings. 1994. Session VIII, Official Report, Trivandrum: Government of Kerala, Vol. XC, No. 7.
20. Kerala Legislative Assembly Proceedings.1958. Session II, Official Report, Trivandrum: Government of Kerala, Vol. V, No. 2.
21. KKSS. 2016. 'A Brief History of Tali Temple Movement' http://mathrusamithy.com/history.php (accessed October 15, 2016).
22. Krishnamoorthy, C.R. 1974. Report on the Financial Position and Other Allied Matters of the Travancore Devaswom Board, Trivandrum: Kerala Government Press.
23. M. Muralidharan Nair vs. State of Kerala. AIR 1990 Ker 25.
24. M.P. Gopalakrishnan Nair vs. State of Kerala AIR 2005 SCR 712.
25. Madhavapilla, P.K. 1961. 'Kottiyoor Jathayodoppam etanum divasangal' (Malayalam) *Navayugam,* 11 (12): 7-8.
26. MHRCE Amendment Act 1981. Kerala Gazette Extraordinary No 75 dated 28/01/1981.
27. MHRCE Amendment Act 2008. Kerala Gazette Extraordinary No 2709 dated 19/12/2008.
28. Mukundan, C.M. 2001. 'Brahmanisation Through Community *Upanayanam*' http:// www.ambedkar.org/News/Brahminization through.htm (accessed September 12, 2016).
29. Nair, Gatotkacha. 2011. 'Communism and Land Reforms Movements in Kerala', *Haindava Keralam*, http://www.haindavakeralam.com/communism-and-land-reforms-hk6744 (accessed October 11, 2016).

30. Nair, Preetha. S. 1992. 'Role of the Kerala Temple in Socio-Economic Articulation: A Structural Functional Analysis'. Unpublished M Phil Thesis, Jawaharlal Nehru University.
31. Nair, Sankaran, K.P.1983. Report of Kerala Devaswom Administrative Reforms Commission, Trivandrum: Government of Kerala.
32. Namboodiripad, E.M.S. 1994. *The Communist Party in Kerala: Six Decades of Struggle and Advancement.* New Delhi: National Book Centre.
33. Namboodiripad, E.M.S. 1993. *From Bourgeois Atheism to Dialectical Materialism*, Trivandrum: Chintha.
34. Narayanan, M.G.S. 2013. *Perumals of Kerala. Brahmin Oligarchy and Ritual Monarchy: Political and Social Condition of Kerala Under the Cera Perumals of Makotai CAD 800-1124.* Thrissur: Cosmo Books.
35. N. Adithayan vs. Travancore Devaswom Board, AIR 1996 Ker 169.
36. Parvathy, A. 2003. *Hindutva: Ideology and Politics*, Delhi: Deep and Deep.
37. Pavanan, 1958. 'Keralathile Prathipaksham Hindu mathathinte asthithwangale nishedhikkunnu' (Malayalam) *Navayugam* July 6(8): 5-6.
38. Pillai, Sreedhar. 2013. 'Crossed Swords', *India Today* http://indiatoday.intoday.in/story/nilakkal-in-kerala-set-for-a-hindu-christian-confrontation/1/371657.html (accessed October 5, 2016).
39. Radhakrishnan, M.G. 1999. 'The New Nampoothiris', *India Today* January 25.
40. Radhakrishnan, P. 1989. *Peasant Struggles, Land Reforms and Social Change: Malabar 1836-1989.* New Delhi: Sage.
41. Rajagopal, P.K. 1995. 'Politics of Temple Administration in Kerala'. Unpublished Ph D Thesis, University Kerala.
42. Ramachandran, T.K. and P.T. John. 2005. 'The Sangh Parivar's Initiatives in the Tribal Belts of Wayanad, Kerala' in Anand Teltumbde (ed.), *Hindutva and Dalits*, pp. 300-04, Kolkata: Samya.
43. Report of the Devaswom Separation Committee with the Dissenting Minutes of Mr. P.K. Narayana Pillai, 1921, Trivandrum: Government of Travancore.
44. Sadasivan S.N. 2000. *A Social History of India,* New Delhi: APH Publishing House.
45. Sankaran Nair, K.P. 1984. Report of Kerala Devaswom Administrative Reforms Commission, Trivandrum: Government of Kerala.
46. Scaria, Suma. 2010. 'Changes in Land Relations: The Political Economy of Land Reforms in a Kerala Village', *Economic and Political Weekly,* 45(26): 191-198.
47. Tarabout, Gilles. 2016. 'Birth vs Merit: Kerala Temple Priests and Court' in Daniela Berti, Gilles Tarabout, and Raphaël Voix (eds), *Filing*

Religion: State, Hinduism, and Courts of Law, pp. 3-33, New Delhi: Oxford University Press.
48. TCHRI Act 1950, Travancore Cochin Gazette dated 21/11/1950.
49. TCHRI Amendment Act 1958, Kerala Gazette Extraordinary No. 172 dated 24/07/1958.
50. TCHRI Amendment Act 1974, Kerala Gazette Extraordinary No. 761 dated 05/11/1974.
51. TCHRI Amendment Act 1990, Kerala Gazette Extraordinary No. 101 dated 23/01/1991.
52. TCHRI Amendment Act 1999, Kerala Gazette Extraordinary No. 436 dated 04/03/1999.
53. TCHRI Amendment Act 2007, Kerala Gazette Extraordinary No. 694 dated 12/04/2007.
54. TCHRI Amendment Ordinance 1984.
55. Tharamel Krishnan vs. GDMC AIR 1978 Ker 68.
56. The Kerala Animals and Birds Sacrifices Prohibition Act 1968, Kerala Gazette Extraordinary No. 226 dated 17/09/1968
57. Thiruppuvaram Payment Abolition Act 1969, Kerala Gazette Extraordinary No 98 dated 09/04/1969.
58. Travancore Cochin Gazette Extraordinary, 1949, Trivandrum: Government of United State of Travancore Cochin, Register No. M4634.
59. Travancore Cochin Legislative Assembly Proceedings, 1950, Session I, Official Report, Trivandrum: Government of United State of Travancore Cochin, Vol.1, No. 26.
60. Vadakkan, Joseph. 1952. *Yeshukristu Moscovilo?* (Malayalam), Aluva: S.H. League Apostolic Seminary.
61. Veluthat, Kesavan. 1993. 'Religious Symbols in Political Legitimation: The Case of Early Medieval South India', *Social Scientist,* 21 (1): 23-33.
62. Vinodan, T.K. 1990. 'Dissemination of Marxist Ideas in Kerala', Unpublished M Phil Thesis, Jawaharlal Nehru University.

List of Contributors

Anu Muhammad is a Professor of Economics at Jahangirnagar University, Dhaka, Bangladesh. He has been teaching economics since 1982 and also taught Anthropology from 1991 to 2005. His research interests include: Globalization, Social Justice and Transformation, Gender, NGO and Energy. He is a theoretical contributor and activist in different issues of imperial domination, inequality, workers' rights, injustice, deprivation, environment and natural resources. Professor Muhammad had been visiting scholar in Columbia University, USA (1993) and Manitoba University, Canada (2001). He is the Member Secretary of 'National Committee to Protect Oil Gas, Mineral Resources, Port and Power, Bangladesh' a national alliance for protecting natural resources and public interest. He is the editor of *Sarbojonkotha* (Public Voice) a Bangla journal on socio-economic issues since November 2014. His works include *Development or Destruction, Essays on Global Hegemony, Corporate Grabbing and Bangladesh*; *Bangladeshe Unnayan Shankat Ebang NGO Model* (Crisis of Development and the NGO Model in Bangladesh); *Bangladesher Kotipati, Madhyabitto O Sramik* (Multimillionaires, Middle Class and Workers); *Dharma, Rashtra ebong Gonotantrik Andolon* (Religion, State and Democratic Struggle); *Rashtra O Rajniti: Bangladesher Dui Doshok* (State and Politics: Two Decades of Bangladesh); *Atonker Somaj Sontraser Arthiniti* (Society of Fear, Economy of Violence); *Bangladesher Tel-Gas: Kar Sompod Kar Bipod* (Oil and Gas in Bangladesh: Whose Resource Whose Liability); *Biswaner Boiporitya* (Contrariety of Globalization); *Phulbari Kansat Garments; Amra 99%* (We are 99%); *Pujir antorgoto probonota,* (Inherent Trends of Capital); *Issor, punji o manush* (God, Capital and People).

Anuja Agrawal is Associate Professor at the Department of Sociology, Delhi School of Economics, University of Delhi. She is the author of *Chaste Wives and Prostitute Sisters: Patriarchy and Prostitution Among the Bedias of India* (2008) and editor of *Migrant Women and Work* (2006). She writes on a wide range of issues especially in the fields of kinship, marriage and gender studies.

Dhritiman Chakraborty is currently working on his doctoral thesis, "Dilemmas of Postcolonial Development in India: An Enquiry into the Politics of Two Dissident Movements" from the Centre for Studies in Social Sciences, Calcutta (CSSSC). He is focusing on the Singur movement and the anti-POSCO movement in India. His interests include explorations of Postcolonial Political in India, social anthropology and political philosophy in the postcolonial contexts. His publications mainly deal with subaltern forms of resistance in India and possible ways of rendering these singular acts of political. He has worked on a project on 'Folk Political and Gramsci' to study folk forms in North Bengal, India. He has jointly edited a book on American Studies after 9/11 from Authors Press (2014). He is an editorial associate of *Kairos: A Journal of Critical Symposium*, available at www.kairostext.in.

Manas Ranjan Bhowmik is Assistant Professor of Economics in the Ramakrishna Mission Vidyamandira College in West Bengal. Marxism with its polymorphous forms has enamoured his interest and issues of non-capital, alternative economic systems, cooperatives have mainly dominated his endeavours. He has been conducting research on handloom weaving cooperatives and working on Marxian political economy for almost a decade. He is presently conducting field visits in rural West Bengal in order to comprehend functioning of cooperatives.

Nirmala V.U. is pursuing her PhD at the Centre for Political Studies, Jawaharlal Nehru University, New Delhi. She was formerly associated with the Department of Political Science, University of Calicut as Lecturer in Political Science. Her areas of research interest include Religion and Politics, Civil Society and Political Parties, Environmentalism, and Left Politics.

Pushpesh Kumar teaches at the Department of Sociology, University of Hyderabad. His areas of interest include gender, sexuality, kinship and family, globalization and cultural change and pedagogical issues, He has published extensively in reputed national and international journals.

Rachna Chaudhary comes with a disciplinary training in Political Science. She has pursued her higher education from the University of Delhi. Her doctoral work is in the area of feminist jurisprudence and criminology. She has been teaching since 1998 and is presently an Associate Professor in Gender Studies at Ambedkar University Delhi. Her other research interests include Masculinity Studies, Disability Studies, Gender and Work, and Sexuality Studies. Currently, she is working on a project on Women in Police with focus on Delhi Police and is also a collaborator on the Indian Feminist Judgment Project.

Radhika Desai is Professor, Department of Political Studies and Director, Geopolitical Economy Research Group, University of Manitoba, Winnipeg, Canada. She has written *Geopolitical Economy: After US Hegemony, Globalization and Empire* (2013), *Slouching Towards Ayodhya: From Congress to Hindutva in Indian Politics* (2nd ed, 2004) and *Intellectuals and Socialism: 'Social Democrats' and the Labour Party* (1994). She has edited or co-edited *Russia, Ukraine and Contemporary Imperialism* (2016), *Theoretical Engagements in Geopolitical Economy* (2015), *Analytical Gains from Geopolitical Economy* (2015), *Revitalizing Marxist Theory for Today's Capitalism* (2010) and *Developmental and Cultural Nationalisms* (2009). Her articles and book chapters appear in international scholarly journals and edited volumes. With Alan Freeman, she co-edits the Geopolitical Economy book series with Manchester University Press and the Future of Capitalism book series with Pluto Press.

Radhika Krishnan is currently teaching in the Department of Humanities at the International Institute of Information Technology (IIIT), Hyderabad. She has been a Fellow at the Indian Institute of Advanced Study (IIAS) in Shimla, India. Earlier, she was a post-doctoral fellow at the Centre at

Concurrences in Colonial and Post-Colonial Studies at Linnaeus University in Sweden, where she worked on the Joseph Stephens' Archives. She has also worked with the research and advocacy group at the Centre for Science and Environment in New Delhi for several years.

Ravi Kumar teaches Sociology at South Asian University, New Delhi. His works include [co-edited, 2018] *Sociology and Social Anthropology in South Asia: Histories and Practices*, New Delhi: Orient Blackswan; [edited, 2016] *Contemporary Readings in Marxism: A Critical Introduction*, New Delhi: Aakar Books; [edited, 2015] *Neoliberalism, Critical Pedagogy and Education*, New Delhi and London: Routledge; [co-edited with Savyasaachi, 2014] *Social Movements: Transformative Shifts and Turning Points*, New Delhi: Routledge. His area of research includes political economy of identity politics, social movements, neoliberal impact on education and processes of knowledge production. He is Associate Editor of *Society and Culture in South Asia* (Sage). He co-edits book series titled *Social Movements, Dissent and Transformative Action* (Routledge: Delhi) and *Conversations on/for South Asia* (Aakar Books: Delhi).

Salimullah Khan teaches at the University of Liberal Arts Bangladesh, Dhaka and directs its Centre for Advanced Theory. He is the editor of the two journals of the Centre, namely *Occasional Papers in Theory* and *Apostrophe: Working Papers of the Centre for Advanced Theory*. Salimullah Khan graduated in legal studies from the Dhaka University and earned his doctorate in Economics at the New School for Social Research, New York. His publications include *Silence: On Crimes of Power* (Dhaka, 2009). Periodicals he edited include *Praxis Journal*, *Stanford Journal of Law*, *Artha* and *Ahmed Sofa Bidyaloy*. He translated into Bengali many works including some by Plato, Rosa Luxemburg, Antonio Gramsci, Dorothee Soelle, Pentii Sarikoski, Jacques Lacan and Frantz Fanon.

Shubhanga Pandey is the Deputy Associate Editor of *Himal Southasian*, which is based in Colombo. Trained in astrophysics, he began his journalism in 2013. His writings on politics and culture have been published in *Jacobin*, *The Caravan*, *World Politics Review*, and *The Record*, among others. He tweets as @shubhangap.

V. Krishna Ananth is Chair and Professor of History, School of Liberal Arts and Basic Sciences, SRM University, Amaravati. He did his PhD from the Centre for Historical Studies, Jawaharlal Nehru University, New Delhi. He taught History at Sikkim University (2012-18); was with *The Hindu* (1991-2004) contributing editorials and op-ed articles on national politics. His works include *The Indian Constitution and Social Revolution: Right to Property Since Independence* (SAGE 2015) and *India Since Independence: Making Sense of Indian Politics* (Pearson Longman, 2009). He was a fellow at the Nehru Memorial Museum and Library, New Delhi between May 2009 and April 2011. He specializes in contemporary history apart from the History of Modern Europe.